Understanding and Using Statistics in Psychology

Understanding and Using Statistics in Psychology

A Practical Introduction

or, how I came to know and love the standard error

Jeremy Miles and Philip Banyard

SAGE Publications
Los Angeles ▪ London ▪ New Delhi ▪ Singapore

First published 2007

SAGE Publications Ltd
1 Oliver's Yard
55 City Road
London EC1Y 1SP

SAGE Publications Inc.
2455 Teller Road
Thousand Oaks, California 91320

SAGE Publications India Pvt Ltd
B 1/I 1 Mohan Cooperative Industrial Area
Mathura Road, New Delhi 110 044
India

SAGE Publications Asia-Pacific Pte Ltd
33 Pekin Street #02-01
Far East Square
Singapore 048763

Library of Congress Control Number: 2006929861

British Library Cataloguing in Publication data

A catalogue record for this book is available from the British Library

ISBN 978-0-7619-4396-9
ISBN 978-0-7619-4397-6 (pbk)

Typeset by C&M Digitals (P) Ltd, Chennai, India
Printed in Great Britain by The Alden Press, Witney
Printed on paper from sustainable resources

Contents

Acknowledgements

We would like to acknowledge the support of our colleagues in the Psychology Division at Nottingham Trent University and the Health Sciences Department at the University of York who provide a positive and friendly working environment. We would also like to thank the many people who commented on the drafts and so helped in the development of this text. If we are successful in selling the film rights we promise to give them all a walk-on part. We would also like to acknowledge the support and indulgence of Michael Carmichael and Claire Reeve at Sage (and we promised not to mention the thumbscrews). They can be in the film as well if they like.

We would like to give name checks (in no particular order) to Nick Neave, (University of Northumbria at Newcastle), Peter White (Southampton University), Keith Bender (Royal Perth Hospital), Linden Ball (University of Lancaster), James Roney (University of California, Santa Barbara), Barry Wright (Selby and York Primary Care Trust), Charles Hulme (University of York), Mark Torrance (Staffordshire University) and Martin Dorahy (Queen's University, Belfast) for allowing us to use and abuse their painstakingly collected data.

Jeremy would like to thank Susanne, Alex and Daniel for allowing him to spend hours at a computer writing this text and generally ignoring them. Phil would like to thank Mark Shevlin whose reluctance to tear himself away from the bookies and collaborate with Jeremy gave him the opportunity to be the support act on this text. Phil would also like to give name checks to the darts players of the Gladstone in Carrington, the loyal supporters of Nottingham Forest and to Jeremy for writing most of this and not laughing at him when he didn't understand something.

1

Introduction: how to get started with statistics

What's in this chapter?

- The misuse of statistics
- Computers and statistics
- How to use this text
- Which chapter do you want?

INTRODUCTION

This chapter explains why we need statistics and why you should love them. It explains why it is important to understand statistics, which is principally so that we don't get fooled by numbers. It also provides a guide to how this book is best used. We realise that most readers will go to the chapter that best suits their immediate needs and are only reading this if it is the last book in their bag and their train has been indefinitely delayed. If you are this position then we hope it gets better soon.

STUDYING STATISTICS IS GREAT

This heading is not an indication of madness on the part of the authors. Statistics really is great and it is a remarkable observation that when students finish their statistics courses after much pain and gnashing of teeth they often come to this conclusion as well. It is the most useful thing you will learn on your degree. Give us a minute (or a couple or paragraphs) and we will attempt to convince you that this statement is not as deranged as it may seem.

Tip: Statistics and statistics

Rather confusingly, the word 'statistics' means two things. Originally, 'statistics' were numbers. The mean of a sample, for example, is a statistic. However, the study of those statistics gave rise to an academic subject, also called 'statistics'. Hence we can say: 'Statistics are great, I love them' and 'Statistics is great, I love it'. Both sentences are grammatically correct, but have different meanings. The first is talking about numbers, the second is talking about the subject.

We learn about statistics because we want to find stuff out. We want to find out two sorts of things. First, we want to find out what our results tell us, and we can do this by using statistics to analyse data. When we analyse our data, and see what they are telling us, we find stuff out. Sometimes we shed light on a problem, sometimes we don't. Whichever we do, we make a contribution to knowledge, even if that knowledge is only 'don't try to do it this way, it won't work'. If we don't do statistical analysis on our data, we will not be able to draw appropriate conclusions. In short, if we don't do statistics, we won't know what works. This text is aimed at illuminating how statistics work and what they tell us.

Tip: Data

'Data' is the plural of the singular term 'datum'. You should write 'data are analysed' and 'data have been entered into the computer', not 'data is …' or 'data has been …'. Be sure to point out when your lecturers make this mistake. Lecturers enjoy it when students point out this sort of simple error.

Second, we want to know about the statistics we get from other people. This is most important because we are bombarded with statistical data every day and they are often used to confuse rather than to clarify. There is a famous quote attributed to Andrew Lang: 'He uses statistics like a drunk uses a lamppost – more for support than for illumination.' We need to know when people are trying to illuminate what they have found, and when they are trying to simply support their preformed opinions.

Consider the following extract:

The number of automatic plant shutdowns (scrams) remained at a median of zero for the second year running, with 61% of plants experiencing no scrams.

(*Nuclear Europe Worldscan*, July/August 1999)

Do you know anything more about nuclear plants after reading that? It is likely that whoever wrote this was using statistics for support rather than for illumination. (Many more examples can be found in *Chance News*, at http://www.dartmouth.edu/~chance/chance_news/news.html).

THE MISUSE OF STATISTICS

Perhaps the most famous quote about statistics is commonly attributed to British Prime Minister, Benjamin Disraeli,[1] who is reported to have said:

There are three kinds of lies: lies, damned lies and statistics.

Less well known is the comment attributed to another British Prime Minister, Winston Churchill, who said:

When I call for statistics about the rate of infant mortality, what I want is proof that fewer babies died when I was Prime Minister than when anyone else was Prime Minister. That is a political statistic.

It is a popular view that statistics can be made to say anything you want and therefore they are all worthless. While it is clearly true that people will selectively present data to

---

[1] There's actually a bit of controversy about who *really* said this. Leonard Henry Courtney (1832–1918) wrote it down, in an essay in *The National Review* in 1895: 'After all, facts are facts, and although we may quote one to another with a chuckle, the words of the Wise Statesman, "Lies – damned lies – and statistics," still there are some easy figures the simplest must understand, and the astutest cannot wriggle out of.' Mark Twain quoted it in his autobiography: writing: 'the remark attributed to Disraeli would often apply with justice and force: "There are three kinds of lies: lies, damned lies and statistics"'. It seems that Twain thought that Courtney was quoting Disraeli when he wrote 'the Wise Statesman', but Courtney was referring to a hypothetical wise statesman, not a specific one. Rather spoiling the whole quote, it has been suggested that the dashes are parenthetical, and Courtney was trying to say something like 'Lies (damned lies!) and statistics'. Most people haven't heard of Courtney, so they say that it was either Twain or Disraeli who said it. So that's clear then.

misrepresent what is actually happening, it is not true that statistics are therefore worthless. If we have a better understanding of where data come from and how they are being presented then we will not be fooled by the politicians, advertisers, journalists, homeopaths and assorted other charlatans who try to confuse and fool us.

	Tip
	One of the reasons why statistics sometimes appear difficult is that they are often counter–intuitive. Think about your friends, for example: half of them are below average. Or, in a wider context, if you have the view that the average car driver is ignorant and thoughtless, then by definition half of them are *even more* ignorant and thoughtless than that. Then there was the man who drowned crossing a stream with an average depth of 6 inches (attributed to W.I.E. Gates).

IS STATISTICS HARD AND BORING?

When students find out that they have to learn about statistics as part of their course, they are often somewhat dismayed. They think that statistics is likely to be hard, and is also likely to be boring. In this text we will try and make it not quite so hard and not quite so boring, but you have to be the judge of how successful we are.

We have made this text as clear as we can and as straightforward as we can, but we have not simplified it so much that we skip over important bits. Albert Einstein wrote, 'Everything should be made as simple as possible, but not simpler', and we have tried to follow this principle.

One way to make statistics less hard is to provide a set of clear and explicit instructions, much like a cookbook. For example, if you want to make mashed potatoes, you can follow a set of instructions like this:

1. Wash and peel potatoes.
2. Cut larger potatoes in half.
3. Put potatoes in saucepan of hot water and boil for 20 minutes.
4. Drain the potatoes.
5. Add milk, salt, butter to saucepan.
6. Mash, with a potato masher, using an up-and-down motion.

This isn't hard. It just involves following a set of rules, and doing what they say. It isn't very interesting, and there is no room for creativity or flexibility. We don't expect you to understand anything about why you do what you do. We do not try to explain to you anything about the potatoes, or the cooking process, we just expect you to follow the rules. If you had to follow instructions like this every time you made a meal you would find it very dull, however, and would probably just send out for a kebab.

A bigger problem would be that if something went wrong with the cooking, you would be in no state to fix it because you don't know what is happening and why. The cookbook approach to statistics might get you to the right answer but you will only have a limited understanding of how you got there. The problem with this is that it is difficult to discuss the quality of your data and the strength of your conclusions. The cookbook approach is not so hard to do, but it doesn't help your understanding.

The approach in this text is to give you the cookbook recipe but also to tell you why it is done this way and what to do in a wide range of circumstances. We hope this allows you to still get to the right result fairly quickly but also to understand how you got there. Staying with the cooking analogy, we will tell you a bit about potatoes and the general process of cooking. 'Too much detail!', you might cry, but you'll thank us for it later.

 Tip

Statistics can be off-putting because of the terms and equations that appear all over the pages like a rash. Don't be put off. The equations are much more straightforward than they look, and if you can do multiplication and subtraction you should be fine. For example, the mean score is commonly written as $\bar{x}$, and once you get used to this and some of the other shorthand then it will become clearer. Imagine you are in a foreign country with a language you can't speak. You don't need to know the whole language, just a few key phrases like 'two beers, please' and 'where's the toilet?'. It is the same with statistics, so just get comfortable with a few key terms and the Land of Statistics will be there for you to explore.

There is another way to deal with statistics, and that is the way that we commonly deal with technology. We open the box, connect everything up and puzzle our way through the various controls. We will only look at the instructions at the point where it either refuses to work or we have broken it. Let's face it, instructions are for wimps! We anticipate that many readers will have adopted this strategy and will be reading this book because their analysis has just gone horribly wrong. It clearly does not help to suggest that this was probably not the best strategy, but all is not lost and the last chapter, with its checklist of important points, will hopefully diagnose your problem and tell you where to go in the text to find the answer.

COMPUTERS AND STATISTICS

Computers have made statistics much harder.

Well, they haven't really, but they have made *learning* about statistics much harder. And they have done this by making it easier to do hard things.

OK, we know that this is a statistics book, which you were expecting to be a bit tricky, at least in places. And you are reading nonsense like this before you have even got to the statistics, so let us explain. When we were students (and computers were the size of an Eddie Stobart truck), learning about statistics primarily involved learning about lots of different formulae. We were presented with formulae and we had to apply them and use them. The majority of the time that people spent doing statistics was spent working through the formulae that were given in books. This wasn't difficult, except that it was difficult to find the time to do it. Some of the statistical techniques that we will cover in this text would take hours or days to carry out. Some techniques were never used, because it was not physically possible to do them. Now we use computers. Computers have made it much easier to find the time to do statistical analysis, because they are much faster. They will do in seconds an analysis that would have taken days in the past.

Our desktop computers can now take all of the long, boring bits away from us. The parts of doing statistics that were boring (they weren't hard, remember, they just involved following a recipe to the letter) aren't there any more. What this means is that there is lots more time to spend on the parts of statistics which are not boring, but which may be a little harder. In the past, we spent a lot of time talking about how statistics were calculated, and considerably less time thinking about what they actually *meant*. Today we can spend much more time thinking about what they *mean*. Spending time thinking about what our analysis means is a good thing, because that is what we are interested in. We are not interested in statistics *per se*, we are interested in what those statistics can tell us.

The double-edged sword that is SPSS

Throughout this book, we are going to assume that if you are using a computer, it will be running SPSS.

There is a downside to computers in that they allow us to do some very complex tasks without ever understanding what we are doing. If you put your data into SPSS you can click your way happily through the various menus until you appear to get a statistical analysis. The problem is whether you have carried out the *appropriate* analysis. SPSS is a very clever program in that it can carry out some amazing calculations, but it is not clever in terms of understanding what it is doing. It won't suddenly say to you, 'Look, are you sure you want to do a regression on these data?', because it doesn't *know* you are doing a regression and even if it did it wouldn't care. The other problem with SPSS for the happy clicker is that it generates bucketloads of output with numerous test results (Roy's largest root is our favourite) and you need to have some idea of what you are doing so that you can understand this output.

HOW TO USE THIS TEXT

This text introduces the basic principles of statistical analysis and works through examples of the most commonly used tests in undergraduate psychology projects. We have attempted to provide the recipe for conducting the tests and also to give the rationale behind the tests (boil the potatoes for 20 minutes, because this makes them soft). We have added some tips and asides to help you through the text and some simple tests so that you can assess your progress.

You don't have to be a mathematician to work through the examples and understand the process of statistical analysis. Although the equations might appear complex, the mathematical principles for calculation are pretty straightforward. As long as you have a calculator with all the standard keys (+, −, ×, ÷) plus $\sqrt{}$ and x^2 you will be fine (oh, we do use the $\boxed{\ln}$ button once or twice too).

At the end of each chapter we tell you how to carry out the calculations in SPSS. If you understand what you are doing before you tackle SPSS, then SPSS is very straightforward. (If you don't, you will struggle, because you won't know what you want, and you won't know what SPSS is doing.)

The final chapters of the book help you complete your research report by outlining the key features that are required in the write-up and the key issues that you need to deal with in the analysis.

Every chapter tells a story and they can be read in any order. If you have an immediate problem with, for example, regression, then you might go straight to Chapter 8 and work your way through the tests. Though having said that, it might well make most sense to start at the beginning and work your way through to the end. The reason for this is that we look at some general principles of tests in the first few chapters which then keep coming up in the later chapters. Have it your own way, though.

To help you through the chapters we have added some features to break up the story, help you take a breath and ease you over the difficult bits. You will find:

- *Tips.* These will commonly suggest shortcuts or ways to think about the material.
- *Optional extras.* There is always some debate about how much you really need to know. We have tried to write this text on a 'need to know' basis, but there are also loads of other things you might *like* to know. We have therefore put in some optional extras that have, for example, other possible tests, or fascinating (yes, really) pieces of information about statistics or statisticians.
- *Common mistakes.* There are a number of common traps that people fall into with statistics. Many of these have arisen because people have learnt how to use statistics by developing some simple 'rules of thumb' that work *most* of the time, but not *all* of the time. We have tried to point out these common traps so you don't fall into them.
- *Steps.* Where we use statistical tests we have broken them down in steps to make the process clearer and, we hope, to help you carry them out more efficiently.
- *Test yourself.* Practice makes perfect, so we have included a few questions for you to try, and just to be nice we have also included the answers. Some of the questions are a straight test of what you have learnt during the chapter, and some will help you tease out what the test is all about.
- *Using SPSS.* At the end of the chapters we have included simple instructions for doing the tests in SPSS, complete with screen dumps. The bluffing student might be tempted to go just to this section, but be careful you are sure what it all means as SPSS can confuse as well as illuminate.

- *Key terms.* We have identified the key terms in each chapter by **emboldening** them and listing them at the beginning of the chapter. Impress your tutors by learning these terms and using them liberally in any conversation with them. Understanding them is optional, of course.
- *Introductions and summaries.* At the beginning and end of each chapter we set the scene and briefly review what we have dealt with.

WHICH CHAPTER DO YOU WANT?

We like to think that students will buy this book at the beginning of their course, read it all of the way through (possibly making notes), as they do the course, and then they will simply refer back to the parts that they need. If you are like most students, this isn't what you will do. Instead, you will pick up the book in the week before your assignment is due, try to find which part you need and then read and try to understand that part. Of course, that will be harder, so to help you we've put signposts back to other parts that you might need to know about.

In this section, we'll try to help you to understand which part of the book you need to read, based on what you need to know. Find the highest–level question that matches most closely to your question, and then answer the subsequent questions.

	Tip
	Read all the questions and see which is the closest match to your question. Don't stop when you get to the first one that matches.

1. I'm looking for a difference between two (or more) groups or treatments.
   (a) I have two or more treatments, and each is applied to a different group of people (i.e. an independent samples, independent groups or between-participants design).
      (i) My outcome measure is continuous (see page 13) and approximately normally distributed (or my sample size is large).
      You need to use an independent samples t-test (page 137) if you have two groups, or ANOVA if you have more than two (page 238).
      (ii) My outcome measure is ordinal (see page 13) or my distribution is non-normal (and my sample size is not large).
      You need to use a Mann-Whitney U test (see page 155).
      (iii) My outcome is categorical or nominal (see pages 13 and 170–71).
      You need to use a χ^2 (chi-square) test.
   (b) I have two or more treatments, applied to the same people (i.e. a repeated measures or within-participants design).

(i)   My outcome measure is continuous (see page 13) and the differences in the scores are approximately normally distributed (or my sample size is large).
You need to use a repeated measures t-test (see page 113).

(ii)   My outcome measure is ordinal (see Chapter 2) or the differences in the scores are non-normal (and my sample size is not large).
You need to use a Wilcoxon test (see page 120).

(iii) My outcome is categorical or nominal (see page 13). If you have two possible outcomes, you can use a sign test.

2. I'm looking for a relationship between two measures.

(a) Both of my measures are continuous and approximately normally distributed.

(i)   I want to know what value of an outcome variable I would expect, given a particular value on a predictor variable.
You need to use regression (see page 197).

(ii)   I want to know the strength of the (linear) relationship between my two measures.
You need to use a Pearson (product moment) correlation (see page 214).

(b) One or both of my measures is either ordinal (see page 13) or is highly non-normal.

(i)   I want to know the strength of the (linear) relationship between my two measures.
You need to use a Spearman (rank) correlation (see page 221).

(c) At least one of my measures is categorical.
This is the same as looking for a difference between groups. Go to Question 1.

3. I'm looking to see if two (or more) measures of the same thing agree.

(a) I've got a multiple item questionnaire, and I want to see if the items seem to be measuring the same thing.
You need coefficient alpha (see page 281).

(b) I've got two measures of the same thing, and I want to see if they are giving the same score.

(i)   My measures are continuous.
You need to use the limits of agreement measure (see page 274).

(ii)   My measures are categorical.
You need to use Cohen's kappa (see page 286).

(iii) My measures are ordinal.
This is a difficult one. If there aren't many possibly values, you could use kappa.

If your question isn't here, there are three possibilities:

1. We don't cover that technique, because it is too advanced for this book.
2. No technique exists that can answer your question.
3. Your question isn't analysable. (That's horribly easy to do.)

WEBSITE

You can find further advice in the blog relating to the book, which you'll find at http://www.jeremymiles.co.uk/learningstats. If you still struggle, then send us a question, and if it's clear and interesting, we'll try to answer it (in the same place). We can't promise anything though.

SUMMARY

Statistics are great! Statistics are fun! They are interesting and not so difficult as you might think. They are also an essential component of almost any information source, so if you know how they work you are ahead of the game. Enjoy.

2

Descriptive statistics

What's in this chapter?

- Levels of measurement
- The normal distribution
- Measures of dispersion
- Measures of central tendency
- Graphical representations
- Using SPSS

KEY TERMS

binary measures
boxplot
categorical measures
ceiling effect
central tendency
continuous measures
descriptive statistics
discrete measures
dispersion
distribution
exploratory data analysis
floor effect
frequencies
histogram
inter-quartile range

interval measures
kurtosis
mean
median
mode
nominal measures
normal distribution
ordinal measures
outliers
range
ratio measures
skew
standard deviation
variable

INTRODUCTION

The purpose of descriptive statistical analysis is (you probably won't be surprised to hear) to describe the data that you have. Sometimes people distinguish between **descriptive statistics** and **exploratory data analysis**. Exploratory data analysis helps *you* to understand what is happening in your data, while descriptive statistics help you to explain to *other people* what is happening in your data. While these two are closely related, they are not quite the same thing, and the best way of looking for something is not necessarily the best way of presenting it to others.

Common Mistake

You should bear in mind that descriptive statistics do just what they say they will do – they describe the data that you have. They don't tell you anything about the data that you don't have. For example, if you carry out a study and find that the average number of times students in your study are pecked by ducks is once per year, you cannot conclude that all students are pecked by ducks once per year. This would be going beyond the information that you had.

Optional Extra: *Harry Potter* and the critics

Chance News 10.11 (http://www.dartmouth.edu/~chance/chance_news/recent_news/chance_news_10.11. html) cites an article by Mary Carmichael (*Newsweek,* 26 November 2001 p. 10), entitled 'Harry Potter: What the real critics thought':

> 'Real critics,' of course, refers to the kids who couldn't get enough of the Harry Potter movie, not the professional reviewers who panned it as 'sugary and overstuffed.'

> The article reports that: 'On average, the fifth graders Newsweek talked to wanted to see it 100,050,593 more times each. (Not counting those who said they'd see it more than 10 times, the average dropped to a reasonable three.)'

What can you say about the data based on these summaries?

How many children do you think were asked?

What did they say?

Write down your answers now, and when you've finished reading this chapter, compare them with ours (see page 46).

LEVELS OF MEASUREMENT

Before we can begin to describe data, we need to decide what sort of data we have. This seems like a very obvious thing to say, but it is easy to make mistakes. Different sorts of data need to be summarised in different ways.

When we measure something, we are assigning numbers to individuals (where an individual is usually, but not always, a person). A measurement is usually called a **variable**. A variable is anything that can vary (or change) between individuals. There are two main kinds of variables: **categorical measures** and **continuous measures**.

Categorical measures

When we are talking about attributes, we can put each individual in a category. It is an activity that we do in our daily lives. We might categorise a person as mean or funny or male or a 4 × 4 owner. When we see a bird, we probably categorise it. Some people, such as the authors, will put the bird into one of four or five simple categories (for example, small brown bird, seagull, pigeon, large bird). Bird spotters, however, will categorise a bird in one of a thousand categories ('oh look, there goes a lesser spotted split-toed tufted great bustard').

These data are also called categorical, qualitative or classification variables. They come in three different kinds:

- **Binary**, where there are two possible categories (e.g. female/male, smoker/non-smoker).
- **Nominal**, where there are three or more possible categories, but there is no natural order to the categories. For example, if people are asked where they were born, they can be classified as 'England', 'Scotland', 'Wales', 'N. Ireland', or 'elsewhere'. Even though, for convenience, we may use numbers to refer to these categories, the order does not mean anything. Telephone numbers are another example of nominal categories: just because my phone number is larger than your phone number doesn't make my phone any better than yours, and if you dial my phone number with one digit wrong, you won't find someone similar to me answering the phone.
- **Ordinal**, when the categories have an order. If people are asked to rate their health as 'good', 'fairly good' or 'poor', they fall into one of three categories, but the categories are in an order.

Continuous measures

Continuous measures give you a score for each individual person. They can be classified in two ways: interval or ratio, and continuous or discrete.

Interval versus ratio

Interval measures have the same interval between each score. In other words the difference between 6 and 7 is the same as the difference between 8 and 9 – one unit. So 7 seconds comes 1 second after 6, and 9 seconds comes 1 second after 8. Blindingly obvious, you say, but this does not happen with ordinal measures even when they are presented as numbers. If we imagine the final list of people who completed a marathon, it might be that the people who came 6th and 7th crossed the line almost together and so were only half a second apart, but the people who came 8th and 9th were miles away from each other so crossed the line several minutes apart. On the final order, however, they appear as next to each other and the same distance apart as the 6th and 7th runner.

Ratio measures are a special type of interval measure. They are a true, and meaningful, zero point, whereas interval measures are not. Temperature in Fahrenheit or Celsius is an interval measure, because 0 degrees is an arbitrary point – we could have made anywhere at all zero (in fact, when Celsius devised his original scale, he made the freezing point of water 100 degrees, and boiling point 0 degrees). Zero degrees Celsius does not mean no heat, it just refers to the point we chose to start counting from. On the other hand, temperature on the kelvin scale is a ratio measure, because 0 k is the lowest possible temperature (equivalent to – 273°C, in case you were wondering). However, it is not commonly used. In psychology, ratio data are relatively rare, and we don't care very often about whether data are interval or ratio.

Discrete versus continuous

Continuous measures may (theoretically) take any value. Although people usually give their height to a full number of inches (e.g. 5 feet 10 inches), they could give a very large number of decimal places – say, 5 feet 10.23431287 inches. **Discrete measures** can usually only take whole numbers so cannot be divided any more finely. If we ask how many brothers you have, or how many times you went to the library in the last month, you have to give a whole number as the answer.

Test yourself 1

What level of measurement are the following variables?:

1. Shoe size
2. Height
3. Phone number
4. Degrees Celsius
5. Position in top 40
6. Number of CD sales
7. Cash earned from CD sales
8. Length of headache (minutes)
9. Health rating (1 = Poor, 2 = OK, 3 = Good)
10. Shoe colour (1 = Black, 2 = Brown, 3 = Blue, 4 = Other)
11. Sex (1 = Female, 2 = Male)
12. Number of times pecked by a duck
13. IQ
14. Blood pressure

Answers are given at the end of the chapter.

Luckily for us, in psychology we don't need to distinguish between discrete and continuous measures very often. In fact, as long as the numbers we are talking about are reasonably high, we can safely treat our variables as continuous.

Optional Extra: Continuous measures that might really be ordinal

There is an extra kind of data, that you might encounter, and that is continuous data which do not satisfy the interval assumption. For example, the Satisfaction With Life Scale (Diener, Emmons, Larsen & Griffin, 1985) contains five questions (e.g. 'The conditions of my life are excellent', 'So far, I have gotten [sic] the important things from life'), which you answer on a scale from 1 (strongly disagree) to 7 (strongly agree). Each person therefore has a score from 5 to 35. It's not quite continuous, in the strict sense of the word, but it is very close. We treat height as continuous, but people tend to give their height in whole inches, from (say) 5 feet 0 inches to 6 feet 6 inches. This has 30 divisions, the same as our scale.

Should we treat this scale as interval? If we do this, we are saying that the difference between a person who scores 5 and a person who scores 10 (5 points) is the same difference as the difference between a person who scores 30 and one who scores 35 – and by difference, we don't mean five more points, we mean the same amount more quality of life, and we are not sure what that means.

Should we treat this scale as ordinal? If we do, we are saying that a higher score just means a higher score. If one person scores 10, and another scores 20, we can just say that the person who scored 20 scored 'higher'. If a third person scores 21, we can only say that they scored higher still. We cannot say anything about the size of the gap from 10 to 20, and from 20 to 21. We can just say that it is higher. This doesn't seem very sensible either. So what are we to do?

One option is to use sophisticated (and difficult) methods that can deal with ordinal data more appropriately, and treat these data as a special kind of continuous data. These are, frankly, so difficult and frightening that we're not going to even give you a reference (they even frighten us). Anyway, these methods usually can't be used for variables that have more than (about) nine categories.

The solution, used by almost everyone, almost all of the time, is to treat the measures as if they are continuous. It isn't ideal, but it doesn't actually seem to cause any problems.

DESCRIBING DATA

We carry out a study and collect the data. We then want to describe the data that we have collected. The first thing to describe is the distribution of the data, to show the kinds of numbers that we have.

Table 2.1 shows the extraversion scores of 100 students. We could present these data just as they are. This would not be very useful, but it would be very accurate.

Table 2.1 *Extraversion scores of 100 students*

11	11	20	16	14	13	7	26	15	11
17	16	8	24	18	13	25	13	19	17
20	17	22	16	20	10	13	20	19	29
13	14	20	15	25	19	23	17	16	17
20	23	18	10	9	14	24	11	17	17
13	23	14	24	17	14	15	38	14	21
26	15	22	7	14	25	10	15	18	14
16	19	14	18	23	17	15	10	11	20
17	15	25	26	22	26	5	14	17	8
16	12	17	10	15	17	8	20	13	5

For the first time we come across the problem of summarising our data, and presenting our data accurately. Generally we will find that the more accurately we present our data, the less we summarise them, and the more space they take up. For example, in Table 2.1 we have presented our data very accurately but have failed to summarise them at all. We want a way of presenting the data that does not overwhelm the reader who is trying to see what is going on. Table 2.1 would be a very accurate way of describing the data. No one could argue that you were trying to deceive them, or that you have not given sufficient information. The problem is that hardly anyone will be able to read anything useful from that table.

One way to make more sense of the data and summarise them is to present a table of **frequencies**. This is shown in Table 2.2, and already you can start to see some patterns in

Table 2.2 *Frequency scores of information from Table 2.1*

Score	Number	Percentage
5	2	2.0
7	2	2.0
8	3	3.0
9	1	1.0
10	5	5.0
11	5	5.0
12	1	1.0
13	7	7.0
14	10	10.0
15	8	8.0
16	6	6.0
17	13	13.0
18	4	4.0
19	4	4.0
20	8	8.0
21	1	1.0
22	3	3.0
23	4	4.0
24	3	3.0
25	4	4.0
26	4	4.0
29	1	1.0
38	1	1.0

the data. For example, you can see that the high and low scores (extreme scores) have only a few individuals, whereas the middle scores (14, 15, 16, 17) have the most individuals.

You'll notice that the percentage scores are the same as the number of people. This has only happened because we had 100 people in the dataset, and usually the numbers would be different.

Charts

A chart can be a useful way to display data. Look at Figures 2.1, 2.2 and 2.3, and decide which one you think best represents the data.

Figure 2.1 shows a **histogram** with a bin size of 1, which means that there is one score represented in each bar. This chart represents exactly the information that was shown in Table 2.2.

Figure 2.2 shows a histogram with a bin size of 2, which means we have combined two sets of scores into one bar. We can see that a total of two people scored 4 or 5, and two people scored 6 or 7.

Test yourself 2

Before reading on, try to decide which of those two charts is the better.

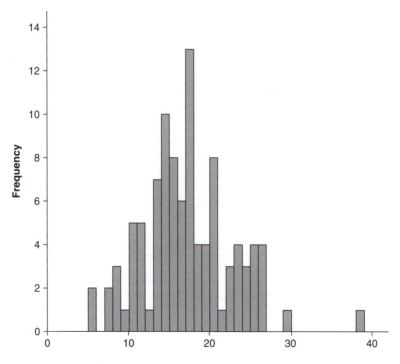

Figure 2.1   Histogram with bin size 1

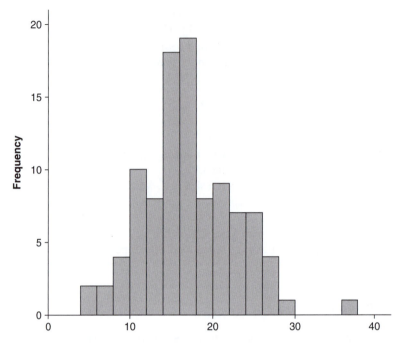

Figure 2.2 Histogram with bin size 2

When we asked you to decide which was better, we raised the issue of summarising our data, and presenting our data accurately. You can't argue with the fact that the first chart is accurate – it contains all of the information in the data. However, if we want to present our data accurately we use a table and present the numbers. A chart is used to present the pattern in our data. Using a bin size of 1 – that is, having each bar represent one point on the scale – leads to a couple of problems. First, when we have a very large number of points, we will have an awful lot of very thin stripes. Second, we are using a graph to show the pattern, and by using small bin sizes we get a very lumpy pattern, so we would rather smooth it a little by using larger bins.

A different way of presenting the data is shown in Figure 2.3. This is a bar chart.

	Tip
	Statisticians have developed a number of formulae to determine the best number of bins. However, the best thing to do is to draw your histogram, see what it looks like, and then if you don't like it, try a different bin size.

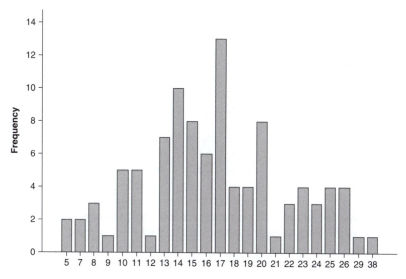

Figure 2.3   Bar chart

Common Mistakes: Draw your distribution in a bar chart

Figure 2.3 shows the same information as in Figure 2.1, except the scale along the x-axis (that's the horizontal one) is not spaced equally. We have treated the scale as if it were a categorical variable, not a continuous one. By doing this, we deceive the reader – it appears as if the highest score is only a little higher than the next highest score. This is not the case – it is considerably higher, as can be seen in the other charts.

Don't draw a bar chart for continuous measures.

Histograms and distributions

Histograms are very important in data analysis, because they allow us to examine the shape of the **distribution** of a variable. The shape is a pattern that forms when a histogram is plotted and is known as the distribution (if we are going to be strict about this, the distribution is defined by the formula that leads to that distribution, but thinking about it as a shape is much easier).

THE NORMAL DISTRIBUTION

One of the most commonly observed distributions is the **normal distribution** (also known as the *Gaussian distribution* even though, surprisingly, it wasn't first described by Gauss).

Optional Extra: Stigler's law of eponymy

Stigler's law of eponymy (Stigler, 1980) states that all statistical concepts which are named after someone, are named after someone who did not discover them. Gauss was not the first to mention the normal (or Gaussian) distribution – it was first used by De Moivre in 1733. Gauss first mentioned it in 1809, but claimed to have used it since 1794. It still got named after Gauss though.

The sharper-eyed amongst you will have noticed that for Stigler's law of eponymy to be correct, Stigler should not have first noted it. And, of course, he didn't.

A very large number of naturally occurring variables are normally distributed, and there are good reasons for this to be the case (we'll see why in the next chapter). A large number of statistical tests make the assumption that the data form a normal distribution. The histogram in Figure 2.4 shows a normal distribution.

A normal distribution is symmetrical and bell-shaped. It curves outwards at the top and then inwards nearer the bottom, the tails getting thinner and thinner. Figure 2.4 shows a perfect normal distribution. Your data will never form a perfect normal distribution, but as long as the distribution you have is close to a normal distribution, this probably does not matter too much (we'll be talking about this later on, when it does matter). If the distribution formed by your data is symmetrical, and approximately bell-shaped – that is, thick in the middle and thin at both ends – then you have something close to a normal distribution.

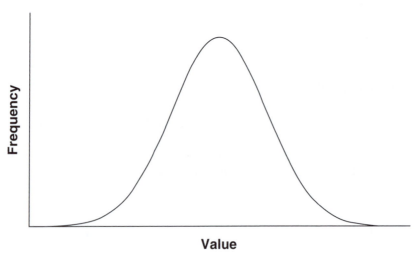

Figure 2.4 Histogram showing the shape of a normal distribution

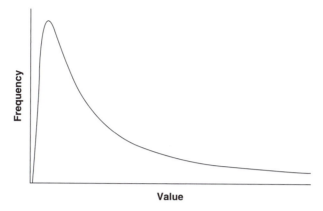

Figure 2.5   Histogram showing positively skewed distribution

Common Mistakes: What's normal?

When we talk about a normal distribution, we are using the word 'normal' as a technical term, with a special meaning. You cannot, therefore, refer to a usual distribution, a regular distribution, a standard distribution or an even distribution.

Throughout this book, we will come across some more examples of seemingly common words that have been requisitioned by statistics, and which you need to be careful with.

DEPARTING FROM NORMALITY

Some distributions are nearly normal but not quite. Look at Figures 2.5 and 2.6. Neither of these distributions is normal, but they are non-normal in quite different ways. Figure 2.5 does not have the characteristic symmetrical bell shape: it is the wrong shape. The second, on the other hand, looks to be approximately the correct shape, but has one or two pesky people on the right-hand side, who do not seem to be fitting in with the rest of the group. We will have a look at these two reasons for non-normality in turn.

Tip: Why does it matter if a distribution is normal or not?

The reason why we try and see the distributions as normal is that we have mathematical equations that can be used to draw a normal distribution. And we can use these equations in statistical tests.

A lot of tests depend on the data being from a normal distribution. That is why statisticians are often delighted to observe a normal distribution.

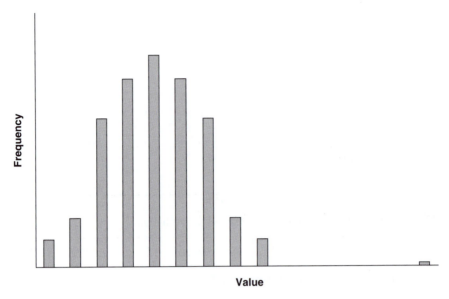

Figure 2.6   Histogram showing normal distribution with an outlier

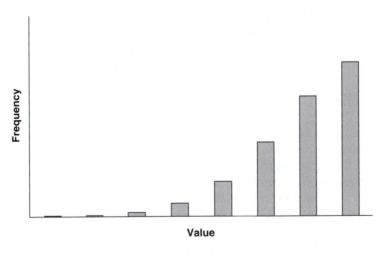

Figure 2.7   Histogram showing negatively skewed distribution

Wrong shape

If a distribution is the wrong shape, it can be the wrong shape for two reasons. First it can be the wrong shape because it is not symmetrical – this is called **skew**. Second it can be the wrong shape because it is not the characteristic bell shape – this is called **kurtosis**.

Skew

A non-symmetrical distribution is said to be *skewed*. Figures 2.5 and 2.7 both show distributions which are non-symmetrical. Figure 2.5 shows *positive* skew: this is where the curve rises rapidly and then drops off slowly. Figure 2.7 shows *negative* skew, where the curve rises slowly and then decreases rapidly. Skew, as we shall see later on, has some serious implications for some types of data analysis.

Tip: Positive and negative skew

Negative skew starts off flat, like a minus sign. Positive skew starts off going up, like part of a plus sign.

Skew often happens because of a **floor effect** or a **ceiling effect**. A floor effect occurs when only few of your subjects are strong enough to get off the floor. If you are interested in measuring how strong people are, you can give them weights to lift up. If your weights are too heavy most of the people will not get the weights off the floor, but some can lift very heavy weights, and you will find that you get a positively skewed distribution, as shown in Figure 2.8. Or if you set a maths test that is too hard then most of the class will

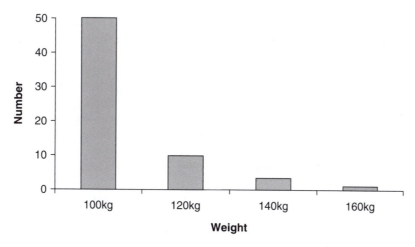

Figure 2.8   Histogram showing how many people lift different weights and illustrating a floor effect, which leads to positive skew

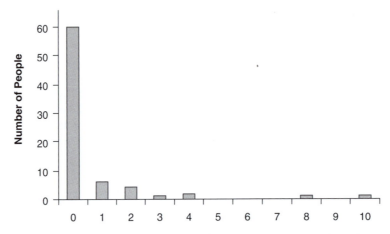

Figure 2.9   Histogram showing the number of times a group of people have been arrested

get zero and you won't find out very much about who was really bad at maths, and who was just OK.

Floor effects are common in many measures in psychology. For example, if we measure the levels of depression in a 'normal' population, we will find that most people are not very depressed, some are a little depressed and a small number are very depressed. The distribution of depression scores would look something like Figure 2.8. Often we want to measure how many times something has happened – and something cannot have happened less frequently than never. If we were interested in criminal behaviour, we could count the number of times a group of people had been arrested (Figure 2.9). Most people have never been arrested, some people have been arrested once (among them one of the authors), fewer have been arrested twice, and so on.

In a similar way, if you were carrying out a study to see how high people could jump, but found that the only room available was one that had a very low ceiling, you would find that how high people could jump will be influenced by them banging their heads on the ceiling. Figure 2.10 shows the distribution that is found in this experiment. We find that most people cannot jump over a hurdle higher than 80 cm, because they bang their heads on the ceiling. A few short people can jump over such a barrier, before they hit their head. The ceiling effect causes negative skew and a lot of headaches.

Ceiling effects are much less common in psychology, although they sometimes occur – most commonly when we are trying to ask questions to measure the range of some variable, and the questions are all too easy, or too low down the scale. For example, if you

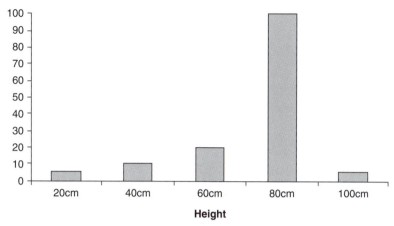

Figure 2.10   Distribution of height of barrier people can jump over, in a room with a very low ceiling. Ceiling effects cause negative skew

wanted to measure the ability of psychology students to do maths, you might give them the following test.

1. 3 + 4
2. 2 × 3
3. 7 − 5
4. 10 / 2
5. 6 × 8

Hopefully they would all answer all of the questions correctly (or at least most of the students would get most of the questions right). This causes a ceiling effect, which, as before, causes a headache.

Kurtosis

Kurtosis is much trickier than skew, and luckily for us, it's usually less of a problem. We'll give a very brief overview. If you are really interested in more, see DeCarlo (1997). Kurtosis occurs when there are either too many people at the extremes of the scale, or not enough people at the extremes, and this makes the distribution non-normal. A distribution is said to be *positively kurtosed* when there are insufficient people in the tails (ends) of the scores to make the distributions normal, and *negatively kurtosed* when there are too many people, too far away, in the tails of the distribution (see Figure 2.11).

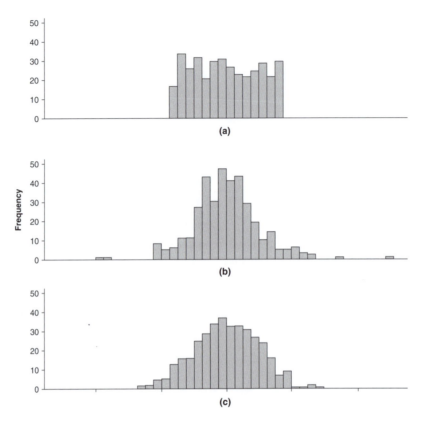

Figure 2.11   Three different distributions randomly sampled from (a) a negatively kurtosed distribution, (b) a positively kurtosed distribution, and (c) a normal distribution

Optional Extra: What's so tricky about kurtosis?

Have a look at the three distributions shown in Figure 2.12. If we told you that the middle distribution was normal, what would you say about the kurtosis of the other two? You might say that the bottom one is positively kurtosed, because there are too few people in the tails. You might say that the top one is negatively kurtosed, because there are too many people in the tails.

You'd be wrong. They are all normally distributed, but they are just spread out differently. When comparing distributions in the terms of kurtosis, it's hard to take into account the different spread, as well as the different shape.

(Continued)

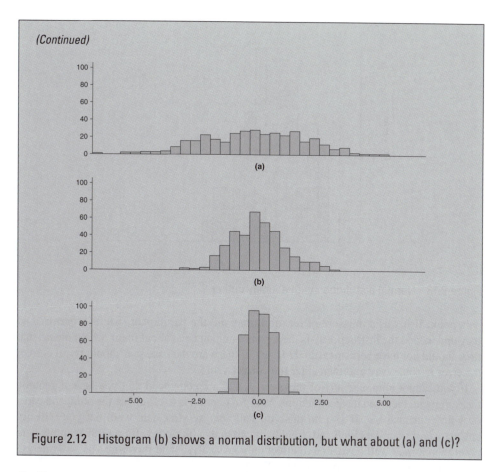

(Continued)

Figure 2.12   Histogram (b) shows a normal distribution, but what about (a) and (c)?

Outliers

Although your distribution is approximately normal, you may find that there are a small number of data points that lie outside the distribution. These are called **outliers**. They are usually easily spotted on a histogram such as that in Figure 2.13. The data seem to be normally distributed, but there is just one awkward person out there on the right-hand side. Outliers are easy to spot but deciding what to do with them can be much trickier. If you have an outlier such as this you should go through some checks before you decide what to do.

First, you should see if you have made an error. The most common cause of outliers is that you are using a computer to analyse your data and you have made an error while entering them. Look for numbers that should not be there. If the maximum score on a test is 10, and someone has scored 66, then you have made a mistake.

If you have checked that you did not make an error, you should now check that any measurement that you took was carried out correctly. Did a piece of equipment malfunction? If you have checked that, you should now decide whether the data point is a 'real'

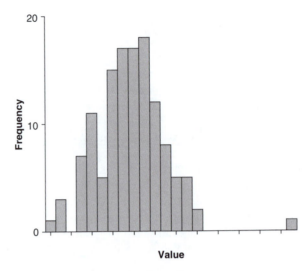

Figure 2.13   Normal distribution with a lonely outlier

data point. If it was a measure of reaction time, did the participant sneeze or yawn? Did they understand the instructions? Is there something unusual about them, which means that they should not have been measured? If any of these are the case you should try to correct the error in some way and then enter the correct value.

If you cannot eliminate any of these errors and are convinced that you have a genuine measurement, then you have a dilemma. Your first option is to eliminate the point and carry on with your analysis. If you do this you will analyse your data well, but you will not analyse *all* of your data well and, frankly, it can look a bit dodgy. If you can keep the data point then it may well have a large effect on your analysis and therefore you will analyse your data badly. Not much of a choice. (Sorry.)

MEASURES OF CENTRAL TENDENCY

Saying **central tendency** is just a posh way of saying 'average'. Average is a tricky word, because it has so many different meanings, so it is usually best to avoid it, and use a more specific word instead.

The mean

The **mean** is what we all think of as the average. Strictly speaking, it is called the *arithmetic mean* because there are other types of mean, though you are very unlikely to come across these.

As you probably know, the mean is calculated by adding up all of the scores and dividing by the number of individual scores. We can write this in equation form as follows:

$$\bar{x} = \frac{\sum x}{N}$$

Whatever it is we have measured and want to know the mean of, whether it is temperature, IQ, or severity of depression, or the time it took to solve a problem, we will just refer to it as x. (We could call it anything we like, such as Derek, but it is easier if we just call it x because that is what statisticians call it.)

The mean of the variable x, is written as $\bar{x}$, and often pronounced 'x-bar.'

Even if you know how to calculate the mean have a look at the above equation to get used to using this sort of equation. On the top of the fraction is the Greek capital letter Σ, or sigma. If you are using a computer and want to type a Σ you can type the letter 's' and change the font to symbol. You will come across this symbol quite often as you study research methods and statistics; it means 'add up' or 'take the sum of'. Σx therefore means 'add up all of the scores in x'.

On the bottom of the fraction, we have the letter N. Again we will come across N quite often. N always refers to the number of people in the sample.

The table below shows the variable x. We are going to find the mean of x.

x	5	6	7	8	9	10

To solve this problem we need to take the equation, and substitute each of the letters and symbols in it, with a number. Then we can work the answer out. We will take this one step at a time. If you think this is easy, that is good, because this is almost the hardest thing we are going to have to do. (And you thought statistics was a difficult subject!)

1. Write down the equation. This is always a good idea as it tells everyone you know what you're doing. $\quad \bar{x} = \frac{\sum x}{N}$

2. Σx means 'the sum of x.' That means add up all of the values in x. We will replace the Σx in the equation, with the sum. $\quad \bar{x} = \frac{5 + 6 + 7 + 8 + 9 + 10}{N}$

3. N means the number of individuals. We find this by counting the scores, and we find there are 6 of them. $\quad \bar{x} = \frac{5 + 6 + 7 + 8 + 9 + 10}{6}$

4. Now we will work out the top row: $5 + 6 + 7 + 8 + 9 + 10 = 45$. $\quad \bar{x} = \frac{45}{6}$

5. Now we work out the fraction that we are left with. $\quad \bar{x} = 7.5$

Assumptions

We often need to make assumptions in everyday life. We assume that everyone else will drive on the left-hand side of the road (or the right-hand side, depending on which country you are in). We assume that when we press a light switch, the light will come on. We assume that if we do enough work and understand enough then we will pass our exams. It's a bit disturbing if our assumptions are wrong. If we find that passing exams is not related to the amount of work we do, but that to pass an exam we actually need to have an uncle who works in the exams office, then our assumption is wrong. Similarly, if we assume everyone will drive on the left, but actually some people drive on the right, again our assumptions are wrong. In both these cases, the things that we say will be wrong. 'Work hard, and you'll pass,' is no longer correct. Assumptions in statistics are much the same as this. For our statistics to be correct, we need to make some assumptions. If these assumptions are wrong (statisticians usually say *violated*), then some of the things we say (the results of our statistical analysis) will be wrong.

However, while our assumptions will usually be broadly correct, they will never be *exactly* correct. People sometimes drive on the wrong side of the road (when parking, for example) and we manage not to crash into them (most of the time). In the same way, if our assumptions about data are wrong, but not too wrong, we need to be aware that our statistics will not be perfectly correct, but as long as the assumptions are not violated to any great extent, we will be OK.

When we calculate and interpret the mean, we are required to make two assumptions about our data.

1. The distribution is symmetrical. This means that there is not much skew, and no outliers on one side. (You can still *calculate* the mean if the distribution is not symmetrical, but *interpreting* it will be difficult because the result will give you a misleading value.)
2. The data are measured at the interval or ratio level. We saw earlier that data can be measured at a number of levels. It would not be sensible to calculate the mean colour of shoes. If we observed that half of the people were wearing blue shoes, and half of the people were wearing yellow shoes, it would make no sense to say that the mean (average) shoe colour was green.

Common Mistake: Garbage in, garbage out

When you use a computer program, it will not check that you are asking for sensible statistics. If you ask for the mean gender, the mean town people live in, and the mean shoe colour, it will give them.

Just don't put them into your report.

Median

The second most common measure of central tendency is the **median**. It is the middle score in a set of scores. The median is used when the mean is not valid, which might be because the data are not symmetrically or normally distributed, or because the data are measured at an ordinal level.

To obtain the median the scores should be placed in ascending order of size, from the smallest to the largest score. When there is an odd number of scores in the distribution, halve the number and take the next whole number up. This is the median. For example if there are 29 scores, the median is the 15th score. If there are an even number of scores, the median is the mean of the two middle scores.

We are going to find the median of the variable x below:

x:	1	14	3	7	5	4	3

The first thing to do is to rearrange the scores, in order, from smallest to largest. The rearranged data are presented below.

x:	1	3	3	4	5	7	14

We have seven data points. If we calculate $7 \div 2 = 3.5$ and we therefore take the next number above 3.5, which is 4. The fourth item is the median, and has the value 4.

Mode

The final measure of central tendency, rarely reported in research, is the **mode**. It is the most frequent score in the distribution or the most common observation among a group of scores. The mode is the best measure of central tendency for categorical data (although it's not even very useful for that).

In the dataset that we analysed in the previous example the number 3 was the only number to appear twice, and hence the mode is 3. In a frequency distribution the mode is very easy to see because it is the highest point of the distribution.

The problem with the mode is that it doesn't tell you very much. For example, imagine that we have a group of 20 females and 5 males. What is the mode? The mode is female. But that just tells us that there were more females than males. It doesn't take much more space to say that there were 20 females and 5 males.

Comparison of mean, median and mode

When deciding which of the three measures of central tendency to use, you should take into account the distribution of the scores. When the distribution is unimodal (i.e. has one mode) and symmetrical, then the mode, median and mean will have very similar values.

The mean is often the best average, for a couple of reasons. First, unlike the median, it uses all of the information available. Every number in the dataset has some influence on the mean. Secondly, the mean also has useful distributional properties (don't worry about what this means, we will cover it later), which the median does not have. The downfall of the mean is that it is affected by skew and by outliers.

Consider the following example. Five psychology students and five biology students were questioned to see how many lectures in research methods and statistics they attended. The results are shown below:

Psychology	Biology
17	20
19	20
19	20
17	20
18	1

Test yourself 3

Which group of students attended the most lectures?

The mean number of lectures attended by the psychology students was 18. The mean number of lectures attended by the biology students was 16.2. Thus it appears at first glance as if the psychology students attend more lectures. However, when we look more closely at the data, it is clear that there is an outlier who is skewing the data. If you were to think that a psychology student would be likely to attend about 18 lectures, you would be right. If you were to think that a biology student would be likely to attend about 16 lectures, you would be wrong.

If instead we use the median, we find that the median for the psychology students is 18, and the median for the biology students is 20. If you thought that the psychology student would be likely to attend 18 lectures, you would be right. If you thought that a biology student would be likely to attend about 20 lectures, you would be right 4 times out of 5. This shows that when the distribution is skewed, the median is a more representative value of central tendency.

When a distribution is skewed, the skewed values have the effect of 'pulling' the mean away from the true value. In a normal (or any symmetrical, unimodal) distribution, the mean, median and mode are all the same. In a skewed distribution, they are not the same.

A survey was carried out in which 100 students were asked how many books they consulted in their statistics module. Table 2.3 shows that 6 students are honest enough to say they never used a book, and that 3 students are making the unbelievable claim that they used 9 books. If we calculate the mode, median and mean, we find that the mode is equal to 1. More students have read 1 book than any other number of books. However, the median is slightly higher, at 2, and the mean is higher again, at 2.88. The histogram in Figure 2.14 shows the frequency plot, with the mode, median and mean marked on it. This separation of the mean, median and mode in the direction of the skew is a consistent effect in a skewed distribution. If the distribution were negatively skewed we would find the effect going in the opposite direction.

Table 2.3 *Frequency table of number of books used by students studying biostatistics*

Number of books	Frequency
0	6
1	25
2	20
3	18
4	12
5	8
6	4
7	2
8	2
9	3

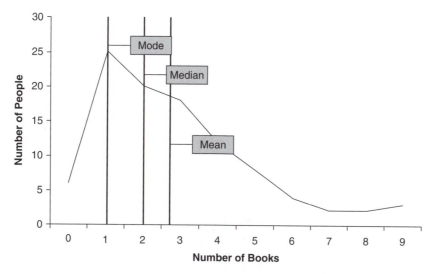

Figure 2.14   Frequency plot of number of books read and number of students. The mode, median and mean are all marked. Note that the median is to the right of the mode, and the mean is to the right of the median. This is to be expected in a skewed distribution

Optional Extra: Lies, damned lies and statistics (again)

One of the most common places to lie in statistics is to selectively choose the mean or median, depending on the argument that you want to present. Politicians are particularly guilty of this, for example when they talk about incomes. The distribution of income is highly skewed – some people don't earn much money, most people earn a moderate amount, and a very small number of people earn absolutely loads. This makes the mean amount of money that people earn rather unrepresentative. If the population of the United Kingdom was 50 million people (it's not, but it makes the sums easier), and one person gets £1 billion (from somewhere) then the mean amount of money that we each have goes up, by £20. So the mean wealth of people in the UK has risen by £20 but, ofcourse, you haven't got £20 more than you had a few minutes ago.

However, if I am a politician, and I want to argue that you are better off, I might use the mean. An example of this was the 1992 Conservative Party election campaign, in which they said 'You'd pay £1,000 more tax a year under Labour' (Figure 2.15).

(Continued)

(Continued)

Figure 2.15   An example of an election campaign using the mean, in an unrepresentative fashion

If the mean is £1,000, this doesn't mean that everyone will pay £1,000. Some people (for example, Richard Branson, the bosses at Sage Publications, Andy Field) will pay a lot more, while others (for example, poverty-stricken textbook authors) may pay no more, but on average, we will pay £1,000 more. A much more representative measure would be the median.

We know that politicians know that the median is the more appropriate measure of income, so when the minimum wage was introduced into the UK, it was based on the median income, not the mean. Child poverty is also defined as being in a family that earns less than 60% of median income.

There are lies, damn lies and statistics, but only if you don't understand statistics. One thing that this book tries to do is let you see through the bullshit that people (and politicians) try to give you. Read this book and be empowered.

Ordinal data

When data are measured on an ordinal scale it becomes something of a tricky issue to decide whether to use the mean or the median, or even the mode. Opinions differ between statisticians, so we have to be careful about what we decide to do.

The problem is that there is a very fuzzy line between what could definitely be called ordinal, and what could definitely be called interval. Some statisticians would argue that things like personality measures and attitude scales can only be considered to be ordinal data. The majority would argue that these can be considered to be interval data and therefore it is OK to use the mean. As we've already said (but it was an optional extra, so you probably skipped it) if you consult most journals you will find that most researchers, most of the time, will treat their data as if they are measured on an interval scale. (There is some research to back this up, but you don't really want to be reading papers about this sort of thing, do you?)

Tip: Dazed and confused

If you can't decide whether your data are ordinal or interval then it might not be due to your lack of knowledge. Some measures can be seen as either. For example, IQ scores are commonly dealt with *as if* they are interval, but some people argue that the data are really collected on an ordinal scale.

MEASURES OF DISPERSION AND SPREAD

When describing a variable it is necessary to describe the central tendency (the mean, median or mode). However, the central tendency doesn't mean a lot without a measure of **dispersion** or spread. An experiment was conducted to examine the effects of a new anti-depressant drug. An experimental group were given a dose of the drug and a control group were given a placebo (which looks like the drug but does not have the active ingredient). Later, both were scored by a psychiatrist on their level of depression. The results are shown in Table 2.4.

Table 2.4 *Mean scores in depression study*

Group	Mean score
Placebo	80
Drug	70

Test yourself 4

Did the drug have an effect on level of depression? How much of an effect was it?

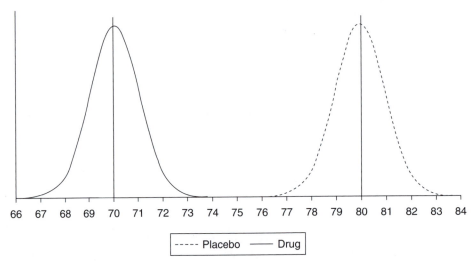

Figure 2.16 Drug group mean 70, placebo 60 group mean 80. When the dispersion is very small, this is a very large difference between the two groups. If you knew what someone's score was, you would know which group they were in.

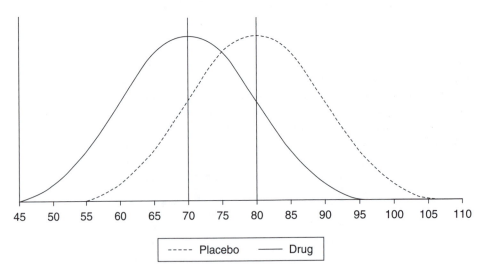

Figure 2.17 As with Figure 2.16, the drug group mean is 70 and the placebo 60 group mean is 80. In this case the dispersion is much larger and the two distributions overlap.

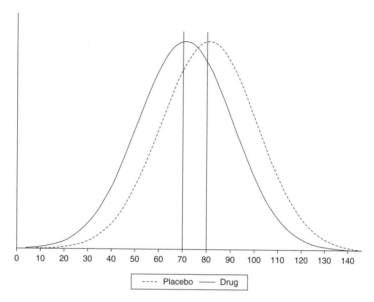

Figure 2.18   Placebo group mean 80, drug group mean 70. When the dispersion is large, the same size difference between the two groups is very hard to distinguish. There is very little difference between the two groups.

Of course, you cannot give a full answer to the question above because we haven't given you any information about the dispersion (spread) of the scores. Have a look at Figures 2.16–2.18. In each of these figures the results are as presented from Table 2.4. The means are the same in each graph. but the graphs look very different because the dispersions of the scores in each one are very different.

What this shows is that it is very hard to interpret a measure of central tendency without also having a measure of dispersion. In Figure 2.16 means are different and the distributions do not overlap, so there is clearly a big difference between the groups. In Figure 2.17 the distributions overlap but the bulk of the experimental groups scored higher than the control group. In Figure 2.18 the overlap is so great that it would not be possible to predict which group an individual was in from looking at their score. Therefore, if you only use the mean score to describe the data the results can be misleading – or, worse, meaningless. We will now look at three different measures of dispersion: the range, the inter-quartile range, and the standard deviation.

Range

The **range** is the simplest measure of dispersion. It is simply the distance between the highest score and the lowest score. It can be expressed as a single number, or sometimes it is expressed as the highest and lowest scores. We will find the range of the following variable *x*:

x:	4	11	17	12	3	15	10	2	8

To find the range we find the lowest value (2) and the highest value (17). Sometimes the range is expressed as a single figure, calculated as:

$$\text{Range} = \text{highest value} - \text{lowest value}$$

Sometimes it is expressed as the range of scores: here the range is from 2 to 17.

The range suffers from one huge problem, in that it is massively affected by any outliers that occur. If one person gets a strange score the range is very distorted and two dispersions that may actually be very similar are suddenly made to appear very different. Because of this, the range is only rarely used in psychological research. It is most commonly used to describe some aspect of a sample which does not need to be summarised with any degree of accuracy. For example 'the ages of the participants ranged from 18 to 48' or 'class sizes ranged from 23 to 36'.

Inter-quartile range

The **inter-quartile range** (IQR) is used with ordinal data or with non-normal distributions. If you use the median as the measure of central tendency then you'll probably use the inter-quartile range as a measure of dispersion.

The inter-quartile range is, you will be surprised to hear, the distance between the upper and lower quartiles. There are three quartiles in a variable – they are the three values that divide the variable into four groups. The first quartile happens one-quarter of the way up the data, which is also the 25th centile. The second quartile is the half-way point, which is the median, and is also the 50th centile. The third quartile is the three-quarter-way point, or the 75th centile.

Common Mistakes

1. People often think of the quartile as being the range of the data – that is that the bottom 25% of people are in the lower quartile. This is not correct.
2. Because the median is the 2nd quartile (and the 50th centile) there is no point presenting both in a table. (A computer will do this if you ask it to.)

To find the inter-quartile range the scores are placed in rank order and counted. The half-way point is the median (as we saw previously). The IQR is the distance between the quarter and three-quarters distance points.

To show how this is calculated, look at Table 2.5. This table shows a variable with 15 values, which have been placed in order. The median is the middle point, which is the 8th value, and is equal to 16. The upper quartile is found one-quarter of the way through the data, which is the 4th point, and is equal to 6. The upper quartile is found at the three-quarter-way point, and is equal to 23. The inter-quartile range is therefore 23 – 6 = 17.

Table 2.5   *Calculation of the inter-quartile range*

Count	Value	
1	2	
2	3	
3	5	
4	6	Lower quartile = 6
5	14	
6	15	
7	16	
8	16	Midpoint – median = 16
9	16	
10	21	
11	22	
12	23	Upper quartile = 23
13	24	
14	33	
15	45	

Unlike the range, the IQR does not go to the ends of the scales, and is therefore not affected by outliers. It also is not affected by skew and kurtosis to any great extent. You might also come across the *semi-inter-quartile range*. This is the inter-quartile range divided by 2.

Standard deviation

The final measure of dispersion that we shall look at is the **standard deviation** (SD). The standard deviation is like the mean, in that it takes all of the values in the dataset into account when it is calculated, and it is also like the mean in that it needs to make some assumptions about the shape of the distribution. To calculate the standard deviation, we must assume that we have a normal distribution.

So, why do we pay the price of making those assumptions? Why not just use the inter-quartile range? The SD can be used in a wide range of further analyses, as we will see later.

The standard deviation is calculated as follows:

$$\sigma = \sqrt{\frac{\sum(x - \bar{x})^2}{N - 1}}$$

 Tip

Don't be put off by the equation. Remember:
$\bar{x}$ is the mean;
Σ means 'add them all up';
σ is the standard deviation;
N is the number of cases.

Let us calculate the SD for the following variable (x):

x:	9	8	7	1	11	10	4	13	4	3	7

Just as when we looked at the mean, we will take the equation and substitute the symbols with numbers, and then we will work it out.

Table 2.6 shows some of the calulations. The main steps are as follows:

Table 2.6   *Calculating* $(\Sigma x - \bar{x})^2$

Case	Score	$\bar{x}$	$x - \bar{x}$	$(x - \bar{x})^2$
1	9	7	2	4
2	8	7	1	1
3	7	7	0	0
4	1	7	−6	36
5	11	7	4	16
6	10	7	3	9
7	4	7	−3	9
8	13	7	6	36
9	4	7	−3	9
10	3	7	−4	16
11	7	7	0	0
Totals	77			136

1. Write down the equation. The x refers to each value, $\bar{x}$ is the mean, the superscript 2 means 'square' and the Σ is the Greek letter sigma, which means 'take the sum of'.

$$\sigma = \sqrt{\frac{\Sigma (x - \bar{x})^2}{N - 1}}$$

2. The first thing to do is draw a table, such as that shown above. The first column (score) contains the individual scores. The second column contains the mean. We looked at the calculation of the mean earlier, so we will just go through the workings on the right-hand side. The mean is 7, so we write the number 7 in the second column.

$$\bar{x} = \frac{9 + 8 + 7 + 11 + 10 + 4 + 13 + 4 + 3 + 7}{11}$$

$$\bar{x} = \frac{77}{11}$$

$$\bar{x} = 7$$

3. The next stage is to calculate $x - \bar{x}$ for each person. The calculations for the first two individuals are calculated on the right, and we have filled in the rest in Table 2.6.

$$9 - 7 = 2$$
$$8 - 7 = 1$$

4. Next we need to calculate $(x - \bar{x})^2$. To do this, we square each of the values that we calculated at stage 3. Again, we have shown the first two cases on the right, and we have filled in the Table 2.6.

$$2^2 = 2 \times 2 = 4$$
$$1^2 = 1 \times 1 = 1$$

5. We can add each of these values together, to find $\Sigma (x - \bar{x})^2$.

$$\Sigma (x - \bar{x})^2 = 4 + 1 + 0 + 36 + 16 + 9 + 9 + 36 + 9 + 16 + 0$$

6. Now we have all of the information to put into the equation. By doing this one small stage at a time, you will be less likely to make a mistake. While I do the calculations on the right, I will give instructions in this column. You can follow one, the other, or both.

$$\sigma = \sqrt{\frac{136}{11 - 1}}$$

7. Calculate $N - 1$.

$$\Sigma (x - \bar{x})^2 = 136$$

$N = 11$ (that's how many rows we have in Table 2.6), so $N - 1 = 10$. This gives the bottom half of the fraction.

$$\sigma = \sqrt{\frac{136}{10}}$$

8. Now divide the top half of the fraction by the bottom half: $136 \div 10 = 13.6$.

9. Find the square root in step 7. (You will almost certainly need a calculator to do this.)
$\sqrt{13.6} = 3.69$.
This is the standard deviation.

$$\sigma = \sqrt{13.6}$$

$$\sigma = 3.69$$

Optional Extra: It's (almost) all Greek to me

The symbol used for the standard deviation is a little confusing, and this arises because there are actually two different forms of the standard deviation. The first is the *sample standard deviation*, which is referred to as *s*, and is calculated using

$$s = \sqrt{\frac{\sum(x - \bar{x})^2}{n}}$$

However, the sample standard deviation suffers from a problem – it is a biased estimator of the population standard deviation. This means that if we took lots of samples from a population, and calculated the standard deviation using the above formula, we would not expect the standard average of each of those standard deviations to match the population standard deviations. The sample standard deviations would, on average, be a bit too low. (In contrast, if we did this with the mean, we would find that the mean of all the means did match the population mean – hence the mean is an *unbiased* estimator).

Instead, we use the unbiased standard deviation, or the *population standard deviation*, which is given by this equation:

$$\sigma = \sqrt{\frac{\sum(x - \bar{x})^2}{n - 1}}$$

Notice that it looks very similar to the previous one, except it has *n* –1 instead of *n*. Because this is a population estimate (we'll discuss this on page 201) it is written with a Greek letter – the lower-case sigma, σ.

In statistics, we never want the (biased) sample standard deviation, we always want the population standard deviation, so whenever we talk about the standard deviation, we are talking about σ, not *s*.

One more thing – if you ever happen to use Excel to calculate a standard deviation, there are two functions available. Stdev() is the standard deviation that we use in statistics, which we have called the population standard deviation and refer to as σ; and stdevp(), very confusingly, is what Excel calls the population standard deviation, but which we call the sample standard deviation, *s*.

BOXPLOTS FOR EXPLORING DATA

We have focused so far on describing data using summary statistics (summary statistics is a posh way of saying 'numbers'). However, there are also a number of graphical techniques that can be used. We'll focus on one of the most useful, the **boxplot**, or box and whisker plot.

We used Table 2.5 to calculate the inter-quartile range. We'll now use it again to draw a boxplot (see Figure 2.19).

The median in a boxplot is represented with a thick line, and the upper and lower quartiles are shown as a box around the median. The whiskers then extend from the box to the highest and the lowest points – *unless* this would mean that the length of the whisker would be more than 1.5 times the length of the box, in which case it extends to the furthest point which means it does not exceed 1.5 times the length of the box. The computer defines that point as an outlier.

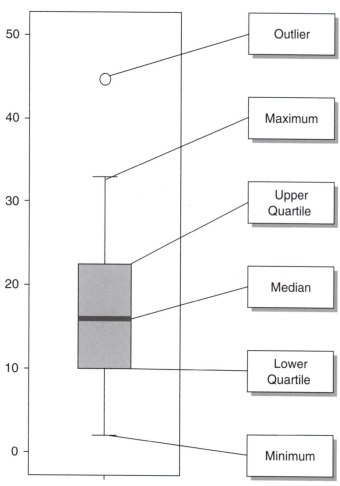

Figure 2.19   Boxplot of the data in Table 2.5

Test yourself 5

Look at the boxplot, showing four variables, in Figure 2.20. Below this are four histograms, showing the same variables. Except we've jumbled up the order. See if you can decide which histogram goes with each boxplot. (The sample sizes are all 100.)

Answers are given at the end of the chapter.

(1)

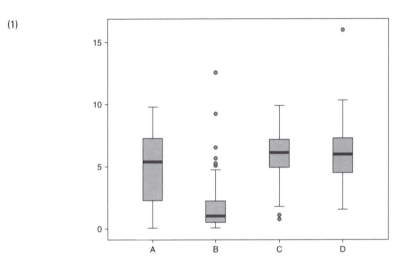

Figure 2.20 Which of the following four distributions goes with each of the four boxplots?

(2)

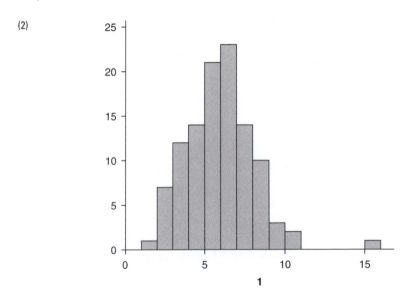

(Continued)

(Continued)

(3)

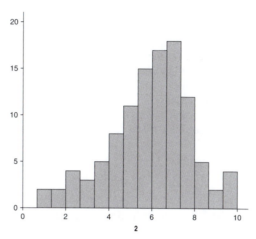

(4)

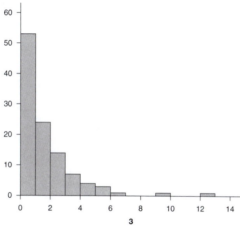

(5)

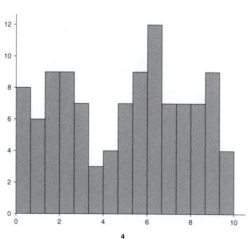

Common Mistakes

1. If you use a computer program, such as SPSS, to draw a boxplot, you will find that it might label the outlier with something like the case number. Whilst this is useful for you – you can find the person in your dataset, it is useless for anyone reading your report – they don't have your data, after all. (It might even be worse than useless – they might think it is something important, which they don't understand.)
2. Notice that we said *the computer defines that point as an outlier*. That doesn't mean *you* have to define it as an outlier. Don't blindly follow the computer – *you* have to decide if it is an outlier.

One final point to note about boxplots, which you may have realised from this exercise – quite simply, they save space. With boxplots, we showed the distribution of four variables using one graph. If we wanted to use histograms, we would need four graphs.

SUMMARY

We've looked at some of the most common techniques that are used to describe statistics. There are a range of measures of central tendency and dispersion and the choice of technique depends on the type of measurement you have and the type of distribution you observe in the data. The principles are straightforward even if the technical terms seem complicated and the equations look off-putting. Concentrate on the principles and everything will fall into place.

Test yourself answers

Harry Potter (page 12)

We don't know how many children were asked or what they said, but here are some data from 20 children that match the statistics the reporters gave:

1,000,000,000	3
1,000,000,000	3
1,000,000	3
10,000	3
1,000	3

500	3
300	3
20	3
3	3
3	3

Some of the children gave extreme answers, which were feasible (to watch the film a billion times would take almost 300,000 years, and that's if you didn't eat, sleep or go to the toilet). We could discard the outliers, because they are clearly not sensible (even watching it 1,000 times will take over 3 months). When we do this, we have a highly skewed distribution, in which case a sensible thing to do would be to take the median, which gives 3.

Test yourself 1

1. Shoe size is a measurement variable, and it is interval, not ratio. We could argue about whether it was discrete or continuous. I would say that it was continuous, because it would be possible to have size 12¼ shoes, but no one would make them.
2. Height is a continuous, ratio measure. If I am 1 metre tall, and you are 2 metres tall, you are twice as tall as me.
3. Phone number is a nominal measure – there is no meaningful order to phone numbers.
4. Degrees celsius is a continuous interval measure – 0°C is not a true zero point.
5. Position in the top 40 is an ordinal measure.
6. Number of CD sales is a discrete, ratio measure.
7. Cash earned from CD sales is a continuous, ratio measure. You could earn 0.001p, you just couldn't spend it.
8. Length of headache is a continuous, ratio measure.
9. Health rating on this scale is an ordered categorical measure.
10. Shoe colour is a nominal measure; shoes can be a number of colours, but they are not in any order.
11. Sex is a binary measure. Gender might be considered to be a continuous measure, you can be more or less masculine or feminine, but you must be male or female.
12. Number of times pecked by a duck is a ratio, discrete measure.
13. IQ is argued about. Most psychologists treat it as a continuous measure, but some people argue that it is actually ordinal. It is not ratio, because you cannot have an IQ of zero.
14. Blood pressure is a continuous measure. We could argue about whether is was ratio or not – it appears to be ratio, because it is measured in millimetres of mercury, but you cannot have a blood pressure of zero, because you would be dead. And if your blood pressure was low, around 20, say, you would be dead as well (or very soon). The zero doesn't really mean anything, so we would treat it as interval.

Test yourself 5

A4. The boxplot shows very short whiskers, relative to the length of the box. This means that the distribution is not very spread out. Histogram 4 is kurtosed; in other words, the distribution has very short tails, and does not spread out very much.

B3. In the boxplot, the median line is not in the middle of the box. This is our first clue that the data are skewed. The second clue is that the whiskers are of very different lengths, meaning that the data extend more in one direction than the other. Finally, there are some outliers at the top. All of these match the distribution shown in histogram 3.

C2. In the boxplot, the median line is in the middle of the box. The whiskers are of equal length. This indicates that the distribution is symmetrical. In addition, the whiskers are a bit longer than the length of the box. This indicates that the distribution has more points in the 'tails' than boxplot A. There are two outliers highlighted by the computer, but in a sample size of 100, this should not surprise us. The distribution shown in histogram 2 is close to a normal distribution, and this is what the boxplot shows us.

D1. Finally, boxplot D looks very similar to C, except that there is an outlier. Boxplot C showed a normal distribution, so we should expect the histogram to show a normal distribution, but also have an outlier, which is exactly what histogram 1 shows.

USING SPSS

The statistics that we have shown in this chapter can all be calculated in SPSS using the Frequencies command. Select: **Analyze** ⇒ Descriptive Statistics ⇒ Frequencies:

Click on the **Statistics** button:

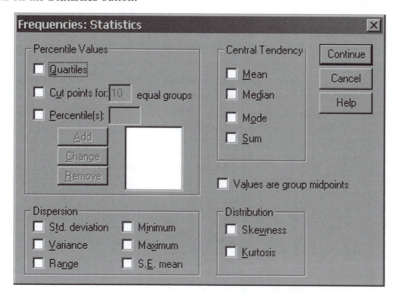

Choose the statistics that are best suited to your data. Click on **Continue**.
Now click on **Charts**:

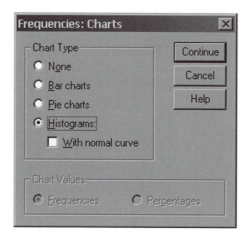

Choose the type of chart you want. (You almost certainly want a histogram).

Note that the output table that is produced shows the difference between exploratory and descriptive statistics. The valid scores are given because there might be scores that are missing or that have been defined as missing values. There are two columns for percentage – percent, and valid percent. This is to help you, the data analyst, understand what is happening. In our data they are the same so don't put them both into your report.

Finally, there is the cumulative percent. Again, this might be useful to you but it probably won't be useful to the reader of your report. If it's not useful to the reader don't put it in your report.

		Frequency	Percent	Valid Percent	Cumulative Percent
Valid	5	2	2.0	2.0	2.0
	7	2	2.0	2.0	4.0
	8	3	3.0	3.0	7.0
	9	1	1.0	1.0	8.0
	10	5	5.0	5.0	13.0
	11	5	5.0	5.0	18.0
	12	1	1.0	1.0	19.0
	13	7	7.0	7.0	26.0
	14	10	10.0	10.0	36.0
	15	8	8.0	8.0	44.0
	16	6	6.0	6.0	50.0
	17	13	13.0	13.0	63.0
	18	4	4.0	4.0	67.0
	19	4	4.0	4.0	71.0
	20	8	8.0	8.0	79.0
	21	1	1.0	1.0	80.0
	22	3	3.0	3.0	83.0
	23	4	4.0	4.0	87.0
	24	3	3.0	3.0	90.0
	25	4	4.0	4.0	94.0
	26	4	4.0	4.0	98.0
	29	1	1.0	1.0	99.0
	38	1	1.0	1.0	100.0
	Total	100	100.0	100.0	

Boxplots are drawn through the **Graphs** command. Select **Graphs** ⇒ **Boxplot**:

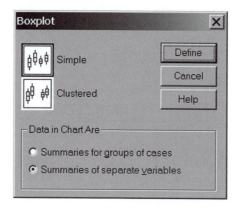

Select **Simple** (this is the default). If you want to draw a boxplot for one or more variables, choose **Summaries of separate variables**. If you want to have separate boxplots for groups of variables, choose **Summaries for groups of cases**. Click on **Define**. Select the variables you want to have in your boxplot:

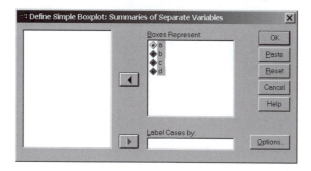

Click **OK**.

3

Samples, populations and the normal distribution

What's in this chapter?

- Samples and populations
- The normal distribution (continued)
- *z*-scores
- The standard error
- Using SPSS

KEY TERMS

central limit theorem
descriptive statistics
generalisations
histogram
inferential statistics
infinity
normal distribution
parameters
population

probability
random sample
representative
sample
sampling distribution of the mean
standard error
uncertainty
variation
volunteer sample
z-score

INTRODUCTION

This chapter is about the tricky task of selecting a sample and making sense of the data you get from it. We often take for granted that the results from one group of people will be similar to those of another group, but why should we? If we carried out our opinion poll in the middle of a shopping centre we might get very different results from those we would get in the Tap Room of the Dog and Partridge. And then there is the matter of the normal distribution. Now read on.

Test yourself 1

To what extent do you believe the claims made in the following two stories? What more information do you need to know if you wanted to evaluate them?

Smoking 'in decline' in Scotland

The number of smokers in Scotland has dropped by nearly 40,000 in a year, according to a national survey.

The 2004 Scottish Household Survey found that 27% of adults smoked, compared to 28% in the previous year.

(BBC News, 4 August, 2005: http://news.bbc.co.uk/1/hi/scotland/4745453.stm)

Survey reveals students' debt fears

Nearly half of this year's freshers say that they would be less inclined to go to university next year when the new top-up fees regime is introduced, according to a new survey.

Students who enter university in September are expecting to spend £28,600 on fees, rent and maintenance during the course of their degrees and most are anticipating a final debt of around £13,680, a NatWest [bank] survey of student finance found.

(The Guardian, 9 August 2005: http://education.guardian.co.uk/students/finance/story/0,,1545658,00.html)

Answers are given at the end of the chapter.

POPULATIONS

In psychology (and in science generally) we are usually interested in making statements that are applicable to large numbers of people. We call this group the **population** (there's another of those occasions where we have a term with a special meaning, which is different from how you might have used it in everyday life. Watch out for these). In every day speech we use the term 'population' to refer to everyone who lives in a given country, but this is only one of many ways to define our research populations. For example, if we wanted to carry out a political opinion poll we would define our population as all people eligible to vote in (say) UK elections. This is a large number of people, but probably only about half of all those people who live in the UK. Sometimes we are only interested in a select group of people and in this case our research population might be, for example, people under the age of 25 with diabetes living in England. The research population can be almost any group of people, but it is important to be clear about how you are defining that population.

We can't study all the people we are interested in because this would be too difficult. There are too many of them, and besides, there is no need. Instead, we take a subset of the population that we are interested in, and we study those people instead. We then try to generalise our results from the sample to the population. We have two branches of statistics: **descriptive statistics**, which is about describing what we have in the sample; and **inferential statistics**, which is about inferring from the sample to the population we are interested in. However, we are getting ahead of ourselves here. Before we can consider inferential statistics, we need to look at ways of getting our sample from our population.

Tip: One step beyond

When we *infer* something, this means we *go beyond* what we know to make an intelligent guess. For example, if we want to know the average height of students in a college we could find the true value by measuring everyone and calculating the mean height. However, we are more likely to measure a few students (a sample) and make an intelligent guess (inference) that the average height of the students we have measured is similar to the average height of all students at the college. We have gone beyond our knowledge to make an intelligent guess.

RANDOM SAMPLING

It is rarely possible to study the whole population of interest, and even when you believe that you have studied the whole population, the population is likely to change in the future, so your research will no longer cover the population. So, instead of examining a population, we study a **sample**. We then make generalisations (extrapolations) from our population to our sample. We infer from our sample to our population, hence the term 'inferential statistics'. However, in order to make these generalisations, we need to make sure, as far as we can, that our sample is an unbiased and **representative** sample of our population. (We also need to make sure that the sample is large enough, but we will come back to that in another chapter.)

Random sampling is the 'gold standard' to which other sampling techniques aspire. To be a **random sample** two conditions have to be satisfied:

1. Every member of the population must have an equal chance of being selected.
2. The selection of any one member of the population should not affect the chances of any other being selected.

To carry out random selection, we need to do something like writing the names of every member of a population on a piece of paper, putting the pieces of paper into a large hat, stirring them around and then pulling out some of the pieces of paper. (Nowadays we would use a computer to do this for us, though this is less fun.)

The second criterion is the one that people often forget about. The chance of selecting one person from your population must not affect the chance of another person being selected. If you select one child from each class in a school you have violated this assumption because when you selected one child you altered the probability of any other child in that class being selected. (The same is true if you select one person from each household, or street, or town, or group of friends.) Alternatively, if you want to obtain a random sample of students in your college or university, you might randomly select flats or houses and then select everyone in each of those houses. Again, you have violated the second criterion. When you selected one person in the flat or house the probability of every other person being selected changed, hence you violated the second criterion.

Common Mistakes: Using random sampling

It is very, very rare for anyone to use random sampling. If you write in your report that you used random sampling then one of the following is true:

(a)   You are lying.
(b)   You don't know what you are talking about.
(c)   Both of the above.

Don't use the term 'random sample'. It is an idea rather than a reality.

In practice it is very difficult to carry out random sampling. Imagine that you want a random sample of students at a university. First you have to get all their names, and select them either from a hat (see above) or using some sort of random number generator on a computer. This is the easy bit. After you have selected them you then have to go and find them all. Some of their addresses will be wrong, some will have left the country, some will have changed their name or even forgotten it. You have more chance of meeting Elvis on the Easter Bunny's knee than you have of finding your entire random sample. It can't be done.

Because random sampling is virtually impossible, we need some other approaches. There are a wide range of approaches to sampling, so many that entire books have been written on the subject (e.g. Kish, 1965; Cochran, 1977), but we don't want to go into that much detail. As a psychology student, or even as a psychology researcher, you are usually confined to volunteer samples of some sort. This commonly means coercing or bribing the most available people to take part in the study.

A **volunteer sample** involves requesting (sometimes through advertising) that individuals take part in a research project. Sometimes you will be active and approach a group of people whom you know to exist and invite them to take part in your study. For example, Vaughan, Morrison and Miller (2003) wanted to look at the illness perceptions of people with multiple sclerosis. To do this they invited people who had been newly diagnosed with multiple sclerosis and referred to a clinic to take part in their research.

On the other hand, Smits, De Boeck and Vansteelandt (2004) were not interested in any special group of people, for the purposes of their study of verbally aggressive behaviour, so they used a group of first-year psychology students at Leuven University, Belgium. (It is an unsurprising coincidence that they worked in Leuven University, Belgium.)

Finally, Swift, Hall, Didcott and Reilly (1998) carried out a study of long-term cannabis users in Australia. The problem with this sort of study is that if you stick a poster up, asking for volunteers who happen to be long-term cannabis users, you probably are not going to get a lot of replies. Instead, Swift, et al. used a **snowball sample**, in which they gained the trust of a small group of users and asked these people to introduce potential other volunteers to the researchers. In this way they gathered participants in the way a snowball gathers more snow when you roll it down a hill.

Each of these studies used a volunteer sample, but what they actually did to obtain their sample was very different. When you are writing your report you need to say more than that you used 'volunteer sampling'. You need to say what you actually did. The key issue with all sample selection is that you need to have a clear statement of your population and a good idea of how representative your sample is.

To understand how we make inferences from samples to populations, we need to have another look at the normal distribution. This might seem unrelated, but at the end of this chapter, we will tie it all together and hopefully make sense of it.

 Tip

The next section is rather long and abstract, which makes it difficult. You don't need to understand this material in order to read the rest of the book, but it does provide a foundation for the rest of the book.

(Continued)

(Continued)

We suggest one of three approaches:

1. Jump straight to the next chapter. If you want to understand why the things we discuss in the next chapter work then come back to this one after you have read it.
2. Read this chapter until it gets to be too much. Then read the other chapters. When you have read those it might help you to understand why this one is important.
3. Read this one all the way through, even the bits that don't make sense. When you get to the next chapters, you might see what they were about.

If you were to read any psychological research it will not mention the information in this chapter. However, the researchers do understand this material, even if it doesn't show.

THE NORMAL DISTRIBUTION

In the previous chapter we looked at the **normal distribution** and we hinted at how important that distribution was. In this chapter we will look at why the normal distribution is important and how it relates to the standard deviation.

Remember from the previous chapter that when we draw a **histogram** of the frequencies of different values they plot a shape, or distribution. Figure 3.1 shows a perfect normal

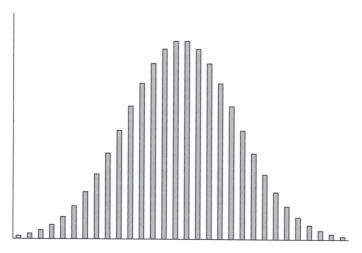

Figure 3.1   A normal distribution

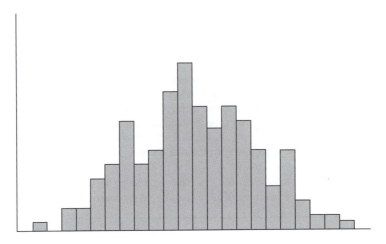

Figure 3.2   An approximate normal distribution

distribution. Many variables that can be measured on continuous scales are (approximately) normally distributed – that is, they form a bell-shaped curve on a histogram. Of course, we cheated to draw that distribution. I calculated the number of individuals who would be in each category, and then drew a graph of it.

What you are much more likely to get is something that approximates a normal distribution but is lumpier, and the fewer people you have the lumpier that distribution is going to be. Figure 3.2 shows data that are approximately normally distributed, with a sample size of 200.

Normal distributions are interesting to us for a number of reasons. The main one is that many statistical tests make the assumption that our data are normally distributed. Of course, you might ask why we should like this distribution above all others, and why statistical tests do assume that we have a normal distribution.

It turns out that normal distributions are rather important things. Let's think about what happens when we roll a die. If we roll it enough times we will get a distribution where every number will appear an equal number of times. This is shown in Figure 3.3. The distribution is flat; this is a uniform distribution.

However, consider what happens when we roll the die twice and find the sum of the two rolls. We can see from Figure 3.4 that the distribution is no longer uniform. This is because there is only one way to get the extreme scores like 12 and 2. To get a score of 12, die one must be a 6 and die two must also be a 6. To get a score of 7, however, there are six possible combinations of the two dice.

If we were to carry out the same exercise for three dice we would find a distribution like Figure 3.5. Now something interesting is happening. The shape of the distribution is no

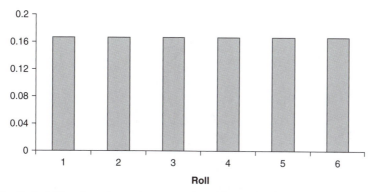

Figure 3.3   Probability of each number occurring, given roll of one die

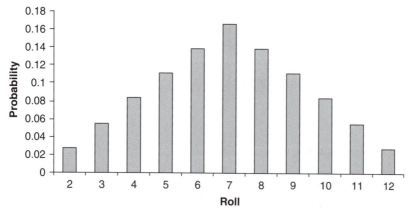

Figure 3.4   Probability of each value occurring, given roll of two dice

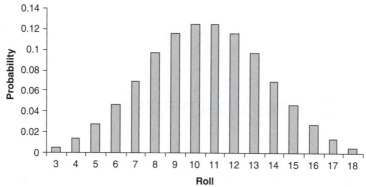

Figure 3.5   Probability of each value occurring, given roll of three dice

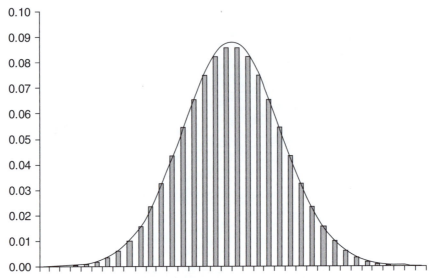

Figure 3.6   Distribution of mean score of 7 dice rolls (bars) and normal distribution with same mean and standard deviation (line)

longer triangular, as it was with two dice, but the sides are becoming curved. And this change in shape is not a coincidence. The distribution is getting closer to a normal distribution. When we use seven dice, the histogram is shown in Figure 3.6, along with a perfect normal distribution. There is some difference between the two (it's hard to see, but there are differences in the middle, and towards the ends) but the two distributions are very similar to one another.

In fact, whenever we add uniform distributions, we get closer to a normal distribution. It is not unfeasible that many final values are arrived at through a series of processes, each of which involved a uniform distribution. Similarly, if we add normal distributions we always end up with normal distributions.

LINE CHARTS, AREAS AND NUMBERS OF PEOPLE

Where we have a histogram represented as a line chart, with a continuous variable on the *x*-axis (and where the *y*-axis represents the frequency density, but we won't worry about that bit), we can calculate the number of people who have any score, or range of scores, by calculating the area of the chart.

Table 3.1   *Test score frequencies*

Score	1	2	3	4	5	6	7	8	9	10
Frequency	10	10	10	10	10	10	10	10	10	10

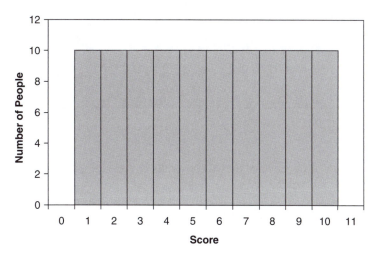

Figure 3.7   Frequency density plot drawn using data in Table 3.1

Let's look at a simple example. Table 3.1 shows the number of people (frequency) who have scored each possible value on a test. Figure 3.7 shows a histogram of those data (it's not very interesting, is it? But soon it will be). If we want to know how many people scored within a particular range of scores, we could count them. For example, if we wanted to know how many people scored 5 or less, we could add up the numbers who scored 1, 2, 3, 4 and 5. This would make 50 people.

However, we could do it in another way. In this type of chart, the area under the curve is equal to the number of people in that area. We've shown this in Figure 3.8. The area we are interested in is 10 units high (on the *y*-axis) and 5 units wide (on the *x*-axis), so the total area is $10 \times 5 = 50$. If 50 people scored 5 or less, and 50 people scored more than 5, then 50% of people scored 5 or less. Therefore the probability that a person scores 5 or less is 0.5.

But what do we do if we have a more complex shape? The answer is the same. We calculate the area under the curve, which will give the number of people, which will give the probability of that range of responses.

Figure 3.9 shows a (slightly) more complex graph. You might remember from school (but don't worry if you don't) that the area of a triangle is given by

$$W \times H \times 0.5$$

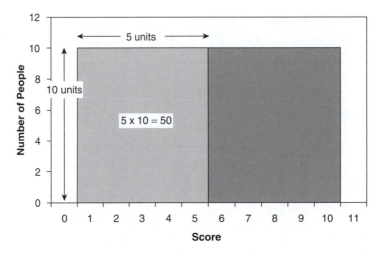

Figure 3.8 Frequency density plot drawn using data in Table 3.1, with the area of people scoring 5 or under highlighted

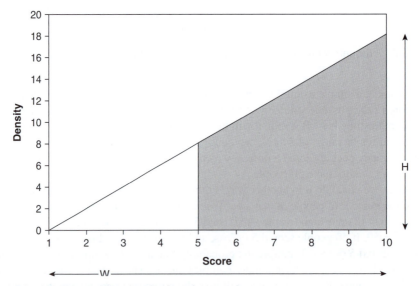

Figure 3.9 A more complex density function graph

where W is the width of the triangle, and H is the height. We have shown W and H for the large triangle on the figure. If we want to know the probability of scoring less than 5, we can, again, use the areas of the shapes. We calculate the area of the large triangle, and the area of the small triangle, and the probability is the area of the small triangle divided by the area of the large triangle.

We can do the same thing with a normal distribution. There is a formula that we use to calculate the area under the curve, for any value taken from the normal distribution, and we can use this to calculate the probability of any range of responses. We'll see how to do this in the next section. (We're not even going to show you the formula, it's a bit nasty, and it involves calculus, and you'll never have to know or use it).

But first, we've not had an optional extra for a while.

Optional Extra: The normal distribution, the area under the curve, and infinity

The graphs that we've been drawing have a definite beginning and end to the x-axis. But the normal distribution goes on to **infinity** in each direction. There is no beginning and end to the x-axis on a normal distribution plot, at least in theory. And infinity (according to Douglas Adams, in *The Restaurant at the End of the Universe* (1980) is: 'Bigger than the biggest thing ever and then some. Much bigger than that in fact, really amazingly immense, a totally stunning size, real "wow, that's big!", time. Infinity is just so big that by comparison, bigness itself looks really titchy. Gigantic multiplied by colossal multiplied by staggeringly huge is the sort of concept we are trying to get across here.'

We can't draw graphs that big. And if we can't draw a graph that big, how do we calculate the area of a shape that goes on for ever? This might seem like a problem, to people like you and us, but to really clever mathematicians, it's not a problem at all. Let's give an example.

Suppose I start to add the numbers:

$$\frac{1}{1} + \frac{1}{2} + \frac{1}{4} + \frac{1}{8} + \frac{1}{16} + \dots$$

where … means keep going for ever. What will I get? The answer is 2. But hold on, you say, when we get to 2, we are going to keep adding more numbers. Yes, we say, and the answer will still be 2. This is similar to the normal distribution – it keeps going for ever, but we know what it adds up to.

If that never crossed your mind as even being a problem, we apologise. (If it had crossed your mind, and you want to know more about infinity, you could read Barrow (2005). Be warned though. It says things like: 'If our Universe is infinite then an infinite number of exact copies of you are, at this very moment, reading an identical sentence on an identical planet somewhere else in the Universe.' And that's just on the cover.)

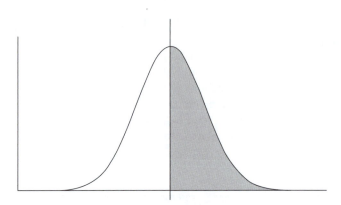

Figure 3.10 Normal distribution with line drawn at the mean, and half the area shaded. Half of people score above the mean, and therefore there is a 50% chance that any person will be above the mean

PROBABILITY AND NORMAL DISTRIBUTIONS

The great advantage òf a normal distribution is that if you know (or can estimate) two values (the mean and the standard deviation) you know everything there is to know about it. This means that we can use the area under the curve to find the **probability** of any value, or range of values.

For example, we know that in a normal distribution half of the scores will lie above the mean and half of the scores will lie below the mean. The shaded area in Figure 3.10 represents half of the scores. If someone asks 'What is the probability that someone will score above the mean', we know that the answer is 0.5. (Meaning that half of us are forever destined to be below average.)

However, we can go further than this, we can find out how likely any score is. This is shown in Figure 3.11. In a normal distribution:

- 95.45% of cases lie within 2 SDs of the mean.
- 47.72% of cases lie between the mean and –2 SDs.
- 49.9% of cases lie between the mean and +3 SDs.
- 2.27% of cases lie more than 2 SDs below the mean.

A score that is presented in terms of the number of standard deviations above the mean is called a *z*-**score**. To calculate a *z*-score, we use the following formula:

$$z = \frac{\text{score} - \text{mean}}{\sigma}$$

(remember that σ is the standard deviation)

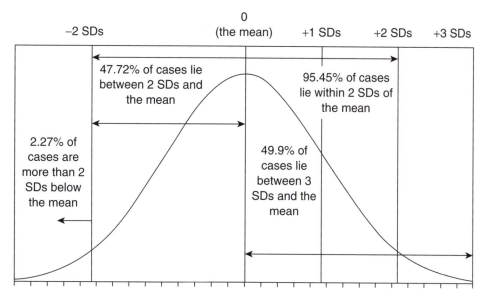

Figure 3.11 Normal distribution showing percentages of people with different ranges of scores

Tip: How to check out a *z*-score

If you have access to MS Excel, you can type the following into a cell: =normsdist(z). Except that instead of z you type the number you are interested in. So if I type = normsdist(2), Excel will give me the value 0.9772. This means that 97.72% of all scores are less than this score.

If you do not have access to Microsoft Excel, there are other programs which are available for free. OpenOffice is available for free, and can be downloaded from http:// www.openof-fice.org

There are also a lot of calculators on the web. For example, if you go to the website http://www-stat.stanford.edu/~naras/jsm/examplebot.html, you will find a useful online calcu-lator. Change the distribution to **Normal Distribution**, type 2 into the first box, at the bottom, and then click Left because we are interested in the proportion of cases to the left (that's below) that value. The program, as you can see, says '0.9772498680518208'. Which is more decimal places than we need, but is the same answer as we had from Excel.

(Continued)

(Continued)

Tables

| Normal Distribution ▾ | ⦿ Probabilities ○ Quantiles |

Mean? `0.0`   **Standard Deviation?** `1.0`

| Left | Between | Right | `2` | |

Answer: 0.9772498680518208

Last modified: Sat Aug 3 13:45:30 PDT 1996

Of course, by the time you read this book, (even by the time we have finished writing this chapter) this page might not be there any more. However, you can find many more of these programs by typing "normal distribution probability calculator" into Google (or whatever your favourite search engine is).

For example, if you look at IQ scores, the tests are designed to give a mean of 100 and a standard deviation of 15. This means that if you have an IQ of 115 you have a score that is 1 standard deviation above the mean and therefore a z-score of +1. On the other hand, if your younger and annoying sibling has an IQ of 70, their score is 2 standard deviations below the mean and they have a z-score of −2. It is that easy. If you look at these scores again and go to Figure 3.11 you can see that your younger sibling's score of −2 is to the left of the mean and only 2% of people are less gifted. If you consult a table, or use a computer program, you can find the proportion of cases in a normal distribution that are likely to occur for any range of scores.

Hold your nerve and read on. It's time to get jiggy with numbers. Table 3.2 shows a brief z-score table. There is a fuller table in the Appendix, though it is usually quicker, easier and better to use a computer or web-based calculator.

Table 3.2   *A shortened z-score table*

z-Score	Proportion scoring lower	% (Rounded to whole number)
3.5	0.9998	100%
3.0	0.9987	100%
2.5	0.9938	99%
2.0	0.9772	98%
1.5	0.9332	93%
1.0	0.8413	84%
0.5	0.6915	69%
0.0	0.5000	50%
−0.5	0.3085	31%
−1.0	0.1587	16%
−1.5	0.0668	7%
−2.0	0.0228	2%
−2.5	0.0062	1%
−3.0	0.0013	0%
−3.5	0.0002	0%

Test yourself 2

Fill in the blanks in the following table:

	Score	Mean	SD	z-Score	% of people above score
1.	10	20	5	−2	98
2.	50	35	15		
3.	12	10		2	
4.	145		15	3	
5.		10	2	0.5	
6.	25		17.3		50
7.		30	5	1	
8.	12		2		84

Answers are given at the end of the chapter.

USING *Z*-SCORES AND THE NORMAL DISTRIBUTION

So far, this discussion has been rather abstract. So let's bring it back down to earth, and try to understand why, as psychologists, we might need to know this information.

If you, as a psychologist, give someone a test of attitude, or ability, or personality, or any other value that can be quantified, you need to know how to interpret that test. Let's say it's a test of binkiness (don't worry about this, we made it up). Your subject gets a score of 17. By itself, this number doesn't mean anything to you or them – but they want to know what it means, and you (as an ethical psychologist) want to tell them. In order to interpret the test, you must find out the mean and standard deviation of the test in the relevant population (this information is provided in the test manual). When we consult the Shevlin Directory of Bogus Scales® we find that the mean score of binkiness is 14 and the standard deviation is 3. You can now calculate the *z*-score:

$$z = \frac{\text{score} - \text{mean}}{\sigma}$$

$$= \frac{17 - 14}{3} = 1$$

You find that your subject has a *z*-score of 1. You can then consult the *z*-score table, and you can tell the person that approximately 84% of people score lower than them on the binkiness scale, and that 16% of people score higher than them.

SAMPLES, POPULATIONS AND ESTIMATES

In many sciences, we know that any sample that we take is likely to be similar to any other sample. If we were chemists, for example, we could go to our local copper sulphate supplier and we could buy some copper sulphate. We would know that this copper sulphate would be the same as any other copper sulphate that we might buy from anywhere. We can therefore make statements about copper sulphate and know them to be true – for example 'Copper sulphate is blue'.

In psychology, we cannot make statements based on one sample, or with such certainty.[1] One group of people is not necessarily the same as another group of people, and all individuals are different from all other individuals. We cannot test the spelling of a seven-year-old, and say 'Seven-year-olds can spell "computer", but they cannot spell "broccoli"'. Instead, we analyse samples and then attempt to make **generalisations** to populations from these samples. Even then we have to be careful because if we test the spelling of a primary school class of seven-year-olds it might be that they can all spell 'broccoli' because they have just done a project on green vegetables and all the other classes in the school can't even draw broccoli, let alone spell it.

The person widely claimed to be the first statistician was John Graunt, who lived in the 17th century.[2] His job was to determine the number of people who were dying at any time from the Black Death.[3] If the number of people dying was particularly high he was to inform the King, who would leave London until the disease had calmed down. Graunt could not count the total number of people dying from the disease at any time because this would have been an impossible job. Instead, he took a sample of mortuaries and visited these. At each mortuary he estimated the number of people who had died of different diseases.[4] From this sample he extrapolated to the number of people dying in London, and informed the King.

While this seems like a simple thing to do, at the time it was revolutionary. People simply did not have the same understanding of probability that we take for granted now. The idea of random variation was not understood, and so generalising from a population to a sample, which takes into account this random variation, would not have been possible. The fact that equal numbers of boys and girls were born was seen by some in the past of proof of the existence of God. It was just too convenient to believe it could happen by chance (see Gigerenzer, Swijtink, Porter, Daston, Beatty & Krueger, 1989, for more on this sort of thing).

---

[1] Actually, you can't do this in chemistry, or other sciences, because there is always uncertainty in the measurements. Psychologists have known this for a long time, but it's only recently that physicists have understood it (Mackenzie, 2004).

[2] It rather depends on what you mean by 'statistician'. You could not study statistics at university until the 20th century.

[3] You probably learned at school that the Black Death was bubonic plague. However, there are some strong suggestions that the characteristics of the Black Death do not match those of bubonic plague. Of course, if it wasn't bubonic plague we don't know what it was, and so we don't know how to cure it if it comes back (see Scott & Duncan, 2004).

[4] The list of causes of death, for 1632, includes: affrighted (1 person), ague (43), burst and rupture (9), dead in the street (6), executed and pressed to death (18), and bit with a mad dog (1).

SAMPLES AND PROBABILITY

For this discussion, we are going to concentrate on the analysis that is carried out for continuous variables. The ideas for categorical variables are not very different and we will cover them later in the book. We thought that there was enough here without any extra information.

Tip: Brace yourself

At this point, we put together the information about sampling and the normal distribution.

Instead of measuring one person we measure a sample of people, and make a statement about this sample. For example, we might measure the spelling ability of seven-year-olds, or the illness beliefs of people suffering from multiple sclerosis. This provides our estimate of the value in the population; if 14% of seven-year-olds in our sample can spell 'broccoli', our best guess at the population value is 14%. But we would like to go slightly beyond that. We want to know how close we are likely to be to the true, population value, and what the true, population value is likely to be.

If we take a sample, from a population and calculate the mean for that sample we are likely to find a value close to the mean for the population. It is very unlikely that we will hit the true (population) mean and we might, if we are very unlucky, find a value far from the true (population) mean. Suppose we are interested in the amount of time students spend thinking about statistics, during the average week. In the population that we are interested in, the mean number of hours that a student spends thinking about statistics is 20.

Common Mistakes: Talking nonsense

People often use data about mean scores to make statements like

The average student thinks about statistics for 20 hours in a week.

This statement encourages people to imagine an 'average student' who doesn't exist. If you present the data in this way you will say things like

The average person owns 0.254 cats and 0.110 budgies.

which are plain daft things to say.

Test yourself 3

Check out the way samples vary by looking at a known set of scores. For example, if you know the weight of everyone in a class of 20 people, you can calculate the average weight of the class. Now take any 10 of the class and calculate their average weight. This is your sample. How different is this from the population average? Repeat the process with a different 10 people and then 10 more. The sample means are likely to be different from each other but to cluster around the population mean.

We take a sample of students, and find the average amount of time that these students spend thinking about statistics. Figure 3.12 shows some different values that we are likely to find. If the true value (the population value) is 20 then we would expect the find values close to 20 in many of our samples. We would not be surprised to find that the value for a sample was about 19. However, as the numbers get further from 20, finding the mean within this range becomes less and less likely. A value of 16 is quite likely, a value of 13 (or lower) is quite unlikely, and finally a value of 11 (or lower) is very unlikely.

We could change the way we present this and instead of using words such as 'quite likely' or 'very unlikely' we could use numbers. Even better, we could use a line to

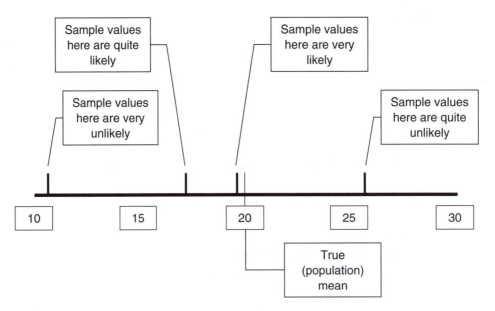

Figure 3.12 Likelihood of selecting different values when the true (population) mean is 20

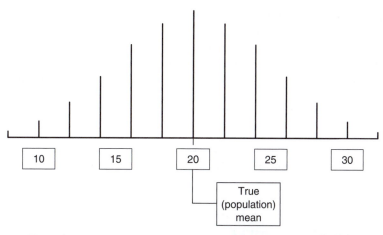

Figure 3.13   The height of the bars represents the probability of obtaining a value in the sample

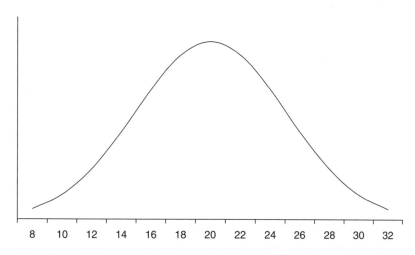

Figure 3.14   Figure 3.13 repeated with smoothed lines drawn to connect the bars

represent the probability of obtaining a particular sample value of the mean (or range of values). Such a graph is shown in Figure 3.13. Have you seen this before somewhere? Is the connection between samples and normal distributions starting to become a bit clearer? This is beginning to look like our old friend, the normal distribution. Just to make it clearer we will join the tops of the bars together, and smooth the line a little. The result of this is shown in Figure 3.14.

Something else to note about this is that the distribution is symmetrical. We are just as likely to underestimate the population mean as we are to overestimate the population mean. This indicates that the mean is unbiased.

This distribution is called the **sampling distribution of the mean** and it appears to be similar to a normal distribution. This is because it *is* similar to a normal distribution.

	Tip
	We are now approaching the hard bit. Take it slowly and it should all make sense, but it may take more than one go to get it all.

CENTRAL LIMIT THEOREM

The **Central limit theorem** tells us that, given some assumptions, the sampling distribution of the mean will form a normal distribution, with a large sample. And this is what we observed in Figure 3.14. (With a smaller sample, the distribution will be *t*-shaped, which we will talk more about in a moment.)

This theorem confuses many students (as well as lecturers). Our statistical tests do not assume that the distribution of the data in the sample is normal. Instead, it assumes that the sampling distribution of the sample means in the population is normal (or *t*-shaped, which is very similar). This is not the same as saying that the distribution in the population is normal.

Now we've got an extra problem because we don't know what the sampling distribution looks like. We have to assume that it is normal, but how do we know? The answer is that we rely on the central limit theorem. This tells us that if the distribution in the sample is approximately normal, then the sampling distribution will be the correct shape. If the sample distribution is not normal, but the sample is large enough, then the sampling distribution will still be normal (or *t*-shaped). The larger the sample, the less we need to worry about whether our sample data are normally distributed or not.[5]

THE STANDARD ERROR

So, where have we got to in trying to decide how close our sample value is to the population value of the mean? We know that values of the sample mean that are close to the population mean are much more likely than values that are further away from the population mean.

We saw above that we can define any normal distribution with two **parameters**: the mean and the standard deviation. We want to know the mean and the standard deviation of the

---

[5] There are some occasions when this is not true – they are beyond the scope of this book, but you could see Wilcox (1997) or Miles (2005).

sampling distribution of the mean. We know that the sample mean is an unbiased estimate of the population mean, so we can use the sample mean as our estimate of the mean of the sampling distribution. What we now need to know is the standard deviation of that sampling distribution. The standard deviation of the sampling distribution of the mean has a special name (which is lucky, because it is a long thing to say each time): it is called the standard error of the mean, or just the **standard error**, which can be shortened further to *se*.

We will come back to the standard error of the mean in the next chapter, but before that we should look at what might affect it. 1. The standard error should be affected by the sample size. The bigger the sample, the closer our sample mean is likely to be to the population mean.

We can demonstrate this by tossing a coin. We know that the true, or population, probability of the coin coming up heads is 0.5. Therefore, if we toss a coin 4 times, we would expect it to come up heads twice, and come up tails twice. However, it will not necessarily come up heads twice half the time. Sometimes you will get three heads, sometimes one, sometimes none.

If you want to be convinced of this, toss a coin 4 times and write down the proportion of times it came up heads. Then repeat the process ten times. When you have ten proportions, calculate the mean and standard deviation. When you have done that, do it again, this time tossing the coin eight times. Then calculate the number of heads that you get.

I did just this, and here's what I found. First, I tossed a coin 4 times, counted the number of heads, and worked out the proportion of heads. I repeated this process 10 times, and this gives me the sampling distribution (Table 3.3). If we take each proportion of heads, and calculate the mean, we find it is 0.45, which is quite close to the true value of 0.5. The standard deviation of these scores is 0.26.

Then I tossed a coin 8 times, counted the number of heads, calculated the proportion, and repeated the process 10 times (Table 3.4). Look at the mean and standard deviation now. The mean is 0.475, and the standard deviation is 0.17. The standard deviation of the distribution has shrunk considerably because my sample size has increased from 4 to 8.[6]

2. The second thing to affect the standard error is the amount of **variation** in our sample. If we have a lot of variation in our sample, there will be more uncertainty in our sample, and so there will be more uncertainty about the population mean.

If I give a test to a random sample of people, and they all get either 3, 4 or 5 questions right, I will be pretty sure that the population mean is somewhere between 3 and 5. If they all get between 10 and 100 questions right the population mean will be between 10 and 100. In the second sample there is more variation, so there is more **uncertainty**.

The equation for the standard error of the mean is very simple:

$$se_{\bar{x}} = \frac{\sigma_x}{\sqrt{N}}$$

Where $se_{\bar{x}}$ is the standard error of the mean of the variable x in our data, σ_x is the standard deviation of the variable x, and N is the number of cases in the sample.

---

[6] Actually, I used a computer to pretend that I had tossed a coin. Statisticians do this when they want to try out statistical procedures.

Table 3.3   *Results from tossing a coin 4 times, repeated 10 times*

	Number of heads	Proportion of heads
1	1	0.25
2	1	0.25
3	3	0.75
4	2	0.5
5	2	0.5
6	3	0.75
7	3	0.75
8	2	0.5
9	0	0
10	1	0.25
Sum	18	0.45

Table 3.4   *Results of tossing a coin 8 times, repeated 10 times*

	Number of heads	Proportion of heads
1	3	0.375
2	4	0.5
3	6	0.75
4	6	0.75
5	3	0.375
6	3	0.375
7	3	0.375
8	2	0.25
9	4	0.5
10	4	0.5
Sum	38	0.485

Optional Extra: Calculate the standard error

To calculate the standard error, we divide by the square root of the sample size. If we want to halve our standard error, what do we need to increase our sample size by?

The answer is 4 times. A four times larger sample will give a standard error half the size. This is a fixed, and boring, fact in research. If your sample was 100 people (which you might think represented quite a reasonable effort on your part), but you wanted to have standard errors that were half the size, you would need to increase your sample size to 400 people. If you want to halve your standard error again, you are going to need a sample size of 1600 people.

So, we know the standard error, which is the standard deviation of the sampling distribution. So what, you might ask? This tells us something very useful – it tells us the amount of uncertainty around the estimator. In other words, it tells us how sure we are about our answer.

SUMMARY

This chapter has looked at some easy matters like sampling and normal distributions, and then put them together to get to grips with some hard bits like sampling distributions. It has looked at the importance of sampling techniques and also the normal distribution. The maths behind the concepts in this chapter forms the foundation of statistical tests. You don't need to understand all the maths to make the statistics work, in the same way that you don't need to know how a car works before you learn to drive it. Mind you, when it breaks down it is handy to have a bit of knowledge so you know where to hit it with your hammer.

Test yourself answers

Test yourself 1

Having read this chapter, you might want to reread the news stories from the start of the chapter, and think again about what further information you might need in order to evaluate the claims.

You can find more information on the students' debts at http://www.natwest.com/ pressroom/index.asp?navid=PRESS_ROOM&pid=99 and more information on the Scottish Household Survey at http://www.scotland.gov.uk/News/Releases/2005/08/04095017.

We really need to know three things. First, how was the sampling done? Was it random, or were steps taken to ensure that it was representative? The information on the student debt survey, which was carried out on behalf of NatWest tells us nothing about the sampling process, other than that the respondents were 'sixth-formers'. The Scottish Household Survey, on the other hand, tells us: 'The survey is designed to provide nationally representative samples of private households and of the adult population in private households.' It also tells us the 'survey is chosen at random'. We are a lot more impressed by the Scottish Household Survey than the NatWest survey (so far).

(You might remember that we said that you would never have a random sample, and now, here we are, saying that these people did have a random sample. Well, we said *you* would never have a random sample. If *you* were the Scottish Executive, then you could get a random sample.)

Second, we would like to know the sample size. We can find this on both of the web pages. The NatWest surveyed a very reasonable 1006 sixth-formers. However, the Scottish Household Survey involved 30,922 interviews.

Third, we would like to know the standard errors. There is no hint of them for the NatWest data, but, they are available for the Scottish Household Survey data. You can even get hold of the dataset from the Scottish Household Survey and find out the standard error yourself (look at http://www.data-archive.ac.uk). We don't think you can get hold of the NatWest survey data.

Test yourself 2

	Score	Mean	SD	z-Score	% of people above score
1.	10	20	5	−2	98
2.	50	35	15	1	16
3.	12	10	1	2	2
4.	145	100	15	3	0
5.	11	10	2	0.5	69
6.	25	25	17.3	0	50
7.	25	30	5	1	16
8.	12	14	2	−1	84

USING SPSS

SPSS provides a number of ways to explore standard errors.

To examine the standard error of a variable (or group of variables), select **Analyze** ⇒ **Descriptive Statistics** ⇒ **Descriptives**. Select the variable, and click on **Options**:

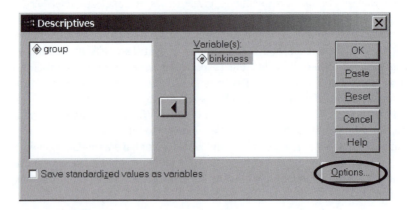

Select **S.E. mean**

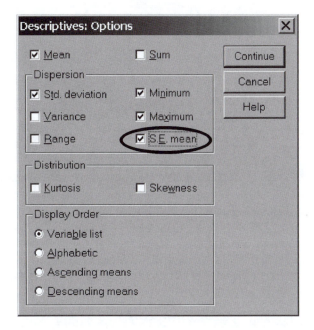

The output is shown below:

Descriptive Statistics

	N	Minimum	Maximum	Mean		Std.
	Statistic	Statistic	Statistic	Statistic	Std. Error	Statistic
binkiness	32	10	85	44.03	3.888	21.992
Valid N (listwise)	32					

If you have two (or more) groups, and you would like to know the standard error of each group, you can use the means procedure. Select **Analyze ⇒ Compare Means ⇒ Means**. Select the continuous variable that you would like to know the standard error of, and put it in the **Dependent List** box (in our case, binkiness). The categorical variable that defines the groups (in our case, group), is put into the **Independent List**:

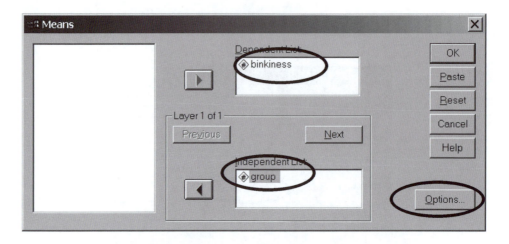

You can then click the **Options** button to decide what information you want displayed. By default, for each group, SPSS will tell you the mean, the number of cases and the standard deviation. You can remove some of these, if you want to. On the left-hand side is the list of additional information that you can request. We want the standard error of the mean, so we'll move that to the right-hand side, and press **Continue** and then **OK**.

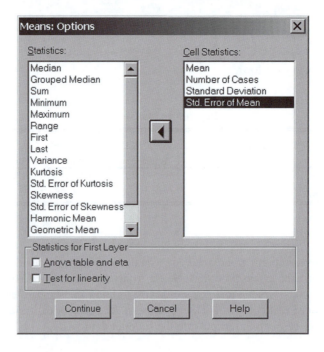

Report

Binkiness

Group	Mean	N	Std. Deviation	Std. Error of Mean
1 Droogs	40.19	16	20.269	5.067
2 Ghawls	47.88	16	23.605	5.901
Total	44.03	32	21.992	3.888

The output is reasonably easy to understand (which is more than we can say about a lot of SPSS output). For both of our groups, the Droogs and the Ghawls, the mean, N (sample size), standard deviation and standard error of the mean are reported. In addition, each of those statistics is reported for the whole sample.

4
Making inferences: confidence limits and statistical significance

What's in this chapter?

- Calculating the standard error
- Probability
- Hypotheses
- *t* distribution
- Degrees of freedom
- Confidence intervals
- Using SPSS

KEY TERMS

alpha
alternative hypothesis
confidence interval
confidence limits
degrees of freedom
descriptive statistics
hypotheses
inference
normal distribution
null hypothesis

one-tailed (or directional) hypothesis
population
probability
standard error
statistically significant
t distribution
two-tailed (or non-directional) hypothesis
type I error
type II error
z-score

INTRODUCTION

This chapter is about the way we make inferences and statements of significance. It is also about how much tolerance there is in our results. By 'tolerance' we mean the how certain we are about our results. For example, when students take A levels they are given a grade from A to U, but there is bound to be some variation in the way the examinations are marked. It is generally agreed, though rarely reported, that the tolerance is about one grade, or just a bit less. So if you achieved BCC in the examinations then your true score is probably somewhere between BBC and CCC. With any measure, we want to know how close our sample estimate has got to the population (true) value, and to do this we use confidence intervals.

Tip: Keeping up

If you have come to this chapter after reading Chapter 3, we are now going to apply the standard error to make inferences from our sample to our population.

On the other hand, if you have skipped Chapter 3, or have jumped straight in here, most of this should make sense – if it doesn't make perfect sense, you should be able to use what we say and apply it, and then you can read Chapter 3 at some point in the future.

INFERENCE

When we used **descriptive statistics** we described the data. It's not that difficult really, the clue is in the word. We can use descriptive statistics to tell us all sorts of useful things about the data such as the central tendency (remember that's the posh way of saying average), the dispersion and the distribution. Sometimes we want to go a little further and ask questions about what the data tell us. In the previous chapter we introduced the term 'inferential statistics'. When we make an **inference** we go beyond what we know and make an intelligent guess. Keep this concept in your mind as you dive deeper into the world of probability and inferential statistics.

THE STANDARD ERROR

At the end of the previous chapter we introduced the **standard error**. This is the name given to the standard deviation of the sampling distribution. That is, if we carry out the same experiment over and over again we will get slightly different results every time. The standard error is the standard deviation of that sample of scores. This might sound confusing, but go back and read it slowly and you'll see that it is really a simple idea that is just complicated by some confusing terms.

The standard error of a variable is given by:

$$se = \frac{\sigma}{\sqrt{N}}$$

where σ is the standard deviation, and N is the number of people. If you want to know how to calculate the standard error, then read on. If this is all too much, skip to the start of the next section. Don't be scared of the calculation. It looks complicated because it has more Greek letters in it than the Athens tourist guide but it doesn't require you to do anything more than a little adding up and multiplying. Most of the work goes into calculating the standard deviation, and if you were paying attention in Chapter 2 we showed how to do that there; nevertheless, we'll go over it briefly again. Remember that the formula for the standard deviation is

$$\sigma = \sqrt{\frac{\sum (x - \bar{x})^2}{N - 1}}$$

where x refers to each score, and $\bar{x}$ is the mean. The symbol $\sum$ is, confusingly, also called Sigma but this is an upper case sigma. It means 'add up all of the cases'.

Table 4.1 shows ten scores for which we want to know the standard error; it also shows some of the calculations we're going to need. We did something similar in Table 2.6. The steps are as follows:

Table 4.1   *Sample scores and calculation of squared differences*

Child number	Score, x	Differences, $\bar{x} - x$	Squared differences, $(\bar{x} - x)^2$
1	18	$17 - 18 = -1$	$-1^2 = 1$
2	34	$17 - 34 = -17$	$17^2 = 289$
3	18	$17 - 18 = -1$	$-1^2 = 1$
4	6	$17 - 6 = 11$	$11^2 = 121$
5	12	$17 - 12 = 5$	$5^2 = 25$
6	15	$17 - 15 = 2$	$2^2 = 4$
7	20	$17 - 20 = -3$	$-3^2 = 9$
8	14	$17 - 14 = 3$	$3^2 = 9$
9	17	$17 - 17 = 0$	$0^2 = 0$
10	16	$17 - 16 = 1$	$1^2 = 1$
Sum, $\sum$	170		460
Mean	17		

1.	Calculate the mean score.	$$\bar{x} = \frac{18 + 34 + 18 + 6 + 12 + 15 + 20 + 14 + 17 + 16}{10}$$ $$= \frac{170}{10} = 17$$
2.	Find the difference between each score and the mean. This gives us $x - \bar{x}$.	See column 3 of Table 4.1.
3.	Square each of these differences. This gives us $(x - \bar{x})^2$.	See column 4 of Table 4.1.
4.	Add up the squared differences.	$\Sigma\,(x - \bar{x})^2 = 1 + 289 + 1 + 121 + 25 + 4 + 9 + 9 + 0 + 1 = 460$
5.	Divide the result of step 4 by $N - 1$, to give the variance.	$\dfrac{\Sigma\,(x - \bar{x})^2}{N - 1} = \dfrac{460}{9} = 51.1$
6.	Find the square root of step 5 (the variance), to give the standard deviation.	$\sigma = \sqrt{\dfrac{\Sigma\,(x - \bar{x})^2}{N - 1}} = \sqrt{51.1} = 7.14$
7.	Steps 1–6 give the top of the expression for the standard error. For the bottom, we take the square root of N.	$se = \dfrac{\sigma}{\sqrt{N}} = \dfrac{7.14}{\sqrt{10}} = \dfrac{7.14}{3.16} = 2.26$

For the data set in Table 4.1, we have therefore found a standard error $se = 2.26$.

PROBABILITY

Now we come again to the tricky concept of **probability**. At first glance there is nothing difficult about the idea of probability but it causes all sorts of problems to people because it is counter-intuitive – it goes against the way we commonly think.

In everyday life we tend to talk about probability in different ways. We might say (if we assume no one is cheating):

- There is a 50:50 chance that the coin will come up heads.
- The coin will come up heads 50% of the time.
- The odds that the coin will come up heads are even.
- The probability that the coin will come up heads is 0.5.

Actually, you might not say that last one, but that's how we talk about probability in statistics. A probability always goes from 0 to 1. An event which has a probability of zero *will not happen, ever, no matter what* (Nottingham Forest winning the Premiership, for example, or the Earth turning into a ball of cheese). An event which has a probability of 1 *will happen, no matter what*. If I jump into the air, I will come back down to the ground again, no matter what.

Imagine that you are having a bet with someone over the toss of a coin. You have bet on tails and your friend has bet on heads. Heads means you have to pay your friend £1. The first toss is heads so you pay up. The second toss is also heads so you pay up again. The third toss is heads, and so is the fourth. You are feeling unlucky but when the next five tosses also come up heads you start to consider another explanation. Maybe your friend is cheating. You begin to calculate the probability of getting so many heads in a row and you work out that it is very small. There have now been 20 heads in a row and your wallet is looking a bit lighter. What are the chances of the next throw being a head? You know that the answer is the same as it was at the start of the exercise – 50:50. Your intuition tells you, however, that the run of heads can't keep going on so you suggest double or quits. Heads again leaves you £40 down. This can't be right, so you make the inferential leap and call your friend a cheat.

You have been considering two **hypotheses** during this costly game. The first hypothesis is that the run of heads is due to chance and your friend is very lucky (this is the null hypothesis), and the second is that your friend has done something to the coin (this is the alternative hypothesis). When the probability of the number of heads occurring by chance becomes too low to be credible you reject the null hypothesis and call your friend a cheat. You haven't *proved* your friend is a cheat, you have made an *inference* based on the probability of the event occurring and made the intelligent guess that you have been done.

But what do we mean by 'too low to be credible' in the previous paragraph? How many times would you have to lose before you got suspicious?

The reason why probability is counter-intuitive is that we like to believe that we *know* things rather than making probability statements about them. Your friend might have been a cheat but they might also have been very lucky. In your mind, however, you are convinced they are a cheat and you will never let them play with your Scalextric again.

HYPOTHESES

When you were wondering about your friend cheating, there were two different possibilities:

1. They weren't cheating.
2. They were cheating.

The first hypothesis, that they weren't cheating, we call the **null hypothesis**. The second, we call the **alternative hypothesis**. From looking at the results of the coin throws, we can never know if they really did cheat or not (though we can torture them to find out for sure). All we can do is estimate the probability that they were cheating. We would like to know the probability that they were cheating. We can't know that (sorry). If we can't know the probability that they were cheating, can we know the probability that they weren't cheating? No, sorry, we can't know that either. What we *can* know is the probability of getting the result, *if* they weren't cheating. (We'll talk more about this later.)

The null hypothesis is often abbreviated to H_0, and the alternative hypothesis to H_1. (We won't do that, though, because you've got enough to remember.)

Optional Extra: Why can't I know the probability they were cheating?

We don't know the probability they were cheating, without taking into account the *prior probability* that they were cheating – that is, the probability that they were going to cheat before the event. This is rather hard (and it relates to the taxi-cab problem on page 88). Basically, if you were playing against your local priest, you would imagine that the probability they were cheating was very low, and so even if they won ten times in a row, you still might say that they weren't cheating. If, however, you were playing against a known conman, you'd think the prior probability that they were going to cheat was very high. Therefore, after the first time you lost, you might conclude that they are probably cheating. Some people think that all probability should be thought of in these ways – they are called *Bayesians*, after Revd Thomas Bayes (who *was* a priest). Bayesians think that all statistics should be done their way. However, we're not going to worry about Bayesians again, until Chapter 11.

Anyhow, let's go ahead, and discover the probability of the result occurring, if you're friend is not cheating. It's very easy.

The probability of a coin coming up heads once is 0.5 – there are two equally likely outcomes, and one of those satisfies the criterion. The probability of a coin coming up heads, if the null hypothesis is true, is 0.5. We can't really accuse your friend of cheating.

If they toss the coin twice, there are four possible outcomes:

1. HH
2. TT
3. HT
4. TH

One of these outcomes suggests that they are cheating, and one out of four is 1/4, which is 0.25.

You might have noticed that there is an easier way to work out these probabilities than writing down all the possible outcomes, and counting them. We use the formula

$$p = \frac{1}{2^k} \quad \text{or equivalently } p - 2^{-k}$$

where k is the number of times they toss the coin. So for one toss we have

$$1/2^1 = 1/2 = 0.5$$

for two

$$1/2^2 = 1/(2 \times 2) = 1/4 = 0.25$$

for three

$$1/2^3 = 1/(2 \times 2 \times 2) = 1/8 = 0.125$$

for ten

$$1/2^{10} = 1/(2 \times 2 \times 2 \times 2 \times 2 \times 2 \times 2 \times 2 \times 2 \times 2) = 1/1024 = 0.00097$$

However, it gets a little trickier than that. Say your friend didn't keep throwing heads, but kept throwing tails. This would make them a bit foolish, but you would still suspect something was going on because it would be just as unlikely to occur. In this case, we need to work out the probability of *either* a large number of heads, *or* a large number of tails in a row.

If we look again at the results of a number of throws, the possible results from 1 toss are H or T. Both of these are equally likely to mean that something fishy is going on, so the probability is 1. For two throws, the possible results are HH, HT, TT, TH. Either HH or TT make us suspicious, and therefore the probability of a fishy result occurring is 2/4, or 0.5.

If we are looking for a suspicious result in one direction only, we call this a **one-tailed (or directional) hypothesis**. If we are looking for a result in either direction, we use a **two-tailed (or non-directional) hypothesis**. We need to modify our formula, so that

$$p = \frac{1}{2^{k-1}} \quad \text{or equivalently } p = 2^{-(k-1)}.$$

(Notice that if we have 1 toss only, the p will equal $2^{-(k-1)}$ which gives $2^{-(1-1)} = 2^0$. In case you didn't know, any number, to the power of 0, is equal to one. (Try it on your calculator, if you don't believe us.)

Because we are usually looking for fishiness in either direction, we should almost always use two-tailed hypotheses, which is why $p = 1$.

STATISTICAL SIGNIFICANCE

So, we've got a probability value (don't forget this is the probability of the result occurring if the null hypothesis is true, *not* the probability that the null hypothesis is true). What cut-off should we use before we decide to reject the null hypothesis? This value is called after the Greek letter alpha, which is written as α.

The short answer to this is 0.05, that is, 1 in 20 or 5%. This is somewhat arbitrary, but it is the convention that is used throughout much of science. One in 20 is deemed rare enough that we can trust it but not so stringent that it is impossible to achieve. You would be disappointed if we didn't tell you that this is a much-debated issue and that we will cover it in more depth in Chapter 11.

When the probability is found to be below 0.05 (or whatever cut-off we are using) it is described as **statistically significant**. Sometimes people just say 'significant', but that is a little confusing. The word 'significant' is another of those that has a special meaning in statistics which is different from its meaning in real life. In real life significant means 'having a meaning', or 'important'. However, a statistically significant result does not necessarily have meaning, and is not necessarily important, it just means that there is a less than 1 in 20 probability that the results would have occurred if the null hypothesis were correct.

A probability cut-off of 0.05 means that your friend would have to toss either heads, or tails (because we are using a two-tailed hypothesis) 6 times in a row, before you rejected the null hypothesis that the results were due to chance. This would have a probability value of 0.031.

Common Mistakes: What you can, and can't, do with a hypothesis

If you find that your *p*-value is below 0.05 (or whatever you choose to use), you reject the null hypothesis. This does *not* mean that you can accept the alternative hypothesis – you cannot say that they are cheating, you can just say that you have evidence that they are cheating.

If you find that your *p*-value is above 0.05, you cannot say that they are not cheating. All you can say is that you have not found evidence that they are cheating. You cannot, therefore, accept the null hypothesis. You can only fail to reject it.

In short (a ✓ means you can say this, a ✗ means you cannot):

✓ Reject the null hypothesis
✓ Fail to reject the null hypothesis
✗ Accept the null hypothesis
✗ Accept the alternative hypothesis
✗ Reject the alternative hypothesis

Test yourself 1: Some more probability puzzles

1. *The birthday problem.* How many people have to be in a room together, before the chances are better than evens that two of them have a birthday on the same day?
2. *The Monty Hall problem.* You are shown three doors. Behind one door is a car, behind the other two doors is a goat. You get to keep the prize that is behind the door that you

choose (for this to work, we assume you want a car more than you want a goat). You choose a door. Another door is opened, to reveal that it has a goat behind it, leaving two doors closed. You can change your choice to the other door. Do you?

3. *The blue taxi/green taxi problem.* A taxi-cab was involved in an accident at night. There are only two taxi companies in the town, the Blue Cab Company, which have 85% of the cabs, and the Green Cab Company, which have 15% of the cabs. A witness said the taxi was green. However, the street was dark, so the police test the witness, to see how often they get the colour correct. The police find the witness can identify the colour correctly 80% of the time. Is it more likely that the taxi was blue, or green?

Answers are given at the end of the chapter.

Type I and type II errors

If we reject our null hypothesis when we find a probability value of 0.05 there is a chance we have made the wrong decision. We have rejected it because there is only a low probability of the result occuring if it (the null hypothesis) is true, but it might actually be true after all. This mistake is called a **type I error** and we estimate the probability of making this error because it is given in our *p*-value. If our *p*-value is 0.05 then we know there is less than a 5% chance of the result occurring if the null hypothesis is true. Conversely we can say there is still a 5% chance of the result occurring if the null hypothesis is true, so if we reject it there is a 5% probability of this decision being an error.

Of course we can sometimes make the other logical error and fail to reject the null hypothesis when it is not true. This is called a **type II error**.

PROBABILITY ESTIMATES

If we want to estimate the statistical significance of our results (that is, the probability of our result occurring if the null hypothesis is true), then we need to get back to the standard error. If we carry out our study a number of times we will get a range of mean scores that make up a sampling distribution. We know that if our sample is large, this distribution will be normal (thanks to central limit theorem – if you didn't read Chapter 3, hang on in there for a minute).

However, we now have to make a confession: there is something we didn't tell you about. If our sample is not large then the distribution is not normal, instead it follows a shape called the *t* **distribution**. However, the *t* distribution is very closely related to the normal distribution. We'll come to the effects of this later.

We know the standard deviation of the sampling distribution of the mean (also known as the standard error – hope you're keeping up). And we saw in Chapter 3 that if we know

the mean, and we know the standard deviation, we know the probability of any value arising. We can then get an answer to the following question, '*If the mean in the population is
a particular value, what is the probability that I would find a value as far from that value
as in my sample, or further?*'

Let's imagine that the data in Table 4.1 are a set of reading scores for a (randomly
selected) group of children from Year 7 in a school. A teacher says to us: 'I think that the
population mean from which your data were sampled is only equal to 14.' Well, the mean
in our sample was 17, which is higher than 14, so it appears that the teacher was wrong.
However, what is the probability of getting a value as high as 17, or higher, if the population mean is 14? Is the probability sufficiently low that we can reject the null hypothesis
that the mean is 14? Or do we not have sufficient evidence to reject that null hypothesis?

Optional Extra: What we didn't say

We said: 'What is the probability of getting a value as high as 17, or higher, if the population
mean is 14?'

We didn't say: 'What is the probability that the population mean is 14 or lower, given that we
found a mean in our sample of 17?'

It's not *very* important, but there is a difference. We'll see why later.

We cannot prove the teacher correct without measuring the whole **population**. However,
we can see if we have enough evidence to demonstrate that she might be wrong. We have
an estimate of the standard deviation of the sampling distribution (the standard error), and
we know the value of the mean in our sample. So we ask: 'What is the probability of getting a value as large (or small) as the value that we have, if the population mean is equal
to 14 (or any other number)?'

When we calculated a *z*-**score**, back on page 67, we used:

$$z = \frac{score - mean}{\sigma}$$

However, we have a complication (only a small one). We do not have a **normal distribution**; instead we have a *t* distribution. This means two things. First, the formula will not
calculate *z*, it will calculate *t*. Second, we don't use σ (the standard deviation); we use our
estimate of the standard deviation, which is the standard error, *se*. So, the equation looks
like this:

$$t = \frac{score - mean}{se}$$

(we told you that it was only a small complication), where the *score* is the value for our mean in the sample, and the *mean* is the value that we suspect in the population. We can simplify this equation a little more, by saying that the difference between the scores we are interested in is called *x*, because it could be anything, so we write:

$$t = \frac{x}{se}$$

This is a very important formula in statistics and it pops up in many different places. If you ever do some advanced statistics in the future, the books, lecturer or computer program might assume that you know this formula. We will not assume that, so we'll remind you when you need it.

Let's work out this formula for our data:

$$t = \frac{\text{score} - \text{mean}}{se} = \frac{17 - 14}{2.26} = \frac{3}{2.26} = 1.33.$$

Our value for *t* is therefore 1.33.

When we had a *z*-score we could look this up in the *z* table and find the probability of getting that score. We do exactly the same with the value of *t*, except instead of using a *z* table we use a *t* table.

Tip: Not your cup of *t*?

A lot of students have problems with the idea of *t* (and similar statistics) because they want it to represent something. They say '*t* is equal to 1.33 – but 1.33 *what*?'. The answer is not 1.33 anything. All we do with this value is compare it with values of *t* that we know about. Imagine how Fahrenheit's peers reacted, when he invented the thermometer. 'Aha', he said, 'the temperature is 45'. And his friends said '45 what? What have we got 45 of?'. He could only say 'degrees' which sounded fairly lame. The value of *t* is similar. You don't have 1.33 of anything. Live with it.

Again, as with *z*, we actually prefer not to use a table and we suggest that if you have any choice you don't either. Instead, use a computer. We've described it again, briefly, in the tip box.

Before we can use a table or a computer to calculate the associated probability, we need to know the **degrees of freedom**. Degrees of freedom are easier to calculate than they are to explain. In this example the **degrees of freedom (df)** can be calculated by the simple formula,

$$\text{df} = N - 1$$

where *N* is the number of participants. In our case df = 10 − 1 = 9.

Tip: Calculate the *p*-value

In the programs Excel and OpenOffice, type the following into a cell (but put your values in rather than the letters):

=tdist(t,df,tails)

where t is your value of *t* from your data, df is the degrees of freedoms and tails is the number of tails in your hypothesis (either 1 or 2). If you get into difficulties then click on the formula bar and it will help you out.

You can also use an online calculator, for example at the website http://www-stat.stanford.edu/~naras/jsm/examplebot.html.

Optional Extra: What is a degree of freedom?

Imagine we play a game. I have some cards with numbers on them, and I am going to put them on the table. You are allowed to remove cards, and replace them with other cards, but the mean of all the cards must remain the same. (It's not a very exciting game, but stick with it.)

But I am going to cheat. Sometimes I am going to glue cards on the table, and then you can't change those cards.

Here's my first card:

The mean is 8. You can't change the card, because if you change the card, you change the mean score. I don't need to glue any cards to the table to make sure you can't change any cards.

I now add a second card:

The mean is 6. You could change the cards for 7 and 5, the mean is still 6. However, I only need to glue one of those cards to the table, and you are stuck – you cannot change the other card, without changing the mean.

(Continued)

(Continued)

Suppose I add a third card:

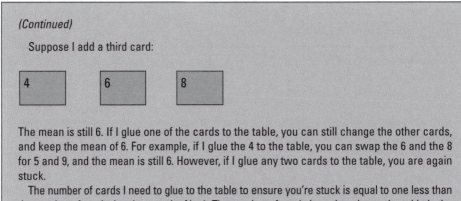

The mean is still 6. If I glue one of the cards to the table, you can still change the other cards, and keep the mean of 6. For example, if I glue the 4 to the table, you can swap the 6 and the 8 for 5 and 9, and the mean is still 6. However, if I glue any two cards to the table, you are again stuck.

The number of cards I need to glue to the table to ensure you're stuck is equal to one less than the number of cards, in other words, $N - 1$. The number of cards I need to glue to the table is the number of degrees of freedom, and it is equal to $N - 1$ (in this case).

Now we know the df we can use a *t*-table or a computer to find the probability of a value as large as 17 arising when the mean is actually 14.

We are asking what proportion of cases lie more than 1.33 SDs above the mean in a *t* distribution with 9 df. The problem is shown in Figure 4.1. We are asking what proportion of the area under the curve is in the shaded area. (Note that we are asking about 1.33 in either direction, because we should have a two-tailed hypothesis.)

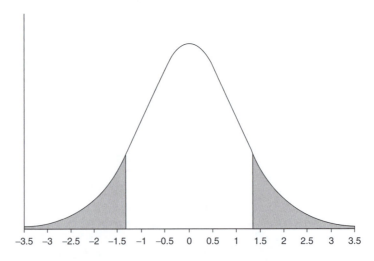

Figure 4.1 *t* distribution with 9 df, showing area above 1.33 (two-tailed)

Table 4.2   *Probabilities associated with t for 8, 9 and 10 df*

t	df		
	8	9	10
0	1.00	1.00	1.00
0.2	0.85	0.85	0.85
0.4	0.70	0.70	0.70
0.6	0.57	0.56	0.56
0.8	0.45	0.44	0.44
1	0.35	0.34	0.34
1.2	0.26	0.26	0.26
1.4	0.20	0.20	0.19
1.6	0.15	0.14	0.14
1.8	0.11	0.11	0.10
2	0.08	0.08	0.07

We have $t = 1.33$ and df $= 9$. Part of the *t*-table is shown in Table 4.2. To use it we first look at the df to see which column to use. We have 9 df so we follow that column down. Our value for t, 1.33, is not represented, so we use the next lowest which gives us a probability of 0.26. We know that this value is higher than the correct *p*-value, but if we are going to be wrong, statisticians prefer to be wrong in a cautious direction. (We could take the next value up for t, which is 1.4, which gives a *p*-value of 0.20, we therefore know that our *p*-value is between 0.20 and 0.26). The better approach is to use a computer which will give a more accurate result. In Excel, we type = tdist (1.33, 9, 2) and we get the value 0.216. This is our probability value, or *p*-value. The tdist() function in Excel needs three values, or arguments, the value for t, which in our case is 1.33, the value for df, which in our case is 9, and the value for the number of tails, either 1 or 2.

We will talk more about the interpretation of probability in Chapter 11, but for now we will consider the hypothesis we were testing, which is the null hypothesis. The probability value associated with the null hypothesis is 0.216 – we would write $p = 0.216$.

Remember that we cannot prove the null hypothesis – all we can do is say that we have found it to be wrong, or that we have not found it to be wrong. We can't say that we have found it to be correct. The very best we can do is say that we have tried our best to prove it wrong, and we have failed. You can reject the null hypothesis, or you can fail to reject the null hypothesis. You can't accept it.

It is tempting to believe that this is the probability that the null hypothesis is correct. It is so tempting to believe this that you can read it in many statistics textbooks (although not as many as in the past). This is wrong. The correct interpretation is: *the probability of a value as high as 17, or higher, occurring in the data, given that the null hypothesis is correct*. Now you can see why many people think that this means the same as the probability of the null hypothesis being correct. The difference is subtle, but it is also important.

So, in conclusion, was the teacher correct? Can we say that the mean score in the population is 14? No, we cannot. We can never say this, unless we were to test the entire population.

This does not mean that the teacher was wrong. We cannot reject (at the 0.05 level) the statement that the mean score in the population is 14.

CONFIDENCE INTERVALS

The *p*-value tells us something about the likelihood of a value being the population mean, which is fine if we have some idea of the value that we want to test as the null hypothesis. Much of the time we don't want to test a value of the null hypothesis; we don't simply want to know whether the population value is equal to some pre-specified value. Instead, we want to know how large a particular value is likely to be in the population.

If we've got two drugs for anxiety to compare we don't just want to know whether one is better than the other, we want to know *how much* better. There may be disadvantages associated with the drug: for example, the better drug may be more expensive, or have a higher probability of producing side-effects.

If we have two ways of testing memory we want to know whether you are likely to remember one more item or ten more items with the better technique. This will make a difference to what we have to say about psychological theory, and may have an effect on whether you win the pub quiz or not.

Luckily, we can use the procedures that we already know about to help us to calculate the values which are the likely range of the population value. This range is called the **confidence interval** and the largest and smallest values in the interval are known as the **confidence limits**. We usually calculate 95% confidence limits (it's quite rare to see anything else) which match the 0.05 significance level which we used in our hypothesis testing. This is equivalent to using α (alpha) = 0.05.

We use very similar logic to significance testing. We know the sample mean, and we know the standard error, which is the standard deviation of the sampling distribution. We need to know the values that cover 95% of the population, in a *t* distribution, with 9 df. This is shown in Figure 4.2, where 2.5% of cases lie in each of the tails, and therefore 95% of cases lie in the centre. We need to know what the value is for *t*, which gives these values.

Calculating confidence intervals

We use either a *t*-table or a computer. Again, the computer is better, but we will show both. The cut-offs are shown in Table 4.3. If we look at the column for *p* = 0.05, and follow it

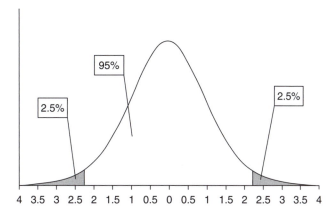

Figure 4.2   *t* distribution with 9 df, showing 2.5% cut-offs

Table 4.3   *t-value cut-offs*

df	*p*			
	0.1	0.05	0.01	0.001
2	2.92	4.30	9.92	31.60
3	2.35	3.18	5.84	12.92
4	2.13	2.78	4.60	8.61
5	2.02	2.57	4.03	6.87
6	1.94	2.45	3.71	5.96
7	1.89	2.36	3.50	5.41
8	1.86	2.31	3.36	5.04
9	1.83	2.26	3.25	4.78
10	1.81	2.23	3.17	4.59
11	1.80	2.20	3.11	4.44
12	1.78	2.18	3.05	4.32
20	1.72	2.09	2.85	3.85
50	1.68	2.01	2.68	3.50
100	1.66	1.98	2.63	3.39
1000	1.65	1.96	2.58	3.30

down to the row where df is equal to 9, we find the cut-off is 2.26. In Excel or OpenOffice, we use the tinv function (which stands for *t* inverse, so called because we want to do the inverse of the usual approach). We type:

$$= \text{tinv } (0.05, 9)$$

which again gives the value 2.26.

I can use this value to work out my confidence interval. To calculate this for my estimate, I use the formula:

$$\text{CI} = \bar{x} \pm t_\alpha \times se$$

Here $\bar{x}$ is just the mean. t_α looks complicated but all this means is that we take α (alpha), which is 0.05, and find the critical value for t in Excel; this value is 2.26. se is the standard error. $\pm$ means 'plus or minus' and tells you that you have to do two calculations, one where you use the plus and get one answer, and one where you use the minus and get another answer. We are working out confidence limits, so using the minus gives our lower confidence limit (LCL) and using the plus gives our upper confidence limit (UCL).

> ## Common Mistakes: Mixing up the standard deviation and the standard error
>
> It is very easy to mix up the standard deviation and the standard error when calculating confidence intervals. Make sure you get it right. The standard deviation is a lot bigger than the standard error, so if you get it wrong, your confidence intervals will be much, much too big.

If we put the numbers into our formula (don't forget that we multiply before we add or subtract), we find:

Lower CL = 17 − 2.26 × 2.26 = 11.89
Upper CL = 17 + 2.26 × 2.26 = 22.11

We would often write: 95% CI = 11.89, 22.11.

Interpreting Confidence Intervals

Just like the p-value, confidence intervals are often misinterpreted. The distinction is subtle, but can be important. What people (even authors of statistics textbooks) often write or think is that there is a 95% chance that the true (population) mean is contained within the confidence intervals.

This is *wrong*. The correct interpretation is that in 95% of studies, the true (population) mean will be contained within the confidence limits.

If you want to know more about this read the 'optional extra' box. If not, then move on.

Optional Extra: What do confidence intervals mean?

Some people think that there is a 95% chance that the true (population) mean is contained within the confidence intervals.

This is wrong. The correct interpretation is that in 95% of studies, the true (population) mean will be contained within the confidence limits.

These seem like very similar statements – and they are. Let's see what the problems are with the first interpretation.

The first problem is rather subtle – if we say that the confidence intervals have a 95% chance of containing the true (population) mean, then we are implying that the population mean is variable – sometimes it's in there, sometimes it's not. But the population mean cannot change – it is fixed. It is either within the confidence intervals, or it isn't.

The second problem is more practical. If I repeat a study, taking repeated random samples, I can calculate the confidence intervals each time. Imagine I carry out two studies measuring the same variables in a different sample of the same population, and I find the following means and confidence intervals:

	Study 1	Study 2
Mean	9.6	10.1
LCL	9.0	9.0
UCL	10.2	11.2

The means are different – but that's OK, we expect that. The first study says that the 95% CI is from 9.0 to 10.2 – we might be tempted to interpret this as meaning that there is a 95% possibility that the true mean is from 9.0 to 10.2, but we will see why this is wrong, when we look at the second study. This says that the confidence interval is from 9.0 to 11.2. Now how can it be true that:

- there is a 95% possibility that the population mean is between 9 and 10.2;
- there is a 95% possibility that the population mean is between 9 and 11.2?

Well, the answer is, it can't. That would be like saying

- you have a 1 in 6 chance of rolling a six on this die;
- you also have a 1 in 6 chance of rolling a five or a six on this die.

However, if we say that in 95% of studies, the confidence intervals will contain the true mean, then there is no such contradiction.

Test yourself 2

Fill in the blanks in the following table:

	Mean	N	Standard deviation	Standard error	$t_{\alpha/2}$	LCL	UCL
1.	10	49	9	1.29	2.01	7.41	12.59
2.	25	100	10				
3.	100	9	6				
4.	200	900	15				
5.	10	10000	2				

And, for the more advanced and enthusiastic, if you want to strain yourself, continue with these:

	Mean	N	Standard deviation	Standard error	$t_{\alpha/2}$	LCL	UCL
6.	16	40		0.79			
7.	50		8	0.67			
8.		9				10.46	13.54
9.		900			1.96	88.36	91.64
10.				0.40		499.21	500.79

Answers are given at the end of the chapter.

Common Mistakes: Using ± for confidence intervals (or standard errors, or standard deviations)

You will sometimes see the mean reported followed by ± some value, for example,

The reading score mean was 17 (±3).

The authors of the statement expect us to know what that means; however, sometimes it means the standard deviation, sometimes it means the standard error, and sometimes it means the confidence interval. It doesn't take a lot more effort to say:

The reading score mean was 17 (σ = 3).

(Continued)

(Continued)

or

The reading score mean was 17 (*se* = 3).

or

The reading score mean was 17 (95% CI = 11.9, 22.1).

So, always do this or the reader won't know what you are talking about.

Drawing confidence intervals

We can draw means and confidence intervals on a graph. This can be a useful way of displaying the information, particularly when we have a large number of groups. Figure 4.3 shows such a graph. The mean is represented by the blob in the middle of the graph, the whiskers extend the length of the confidence intervals.

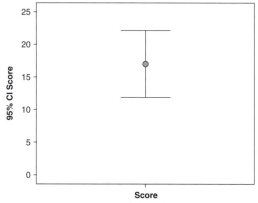

Figure 4.3   Graph showing presentation of mean, with 95% CI

Confidence intervals and statistical significance

Earlier in the chapter, we tested the null hypothesis that the teacher was correct, in that population mean was equal to 14. We found that the *p*-value was equal to 0.216, which was not statistically significant, and therefore we could not say that the teacher is wrong. In other words, the probability that the result would have occurred, if the null hypothesis were true is not less than 0.05 – we therefore know that the result is not statistically significant.

We can also use confidence intervals to find out if we have any evidence that the teacher is wrong. In our example the 95% confidence interval is from 11.89 to 22.11. We know that in 95% of studies, the confidence interval contains the population value.

There's a link there, isn't there? We are using 95% confidence intervals, and 5% as our value for alpha. If, in 95% of studies, the population value will be between 11.89 and 22.11, what is the probability of our result occurring if the null hypothesis (the teacher is correct about the value being 14) is true? In 95% of studies, the true value is contained within the confidence intervals. In 5% of studies, the true value is therefore not contained within the confidence intervals. In 5% of studies, the result will be statistically significant, when the null hypothesis is true. If the confidence intervals contain the null hypothesis, the result is not statistically significant. If the confidence intervals do not contain the null hypothesis, the result is statistically significant. Confidence intervals and statistical significance are therefore two sides of the same coin.

Test yourself 3

In each of the following examples, the null hypothesis is that the mean score is zero. For some of the scores, the confidence intervals and *p*-values match. For others they don't. Which combinations of CIs and p-values are correct, and which are not?

1. 95% CI = 0.65, 1.27, $p = 0.001$.
2. 95% CI = 1.2, 45.3, $p = 0.767$
3. 95% CI = −2.28, 4.22, $p = 0.767$
4. 95% CI = −9.76, 11.58, $p = 0.025$
5. 95% CI = −0.20, 5.95, $p = 0.066$
6. 95% CI = −9.76, 11.58, $p = 0.025$
7. 95% CI = 0.00, 65.4, $p = 0.05$
8. 95% CI = 0.00, 13.2, $p = 0.50$

Answers are given at the end of the chapter.

Common Mistakes: Confidence intervals

1. If your confidence intervals range from −7 to 17, don't write this as CIs = −7 – 17, because it's not clear if that means minus seven to seventeen, or minus seven to minus seventeen. Always use a comma, or write the word 'to'.
2. Small things matter. If you write 0.1 instead of 0.01 in your report, it's a subtle change, but it has big consequences. If you write 'the *p*-value was 0.1, which is statistically significant at the 0.05 level, and therefore the null hypothesis was rejected', the reader will think you don't understand statistical significance. In fact, all you did was make a (very small) error.

SUMMARY

In this chapter we have looked under the bonnet of statistical tests and seen the basic principles of how they work. We have seen how to calculate the standard error and how to calculate confidence intervals. We have also met the concepts of probability and inference, and we're still standing.

So now, you ask, can we embark on our research? Well, no. How often do you have a null hypothesis that the mean score in a population is x (where x is any number you like)? Not very often. We had to go through this chapter to make life easier for ourselves in the future. Our null hypotheses are not about single values, they are about *relationships*; the relationship between the group a person is in (treatment, sex) and the score they get, or the relationship between two measures (reading ability and mathematical ability). But never fear, because we are onto that next.

Test yourself answers

Test yourself 1

1. 23. This means that in more than half of premier league football matches, two people on the pitch (we're including the referee) share a birthday.
2. Yes. It increases your chance of winning the car to 2/3.
3. It's more likely the taxi was blue.

We could discuss those problems for an awful long time, but we won't. We just wanted to show that probability was hard, even when it looks easy. (So imagine what it's like when it is hard.) If you want to know more, type the title of the problem into your favourite internet search engine, and you'll find explanations.

Optional Extra: The Monty Hall problem

The Monty Hall problem is discussed in an interesting way in Chapter 101 of Mark Haddon's book, *The Curious Incident of the Dog in the Night-time* (2003). (The chapters only have prime numbers, which explains the large chapter number.) The book is written from the point of view of a 15-year-old boy who is labelled as having Asperger's syndrome, which is a mild form of autism. It would make a pleasant contrast when you need a break from reading this one.

Test yourself 2

	Mean	N	Standard deviation	Standard error	$t_{\alpha/2}$	LCL	UCL
1.	10	49	9	1.29	2.01	7.41	12.59
2.	25	100	10	1.00	1.98	23.02	26.98
3.	100	9	6	2.00	2.31	95.39	104.61
4.	200	900	15	0.50	1.96	199.02	200.98
5.	10	10000	2	0.02	1.96	9.96	10.04
6.	16	40	5	0.79	2.02	14.40	17.60
7.	50	144	8	0.67	1.98	48.68	51.32
8.	12	9	2	0.67	2.31	10.46	13.54
9.	90	900	25	0.83	1.96	88.36	91.64
10.	500	100	4	0.40	1.98	499.21	500.79

Test yourself 3

1. The lower confidence interval is 0.65, and the upper is 1.27. The null hypothesis (zero) is not contained between these two values, so the result is statistically significant. The p-value of 0.001 is therefore correct.
2. The confidence intervals range from 1.2 to 45.3. Again, zero is not included between these values, so we would expect the result to be statistically significant. The p-value of 0.767 is greater than 0.05, and is not statistically significant. Therefore, this is wrong.
3. The confidence intervals, from −2.28 to 4.22 contain zero, and therefore we would expect the p-value not to be statistically significant. The result of 0.767 is therefore correct.
4. The confidence intervals, from −9.76 to 11.58 contain zero. Therefore, we would expect the result not to be statistically significant. The p-value of 0.025 is less than 0.05, and so is statistically significant. This cannot therefore be correct.
5. The confidence intervals, from −0.20 to 11.58 contain zero, and therefore we would expect the result to be non-significant. The p-value of 0.066 is greater than 0.05, and so is non-significant. This result is therefore correct. (Notice also that the confidence intervals only just contain zero, we would expect the result to be close to statistically significant, and when we examine the p-value, it is).
6. The confidence intervals are from 0.00 to 65.4, and therefore are exactly on the null hypothesis boundary. We would therefore expect the p-value to be exactly 0.05, and it is. This result is therefore correct.
7. Again, the confidence intervals are from 0.00 to 65.4, and therefore are exactly on the null hypothesis boundary. We would therefore expect the p-value to be exactly 0.05, but it is not. This result is therefore wrong.

USING SPSS

To obtain confidence intervals and statistical significance for a single variable, we do a one-sample *t*-test. Select **Analyze** $\Rightarrow$ **Compare Means** $\Rightarrow$ **One-Sample T Test**. The following window appears:

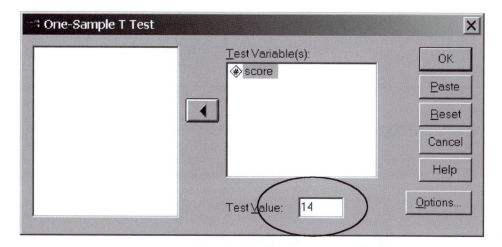

Change the value in **Test Value** to the number you are using for your null hypothesis. (In our example with reading scores this is 14, but it is most commonly zero.) Click OK. The first table presents the summary statistics:

One-Sample Statistics

	N	Mean	Std. Deviation	Std. Error Mean
Score	10	17.0000	7.14920	2.26078

The second table presents the value for *t*, the degrees of freedom, the mean difference (that is, the difference between the score in the sample, and the null hypothesis) and the confidence interval.

One-Sample Test

| | | | | | 95% Confidence Interval of the Difference | |
| | | | | Mean | | |
	t	df	Sig. (2-tailed)	Difference	Lower	Upper
Score	1.327	9	.217	3.00000	-2.1142	8.1142

To draw a chart showing the mean and the 95% confidence intervals, select **Graphs** ⇒ **Error Bar**:

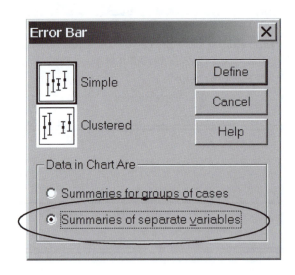

Change the **Data in Chart Are** option to **Summaries of separate variables**, and click **Define**.

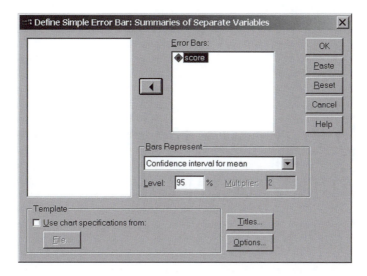

Choose the variable, and press **OK**. This produces the following chart.

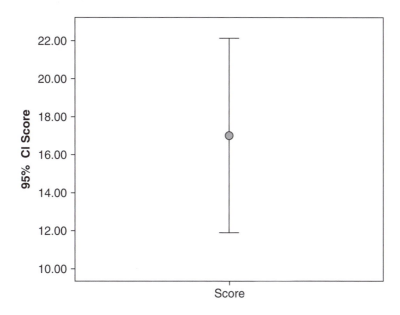

5

Analysing data from repeated measures experiments

What's in this chapter?

- Experimental design
- Repeated measures *t*-test
- Wilcoxon test
- Sign test
- Using SPSS

KEY TERMS

binomial distribution
carry-over effects
confidence interval
continuity correction
continuous scale
correlation
counterbalance
cross-over design
degrees of freedom
experimental design
non-parametric test
normally distributed
parametric test

practice effects
ranking
related design
repeated measures design
robust
sensitisation
sign test
standard deviation
standard error
t-test
variance
Wilcoxon test
within-subjects design

INTRODUCTION

This chapter is about the way we analyse the data we get from experiments that use a repeated measures (or within-subjects) design. We can collect our data and draw our charts, but how do we get to the probability values we dealt with in the previous chapters? There is a school of thought that says that if you can't see the effect in a chart then there probably isn't one there. Statisticians take a different view, however. They scoff at your charts, even if you colour them in nicely. They only look at the numbers. We'll try and find a happy medium between the two approaches but this is a statistics book, so expect more numbers and formulae than charts. In this chapter we will be using standard deviation, standard error, and confidence intervals, which are all covered in Chapter 4. You have been warned.

EXPERIMENTAL DESIGN

There are basically two types of **experimental design**. We can either compare the scores of individuals in one condition against their scores in another condition, or we can compare the scores of one group of people taking one condition against the scores of a different group of people in the other condition. There are variations on this theme, but these two possibilities are the fundamental ones. The first type is called a **repeated measures design**, and is the subject of this chapter.

REPEATED MEASURES DESIGNS

The simplest type of experiment to analyse is a repeated measures study. In this type of study, we have two conditions in which we want to test participants. For example:

- In their classic experiment on levels of processing, Craik and Tulving (1975) wanted to examine the effect of different levels of processing on memory for words. They wanted to make their participants process information at different levels, and see if this affected the participants' recall of the words. Each participant could process a number of words at different levels, and their recall could be compared for different types of processing.
- Neave, Emmett, Moss, Ayton, Scholey and Wesnes (2004) wanted to examine the cognitive and physiological effects of playing cricket (batting) whilst wearing a cricket helmet. They asked teenaged cricketers to have a batting session while wearing a helmet and while not wearing a helmet. They took both physiological measures (such as temperature and body mass) and cognitive measures (such as attention and reaction time).

Repeated measures studies also go under a number of other names:

- *Within-subjects studies (or within-subjects designs).* A **within-subjects design** looks for a change within a group of individuals, rather than between two groups, hence it is within subjects.
- *Related groups* (or related design). A **related design** is one in which the people undergoing two different treatments are closely matched, so that the two groups are not independent, rather they are related. Strictly speaking, a repeated measures design is a type of related design; however, it is very rare to encounter a study where both groups are sufficiently closely matched.
- *Cross-over studies* (or cross-over design). This term mainly tends to be used in medical research, and is not commonly used in psychology. It is called a **cross-over design** because people cross over from one group (say, the helmet group) to the other group (the non-helmet group).

All the names have their own logic and it is a matter of taste which one you choose. You can be sure, however, that whichever one you choose your statistics lecturer will snort with indignation at your choice.

Common Mistakes: Correlational and repeated measures designs

In a repeated measures design we test people twice, using the same measure. In a correlational design we test people twice, sometimes using the same measure. These designs are not the same thing.

A *correlational design* is used when we want to see if people who were high scorers on one test are also high scorers on the second test. We are not interested in whether the scores *overall* have gone up or down. (We will cover the correlational design in more detail in Chapter 8)

A *repeated measures* experimental design is used when we want to see if people, on average, score higher on one occasion than the other. We are not interested whether the people who scored high the first time also scored high the second time.

Make sure you describe your project correctly.

Advantages of repeated measures designs

Repeated measures designs have one huge advantage over the other designs: you don't need as many participants. Getting participants who are willing to take part in your research is difficult. It isn't just difficult for you, it's difficult for everyone. There are a string of papers in psychology that show that research published in journals doesn't tend to use enough people and the people they use are often psychology students sitting in lecture theatres (Banyard & Hunt, 2000).

If we use an experimental design where each person takes part twice, once in one condition, and once in the other condition, we have just halved the number of participants we need. However, it's even better than that. Think again of the Neave et al. study; had we used two separate groups, one with a helmet, and one without a helmet, each person in the helmet-wearing group is compared with what we think that person's score would have been, if they had been in the no-helmet group. But we don't know what their score would have been. We need to estimate it, and we must do this with some uncertainty. If we use a repeated measures design, we *know* what the score of that person in the no-helmet group is so there is no uncertainty. Each person acts as their own (perfectly) matched control, hence we need even fewer people.

Optional Extra: The importance of the correlation

It is often written that an independent group study needs more participants than a repeated measures study, but the question is: how many more? The answer depends on the stability of the thing we are measuring. If we are measuring something very stable, then the **correlation** of the two measures (see Chapter 8) will be very high and the study will need very few people. If we are measuring something which is less stable, then the correlation will be lower, and the relative advantage of repeated measures is reduced.

Let's give a concrete example, which might make more sense of that. Imagine we have some very stable measure, such as weight. A person's weight fluctuates a little over the course of a day. When they eat and drink, it goes up, when they exercise and go to the toilet, it goes down. But it changes by a very small amount, hence the correlation between two measurements is very high (if you are so inclined, weigh yourself, go to the toilet, and weigh yourself again; it's usually hard to see a difference). If I were to do something to people which increased their weight by 5% (in a person who weighed 10 stone, or 140 lbs, that would be about a 7 lb change), it would be very easy to detect that difference. Five per cent heavier is a lot, and you would notice if you were 5% heavier than yesterday.

Now think of something that is relatively unstable, such as level of energetic arousal. People's energetic arousal fluctuates a great deal, sometimes for reasons that we understand, and sometimes it seems to be just random. Yesterday, for example, Phil stayed up late, and so today he is not very energetic. Jeremy had a good night's sleep, and so is feeling energetic today. Tomorrow, Jeremy might wake up feeling tired, and Phil might wake up feeling alert, and there might not be

(Continued)

(Continued)

any obvious reason for this. If we could do something that would make Jeremy and Phil 5% more alert tomorrow, we probably wouldn't notice because sometimes these things just happen. Compare this with something that would make us 5% heavier tomorrow: we certainly would notice this, because these things do not just happen.

There are cases where there can be a negative correlation between the two measures, and when this is so, the repeated measures design is actually worse than the independent groups design. Imagine the situation where we want to examine the effect of different kinds of words on memory. We might have concrete words (e.g. carrot, table) and abstract words (e.g. anger, destiny) and we want to see which type of word is better remembered. We present each participant with a list of words, ask them to learn the words, and then see how many they have remembered. This is a repeated measures design, because each person takes part in both conditions; they learn concrete words and abstract words. It is possible that each person has a maximum number of words (of any type) that they are likely to remember. If this is the case, the more concrete words that they remember, the fewer abstract words they will remember, and vice versa. When this happens, the correlation will be negative, and we will actually be better off using an independent subjects design.

What this means for us, when deciding which design to use, is that the advantage of the repeated measures design increases with the correlation between the two measures. And this has to be taken into account when we consider the disadvantages of the repeated measures design, which we do next.

Disadvantages of repeated measures design

We have said that the repeated measures design is better, because it needs fewer subjects, so why don't we use repeated measures all of the time? The answer is that repeated measures designs bring their own set of problems with them. Keren (1993) has referred to this as 'a methodological dilemma' and points out three types of problems that need to be dealt with.

Practice effects

Practice effects occur when a participant gets better at a task over time. Morrison and Ellis (2000) were interested in looking at the effect of age of acquisition of a word, that is, the age at which children learn it. They wanted to see if the age of acquisition predicted how long it took a participant to start to say the word. Participants were seated at a computer, wearing headphones and a microphone. When a word appeared on the screen, the participants had to say it. This is an unusual and novel task, and it is likely that most people will improve at it over time. If all of the words which people learned when they were young came first it will appear that words with a younger age of acquisition are spoken more quickly; however, this might not be the case. This leads to our first solution: counterbalancing.

When we **counterbalance** we ensure that for half of the participants one group of words comes first, and for the other group of participants the other group of words comes first. Alternatively, we put the words into a different, random order for each participant. Some will receive the words that were acquired early first, some will receive the words that were acquired later first.

Counterbalancing does not solve all of our problems, however. Imagine that you are someone who gets the late-acquired words first. It might be that these words shouldn't take you any longer to say, but because you have just started and are a little confused, they do take longer to say. By the time you get the early-acquired words, you have no problem with the study, and can say these words more quickly. Compare this with someone who gets the early-acquired words first. These are easy, so you say them quickly, and by the time you get to the late-acquired words, you've got the hang of it, so you can say these quickly too. On average, early-acquired words are spoken more quickly than late-acquired words, when in fact there is no real difference between the two. Counterbalancing has not solved our problem, we need a new solution: **practice items**.

Before the real study starts, we give people a set of items that we are not interested in. These are to ensure that the participant has understood the study, and learned the task. Practice effects follow a classic learning curve, that is, improvement is rapid to start with and then levels off, so a small number of trials at the start should get rid of this effect.

Morrison and Ellis used both of these approaches. First, they randomised the order of presentation. Each person saw 220 words, in five blocks of 44. The order of the blocks was randomly determined for each participant. Second, before each participant started, they were given 20 practice items.

Sensitisation

The second problem identified by Keren is **sensitisation**. The participant may perceive that a dependency exists between two measurements, and deliberately keep their answers similar when we are looking for a change. Alternatively, because the participant perceives that the researcher is looking for a change, they might change their answer. In Piaget's classic studies on conservation of number, a researcher would ask a child if two rows of sweets had the same number, then the researcher would spread out the sweets and ask the question again. Children were likely to say that the rows of sweets were not the same. McGarrigle and Donaldson (1974) suggested that this was not because the children didn't understand, but that they perceived that the researcher wouldn't be asking the question again if they expected the same answer. Instead of the researcher rearranging the sweets, McGarrigle and Donaldson used Naughty Teddy who rearranged the sweets. Now it made sense to children that the answer was the same, and they gave the correct answer at a younger age. In this case the problem of sensitisation was solved by Naughty Teddy.

In many cases there is no easy solution, and we cannot, therefore, always use repeated measures design.

Carry-over effects

The third problem identified by Keren is that of **carry-over effects**. A carry-over effect occurs when something about the previous condition is 'carried over' into the next condition. One classic type of carry-over is a drug treatment. If we want to examine the effect of a drug using a repeated measures design, we have to make sure that when an individual changes from the treatment group to the control group there is no remnant of the drug left in their body. The solution to this problem is to include a 'wash-out' period, when the participant stops taking the drug, but before they are assessed in the treatment group.

A second type of carry-over effect is fatigue. A person may get tired and do less well, as the experiment progresses. Counterbalancing is one way of trying to solve this problem, but is not necessarily completely successful, for similar reasons to those we saw when we examined practice effects. It may be that fatigue differentially affects different types of task. For example, if we look again at the Morrison and Ellis study, it may be that when the participant is not fatigued, there would be no difference between the word types. However, when the participant is fatigued, there will be a difference between the words.

The obvious way to avoid this is to allow the participant to rest. Morrison and Ellis split the words into 5 blocks of 44 words, and allowed the participants to rest between studies.

STATISTICAL TESTS FOR REPEATED MEASURES DESIGNS

We will examine three different tests for repeated measures data:

1. The repeated measures *t*-test. This is a parametric test for continuous data.
2. The Wilcoxon test. This is a non-parametric test for ordinal data.
3. The sign test. This is a non-parametric test for categorical data.

The test you choose depends on the data you are testing. The *t*-test is the most powerful, and is the test most likely to spot significant differences in your data. You cannot use it with all repeated measures data, however, and you have to be sure that your data satisfy some conditions before you choose this test. The next choice is commonly the **Wilcoxon test**, which will deal with all data that can be ordered (ordinal data). The **sign test** only deals with data in the form of categories (nominal data). The delight of the sign test is that it is easy to understand and easy to calculate. The down side is that it only deals with crude categories, rather than rich data of ranks or intervals.

The repeated measures *t-test*

To use a repeated measures *t*-test, we need to make two assumptions about our data.

1.   The data are measured on a continuous (interval) level.
2.   The differences between the two scores are normally distributed.

Common Mistakes: Assumptions of the repeated measures *t*-test

The repeated measures *t*-test makes no assumption about the distribution of the scores. It only makes an assumption about the *differences* between the scores. It is possible to have variables which have highly non-normal distributions, but which have normally distributed differences.

The repeated measures *t*-test also makes no assumption about the variances of the variables. That's the independent samples *t*-test, which we cover in the next chapter.

Given a sufficiently large sample, the repeated measures *t*-test is **robust** against violations of both of these assumptions. Above sample sizes of approximately 50, the test becomes very robust to violations of distributional assumptions. It's not difficult to demonstrate this, but it does go beyond the scope of this book. However, if you really, really want to know, email us at *ireallyreallywanttoknow@jeremymiles.co.uk*, and we'll either tell you the answer or write a web page that explains it.

The procedure for carrying out the repeated measures *t*-test is very similar to the procedure that we described in Chapter 4, when we examined statistical significance and confidence intervals:

1.   Calculate the difference between the scores for each person.
2.   Calculate the mean and standard deviation of the difference.
3.   Calculate the standard error of the difference, using the result from step 2.
4.   Calculate the confidence interval for the difference, using the result from step 3.
5.   Calculate the statistical significance of the difference, using the result from step 3.

We shall illustrate this with the data in Table 5.1 from Neave et al. (2004)[1]. Cricketers were asked to rate their body temperature on a 9-point scale, where 1 meant 'not at all hot' and 9

---

[1]We are grateful to Nick Neave for providing these data and allowing us to use them.

Table 5.1   *Raw data showing subjective temperature rating and difference score*

Cricketer	Helmet	No helmet	Difference
1	6.0	7.0	1.0
2	7.0	6.0	−1.0
3	4.5	5.5	1.0
4	6.0	5.0	−1.0
5	6.5	5.0	−1.5
6	6.5	7.0	0.5
7	5.0	6.0	1.0
8	7.0	6.5	−0.5
9	6.0	6.0	0.0
10	7.0	7.0	0.0
11	6.0	7.5	1.5
12	5.5	5.5	0.0
13	7.0	6.5	−0.5
14	6.5	7.0	0.5
15	7.0	6.0	−1.0
16	7.0	6.5	−0.5

meant 'extremely hot', after they had been batting against an automatic bowling machine and running. On one occasion they were wearing a helmet, on the other occasion they were not. (Ignore the right-hand column for the moment.)

First, we should check that the assumptions have been satisfied:

1. The data are measured on a **continuous scale**. If we were going to apply this condition strictly, we might argue that this was not a continuous scale. However, a 9-point scale is sufficiently close to a continuous scale that we would be happy to treat it as such.
2. The difference between the scores is approximately **normally distributed**. To answer this question we need to calculate the differences between the scores (see the right-hand column of Table 5.1), and then use some method to ensure that the distribution is approximately normal.

It might also be helpful to keep an eye on the logic of this exercise. If the helmet has an effect such as making the cricketers feel hotter then they will report higher temperatures with the helmet than they do without. This means that when we work out the difference score by subtracting the with-helmet score from the no-helmet score we will get a negative number. If we get a zero there is obviously no difference and if we get a positive number it means they felt hotter without the helmet. If the helmets are making the cricketers feel hotter we will get a long list of minus values in the difference column, but if there is little effect we will get an even mixture of minus and plus signs.

We can illustrate the differences in a chart. Figure 5.1 shows a histogram of the difference scores. We can see that the distribution is approximately normal, and hence we are happy to carry out a repeated measures *t*-test. You might also notice that seven cricketers have positive differences and six cricketers have negative differences. A first sight of the data suggests that the helmets do not have a clear effect on the perceived temperature of the cricketers.

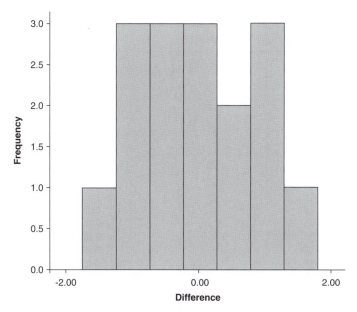

Figure 5.1   Histogram of difference scores, showing approximate normal distribution

Let us now work through our five-step procedure for carrying out the repeated measures *t*-test.

Step 1: Calculate the difference scores.
The first stage of the repeated measures *t*-test is to calculate the differences between the two scores. We have already done this in Table 5.1.

Step 2: Calculate the mean and standard deviation of the difference.
The mean $\bar{x}$ is given by:

$$\bar{x} = \frac{\sum x}{n}.$$

Remember that the symbol Σ means 'add up all the values of', so if we want to know the mean of the difference, we add up all of the scores, and divide by the number of people:

$$\bar{x} = \frac{\begin{array}{c} 1.0 + (-1.0) + 1.0 + (-1.0) + (-1.5) + 0.5 + 1.0 + (-0.5) \\ + 0.0 + 0.0 + 1.5 + 0.0 + (-0.5) + 0.5 + (-1.0) + (-0.5) \end{array}}{16}$$

$$= \frac{-0.5}{16} = -0.03125$$

Table 5.2   *Calculating the standard deviation*

Cricketer	Change (x)	Mean ($\bar{x}$)	$x - \bar{x}$	$(x - \bar{x})^2$
1	1.0	−0.03125	1.031	1.063
2	−1.0		−0.969	0.938
3	1.0		1.031	1.063
4	−1.0		−0.969	0.938
5	−1.5		−1.469	2.157
6	0.5		0.531	0.282
7	1.0		1.031	1.063
8	−0.5		−0.469	0.220
9	0.0		0.031	0.001
10	0.0		0.031	0.001
11	1.5		1.531	2.345
12	0.0		0.031	0.001
13	−0.5		−0.469	0.220
14	0.5		0.531	0.282
15	−1.0		−0.969	0.938
16	−0.5		−0.469	0.220

It's always worth stopping and thinking about your data. What does this mean for the study? Does it make sense? If we found that the difference was 30, we would know that we had made a mistake (because the scale only goes from 1 to 9).

We can see that the mean difference is negative. This means that people were hotter when they were wearing a helmet, which is what we would expect, but we can also see that the difference is 0.03, which, on a scale of 1 to 9, is not a very big difference. And remember there are more people who felt hotter without the helmet than felt hotter with it.

We now turn to the **standard deviation** (σ). Remember that the formula for the standard deviation is:

$$\sigma = \sqrt{\frac{\sum (x - \bar{x})^2}{N - 1}}$$

This looks much harder than it is. On top of the equation we have $\sum(x - \bar{x})^2$ which means 'find the difference between each score and the mean, square them and add them up'.

Let's go back to our data and add some more columns. Look at Table 5.2. It has three additional columns. In the third column, we have written the mean. In the fourth column is the difference between the mean and the change for each person – this is $x - \bar{x}$. In the fifth column are the values of the fourth column, squared – this is $(x - \bar{x})^2$.

We need to find the value $\sum(x - \bar{x})^2$ which is the sum of the values in the fifth column. Forgive us for not showing all of the working, but the total is equal to 11.734.

The next part of the equation is the bottom, which is $N - 1$. N is 16, because we have 16 people, so $N - 1$ is equal to 15.

The standard deviation is therefore:

$$\sigma = \sqrt{\frac{11.874}{15}} = \sqrt{0.782} = 0.884$$

Step 3: Calculate the standard error of the difference.

We calculate the **standard error** in the same way as we calculate the standard error of a single variable:

$$se = \frac{\sigma}{\sqrt{N}}$$

We know σ, the standard deviation, because we have just calculated it. N is still the sample size. So we have

$$se = \frac{\sigma}{\sqrt{N}} = \frac{0.884}{\sqrt{16}} = \frac{0.884}{4} = 0.221$$

The standard error is not very much use on its own, but we use it in the next two steps to calculate the confidence intervals and the probability values.

*Step 4: Calculate the **Confidence Interval**.*

The **confidence interval** tells us about the likely range of the true value of the score. It is given by

$$CI = \bar{x} \pm t_\alpha \times se$$

We already know the value of se, the standard error. We need to know the value of t_α. That sort of symbol probably frightens you a little bit and that's not surprising because it certainly used to frighten us. It's not so bad really and you'll soon be used to it.

We need to know what confidence intervals we are interested in. The answer is almost always the 95% confidence intervals, so α (alpha) is equal to 0.05. We need the cut-off value for t, at the 0.05 level. We can use a table or a computer program to do this (see pages 94–5), but first we need to know the **degrees of freedom** (df). In this case, df = $N-1$, so we have 15 df. With 15 df, the 0.05 cut-off for t is 2.131. The equation has a $\pm$ symbol in it. This means that we calculate the answer twice, once for the lower confidence interval and once for the upper confidence interval.

$$\text{Lower CI} = -0.031 - 2.131 \times 0.221 = -0.502$$
$$\text{Upper CI} = -0.031 + 2.131 \times 0.221 = 0.440$$

Test yourself 1: Interpretation of confidence intervals

We have found a confidence interval from –0.502 to 0.440. What does this mean?

(a)   We are 95% confident that the population effect of removing a helmet is between –0.502 and 0.440.
(b)   This study has found that the effect of removing a helmet is between –0.502 and 0.440. In 95% of studies, this value will contain the population value.

Answer is given at the end of the chapter.

Reporting the confidence intervals

To report this result, you would write: 'When participants played with a helmet their mean temperature rating was 6.281. When they removed the helmet, the mean rating was 6.25 (difference = –0.031; 95% CI = –0.502, 0.440).'

Given that the confidence interval crosses zero, we cannot reject the null hypothesis that there is no difference between the two conditions.

Step 5: Calculate the probability value.

To do this we calculate the value of t, and we then find the probability of a value that large (or larger) occurring, given that the null hypothesis (the null hypothesis being that there is no effect of wearing a helmet) is true.

The formula for the repeated measures t-test is very simple:

$$t = \frac{x}{se}$$

where x is the mean (of the change score) and se is the standard error of that score:

$$t = \frac{-0.03125}{0.221} = -0.141$$

A negative value for t has the same effect as a positive value (it just depends on which condition you subtracted from the other) so we can ignore this, and find that $t = 0.0141$.

Before we can find the probability value associated with t, we need to know the degrees of freedom associated with t. Again, this is given by:

$$df = N - 1 = 16 - 1 = 15$$

Test yourself 2: Hypotheses

Which of the following would it be OK to say?

(a)   We do not reject the null hypothesis.
(b)   We accept the null hypothesis.
(c)   We reject the alternative hypothesis.
(d)   We do not accept the alternative hypothesis.

Answer is given at the end of the chapter.

Test yourself 3: Hypotheses again

What does the *p*-value represent? (You can choose more than one answer.)

(a)   The probability that the null hypothesis is true.
(b)   The probability that the null hypothesis is false.
(c)   The probability that another study would get the same result as this study.
(d)   The probability that another study would not find a difference between the two conditions.
(e)   The probability that we have got the right answer.

Answer is given at the end of the chapter.

We can now use a table or a computer to tell us the probability of getting a value of *t* at least as large as 0.141; when there are 15 df this gives us a value of $p = 0.889$. Because this is higher than 0.05, we cannot reject the null hypothesis that there is no effect of helmet on subjective temperature. If you followed this from the start and kept your eye on the data this probability value will not be a surprise.

We can add the *p*-value to the sentence on the confidence interval: 'When participants played with a helmet their mean temperature rating was 6.281. When they removed the helmet, the mean rating was 6.25 (difference = −0.031; 95% CI = −0.502, 0.440; $p = 0.89$).'

Optional Extra: Reporting the *t*-test

There is some controversy concerning how to report the results of a *t*-test. Some people suggest that you should report the values of *t* and df. We say that the only reason you might want to report the *t* and df is to calculate the *p*-value, they don't mean anything on their own, and we have given the *p*-value.

The Wilcoxon test

When we have data that do not satisfy the assumptions of the repeated measures *t*-test, either because the differences are not normally distributed, or because the measures are ordinal, we can use the Wilcoxon test.

The Wilcoxon test is our first example of a **non-parametric test**. A **parametric test**, such as the *t*-test, makes inferences about population parameters. When we were considering making inferences and statements of significance we talked about the confidence intervals and the population values. A non-parametric test does not try to do this. We cannot make inferences about population parameters so we don't talk about population values with (most) non-parametric tests.

Non-parametric tests use ranks, so if our data has not been measured on an ordinal scale we convert them to an ordinal scale. When we have an ordinal scale, we do not know how far the gaps are between two scores, we just know the *order* of the scores. We know that the winner in a race came first, and they get the prize money; the person that came second does not get any prize money, however close behind they were.

Optional Extra: Two Wilcoxon tests

Frank Wilcoxon was an industrial chemist, who did a little statistics on the side. He developed two statistical tests, which have come to be known as the Wilcoxon rank-sum test and the Wilcoxon signed ranks test. These two names are very similar, and confusing, even to people like us. Fortunately, the rank-sum test is equivalent to another test we will encounter in Chapter 6, called the Mann–Whitney test. The Mann–Whitney test is easier to calculate than the rank-sum test. Because of this, we can ignore the Wilcoxon rank-sum test, and when we talk about the Wilcoxon test, we are talking about the signed ranks test only. You will sometimes see the Wilcoxon rank-sum test called the Wilcoxon–Mann–Whitney test.

The two tests were presented in a paper that was only four pages long (Wilcoxon, 1945).

In their study of the effect of cricket helmets, Neave et al. (2004), took measures of memory, to examine whether the helmet had any effect on cognitive ability. The specific test that we will look at is delayed word recall. Table 5.3 shows the results of this part of the study.

A histogram of the change scores is shown in Figure 5.2. This shows a degree of positive skew, hence we have violated the assumption of the *t*-test. (If the sample were larger, this degree of skew might not concern us; however, with a sample size of 16, we need to be more careful about the assumptions.)

Step 1 when calculating the Wilcoxon test is to rank the change scores (column 4 in Table 5.3) *ignoring the sign*, so if there is a minus sign on the change score, we don't take any notice of it. (See the box for more on ranking.)

Table 5.3 *Delayed word recall scores for helmet condition, no helmet condition, and difference between them*

Cricketer	Helmet	No helmet	Difference
1	7	4	–3
2	7	2	–5
3	3	6	3
4	6	7	1
5	5	10	5
6	5	7	2
7	6	7	1
8	2	4	2
9	0	5	5
10	7	6	–1
11	5	9	4
12	1	5	4
13	5	9	4
14	4	3	–1
15	1	5	4
16	3	5	2

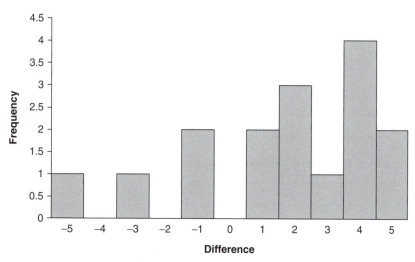

Figure 5.2 Histogram of the change in delayed word recall

Tip: Ranking

As this is the first of the non-parametric tests that we will encounter, this is the first time that we will have to rank. Follow these instructions and you can be sucessful rankers.

Example 1: Ranking without tied scores

To rank data, we give the lowest score the rank 1, the next lowest 2, etc, up to the highest score, which gets the value equal to the number of people in the dataset. Suppose we wish to rank the following data:

| 13 | 14 | 56 | 8 | 4 | 17 | 12 | 92 | 65 | 44 |

The first stage, which is not strictly necessary, but does make things easier, is to sort the numbers into ascending order:

| 4 | 8 | 12 | 13 | 14 | 17 | 44 | 56 | 65 | 92 |

Now we are ready to place the rank with the numbers:

Score	4	8	12	13	14	17	44	56	65	92
Rank	1	2	3	4	5	6	7	8	9	10

You can see that 4 has been given the rank of 1, because it is the lowest number, 8 is given the rank of 2, etc.

Example 2: Ranking with tied scores

We will now introduce a small complication. Suppose there are ties in the data:

| 12 | 14 | 17 | 12 | 11 | 17 | 17 | 17 | 12 | 14 |

Again, the first stage is to sort the data, from lowest to highest.

| 11 | 12 | 12 | 12 | 14 | 14 | 17 | 17 | 17 | 17 |

Let's also number the data from left to right:

Number	1	2	3	4	5	6	7	8	9	10
Score	11	12	12	12	14	14	17	17	17	17

(Continued)

(Continued)

Now the ranks can be assigned to each of the data points. The number 11 is the lowest score, so that is given the rank of 1. The number 12 comes in position 2, 3 and 4; it is therefore given the mean rank of these (which is easy to see, because it is the middle rank), and so is ranked 3. The score of 12 has 'used up' the ranks 2, 3 and 4, so 14 is ranked 5 and 6, which means that 14 is given the rank 5.5. Finally, 17 is ranked 7, 8, 9 and 10, which means that all of the 17s are ranked 8.5. So the ranked data set is as follows:

Score	11	12	12	12	14	14	17	17	17	17
Rank	1	3	3	3	5.5	5.5	8.5	8.5	8.5	8.5

That wasn't too hard was it? Beware, though, because it is very easy to make arithmetic errors in this process.

The ranked change scores, with the signs ignored, are shown in Table 5.4. This tells us about the amount that people changed, but not the direction that they changed in.

Step 2 is to separate out the ranks of the people who scored more without a helmet (they have a positive change score) from the people who scored less without a helmet (they have a negative change score). The separated ranks are shown in Table 5.5.

Table 5.4 *Ranked change scores, ignoring signs*

Cricketer	Difference	Rank (ignoring sign)
1	−3	8.5
2	−5	15.0
3	3	8.5
4	1	2.5
5	5	15.0
6	2	6.0
7	1	2.5
8	2	6.0
9	5	15.0
10	−1	2.5
11	4	11.5
12	4	11.5
13	4	11.5
14	−1	2.5
15	4	11.5
16	2	6.0

Table 5.5 *Positive and negative ranks separated*

Cricketer	Difference	Rank (ignoring sign)	Positive	Negative
1	−3	8.5		8.5
2	−5	15.0		15.0
3	3	8.5	8.5	
4	1	2.5	2.5	
5	5	15.0	15.0	
6	2	6.0	6.0	
7	1	2.5	2.5	
8	2	6.0	6.0	
9	5	15.0	15.0	
10	−1	2.5		2.5
11	4	11.5	11.5	
12	4	11.5	11.5	
13	4	11.5	11.5	
14	−1	2.5		2.5
15	4	11.5	11.5	
16	2	6.0	6.0	

Now we add up the two columns of ranks. (Can you see why it's called the *signed ranks test*?) For the positive ranks the sum is 107.5, for the negative ranks the sum is 28.5. The test statistic for the Wilcoxon test is known as T (that's a capital T, unlike the *t*-test, which has a lower-case *t*) and is given by whichever is the lower of these two values.

In our case $T = 28.5$.

That's all there is to it.

Step 3 is to know the probability associated with this value for T. There are two ways to do this:

1. *We can look it up in a table.* To do this, we need to know the value for T and the sample size. You will find an appropriate table in Appendix 6 at the back of the book. Here we reproduce an excerpt from it, the row for $N = 16$:

		p	
N	0.1	0.05	0.01
16	35	29	19

For our result to be statistically significant, at the given level, the value of T must be below the critical value given in the table. The first column shows the cut-off for the 0.1 level of significance and that is 35. The value for T that we have is below that, so the probability value is less than 0.1. The next column is for 0.05 and this is 29, and the value that we have for T is below that so our *p*-value is less than 0.05. The next column shows the *p*-value for the 0.01 level of significance and this is 19. But our value of T is above 19, so our *p*-value is somewhere between 0.01 and 0.05.

There are times when we can't use a table, for example when the sample size is bigger than the values given in the table. And anyway, wouldn't it be nice to know exactly what the p value was? In this case, as long as our sample size is above 10 we can use the normal approximation.

2. *The normal approximation.* This is a formula which will convert our value of T into a value of z, which as we know (from Chapter 4) we can look up in a normal distribution table, or use a computer, to get the exact p-value. The formula looks like this:

$$z = \frac{T - N(N+1)/4}{\sqrt{N(N+1)(2N+1)/24}}$$

Tip: Don't panic

Once again, although the formula looks intimidating you can maybe work it out in your head or at worst using the calculator in your mobile phone.

We hope you don't mind if we step through that formula quite quickly (it's hardly interesting, is it?)

$$z = \frac{28.5 - 16(16+1)/4}{\sqrt{16(16+1)(2 \times 16 + 1)/24}} = \frac{-39.5}{\sqrt{374}} = \frac{-39.5}{19.33} = -2.04$$

We can look up the probability associated with this value of z, and we find that it is 0.02. However, we must also remember that that value only includes one tail of the distribution – so we need to double the probability value given, giving us a value of 0.04.

Optional Extra: Extra formulae for the Wilcoxon z transformation

The formula for converting Wilcoxon T to z is a slight simplification, and you might encounter two slightly different formulae. First, there is the **continuity correction**. We might need to use a continuity correction because we need to correct for continuity (*Really! – Ed*). The z distribution is continuous – that is, any value at all is possible. However, the Wilcoxon T distribution is not truly continuous, because it can only change in steps. It is hard to see how we could have got a value of 28.413 from our

(Continued)

(Continued)

data, because we added ranks. However, the z calculation assumes that we could have that value (or any other). The continuity correction is very easy: we just add −0.5 to the top of the equation.

So, instead of looking like this:

$$z = \frac{T - N(N+1)/4}{\sqrt{N(N+1)(2N+1)/24}}$$

it looks like this:

$$z = \frac{[T - N(N+1)/4] - 0.5}{\sqrt{N(N+1)(2N+1)/24}}$$

Continuity corrections are a bit controversial in statistics (see what statisticians get excited about?). If we employ a continuity correction, we are sure that our type I error rate is controlled at, or below, 0.05. If we don't, then the type I error rate might be above 0.05. However, the price of using the continuity correction is (always) a slight loss of power. Sheskin (2003) suggests that you should perhaps analyse the data twice, once with and once without the continuity correction. If it makes a difference, then you should collect more data.

The second complication is that the calculation of z assumes that there are no ties in the data – that is, no one had the same score on both occasions. This is true in our data, but if it weren't, we would need to use a further correction. We would add the number of ties, called t, into the equation:

$$z = \frac{[T - N(N+1)/4]}{\sqrt{[N(N+1)(2N+1)/24] - [\Sigma t^3 - \Sigma t]/48}}$$

If we wanted the continuity correction as well, we would use:

$$z = \frac{[T - N(N+1)/4] - 0.5}{\sqrt{[N(N+1)(2N+1)/24] - [\Sigma t^3 - \Sigma t]/48}}$$

Unless you have a large number of ties, this correction is going to have very little effect.

When SPSS calculates the value of z, it does use the correction for the number of ties, but it does not use the continuity correction.

Reporting the Wilcoxon test

When reporting the Wilcoxon test, we might report the means, and the difference between the means, but if we were going to use means, we shouldn't really have done a Wilcoxon test. Instead, we could report the medians, and inter-quartile ranges, for each group.[2] Here's an example of what you might write: 'The median delayed word recall in the helmet group was 5.00 (quartiles 2.25, 6.00) and in the non-helmet group it was 5.50 (quartiles 4.25, 7.00). The difference was statistically significant, Wilcoxon $T = 28.50$, $z = 2.05$, $p = 0.04$.'

Test yourself 4: Probability statements

Which of the following does the probability of 0.04 represent?

(a) The probability that the helmet makes no difference to memory.
(b) The probability that the helmet makes a difference to memory.
(c) The probability of getting a difference this large, or larger, if the helmet makes no difference to memory.
(d) The probability of getting a difference this large, or larger, if the helmet makes a difference to memory.

Answer is given at the end of the chapter.

The sign test

The final test that we shall look at in this chapter is the sign test. The sign test is used when we have nominal data with two categories, and have repeated measures data. You will be glad to hear that it is the easiest statistical test that you will ever carry out. By a long way. Honest.

As an example, we will examine a study carried out by White, Lewith, Hopwood and Prescott (2003). When we carry out evaluations of different treatments we want to ensure that the patients and the people who are evaluating the treatment are not aware of which treatment the patient received. This is referred to as blinding, or masking (recently many people have started to prefer the word masking, although blinding is used more commonly).

If the treatment is a drug, this is easy. You give the patient either the real drug, or some pills which contain no active ingredients. On other occasions, it is much more difficult. Acupuncture is one such case. If I stick a needle in you, you know about it. It is hard to mask the treatment from the patient (it is impossible to mask the treatment from the therapist, but it is possible for a different person to carry out the assessment, who is unaware

---

[2] A rather weird possible problem is that the medians and inter-quartile ranges *can be the same* but the difference can still be statistically significant, according to the test (and the test is right). However, this is so unlikely that you can forget about it.

of which treatment a person had). One approach to this problem is to carry out 'sham acupuncture' where you put the needles in the wrong place. This might be your idea of fun, but it raises an ethical issue as people don't want to have needles put in them if they think the needles aren't going to have any effect (surely this is what happens in accupuncture? *Skeptical – Ed*).

One solution that has been proposed is the 'Streitberger needle'. This is a needle that is a bit like the sort of dagger that is used on stage and in films. As the needle is pushed down it appears that the needle is going into the skin, but actually it is retracting into the handle. The needle causes a slight pricking sensation, and this might convince the patient that a real needle is going into the skin. White et al. carried out an evaluation of the Streitberger needle, comparing it with a normal acupuncture needle. They were interested in whether patients could tell the difference between them. They used 36 patients in the study, and they asked them to score which needle gave the strongest stinging sensation. The results are shown in Table 5.6.

Table 5.6   *Results of White et al.*

Needle type	Number of patients
Normal needle stung more	19
Streitberger needle stung more	14
No difference in needles	3

The test statistic from the sign test is called *S*. Remember we told you that the sign test was the easiest statistical test by far. (Did you believe us?)

We find that 19 people said that one treatment stung more, and 14 people said that the other treatment stung more. *S* is the smaller of these two values, so

$$S = 14.$$

That's it. Now do you believe us?

Common Mistake: *N* in the sign test

In the sign test, *N* is different from in other tests. The sign test uses *N* as the total number of people for whom there was not a tie. Although there were 36 people in the study, 3 of them gave the same rating to each needle type, so *N* = 33.

Of course, we need to know the probability value associated with that value, and to do that we need to either look it up in a statistical table or use a computer.

To use the table in Appendix 7, we need to know two values: *S* and *N*. Choose the appropriate row, which is equal to our *N*. Select the column that matches our value for *S*. Using this we find that the probability value for our result is equal to 0.487. As this result is greater than 0.05, we cannot reject the null hypothesis that the needles are equivalent.

Test yourself 5

Does this *p*-value mean that we have found that there is no difference between the two sets of needles?

Answer is given at the end of the chapter.

If we can't find a table we can use a computer program that has a **binomial distribution** function in it. Luckily, all the programs that we have been using so far have got such a thing. In Excel, we type:

$$= \text{binomdist}(S,N,0.5,1)*2$$

substituting the values 14 for *S*, and 33 for *N*. (We need to multiply by 2, to ensure the probability is two-tailed.)

SUMMARY

We have looked at three ways to analyse data from repeated measures design experiments. The selection of test depends on the data that you have collected. All of the tests give us a probability statement at the end of the process so we can draw some conclusions about our hypothesis. So far so good, though be warned that the experiments we looked at here have very basic designs, with just one independent variable and only two measures of it. Out there in the big, bad world of experimentation there are studies with more variables and more measures. On the good side, you can analyse using the same principles as in this chapter.

Test yourself answers

Test yourself 1

Answer (b).

Test yourself 2

Although these four sound very similar to one another, we should only say that we do not reject the null hypothesis. Both (b) and (c) would be very wrong – this would imply that we have demonstrated that wearing a helmet makes no difference, and this is not the case; we have failed to find a difference, but that does not mean that there is no difference. Answer (d) just sounds a bit weird.

Test yourself 3

We're not above asking the odd trick question (sorry). The *p*-value is the probability of a difference that large occurring, if the null hypothesis is correct. If you selected any answers, go to the back of the class and read Chapter 4 again. Who said life was fair?

Test yourself 4

Answer (c). The probability of getting a difference this large, if there is no effect.

Test yourself 5

No. It means that we have found no evidence of a difference – this does not mean that there is no difference.

USING SPSS

To carry out a repeated measures *t*-test in SPSS select **Analyze** ⇒ **Compare Means** ⇒ **Paired-Samples T Test**. You need to choose two variables, which are paired, on the left-hand side (it says at the bottom which variables you have selected; note that this is a bit fiddly if you have a lot of data). Click the arrow to move the pair to the right, and press **OK**.

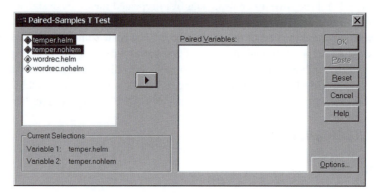

The first table that SPSS gives is some descriptive statistics.

Paired Samples Statistics

		Mean	N	Std. Deviation	Std. Error Mean
Pair 1	temper.helm	6.250	16	.7528	.1882
	temper.nohelm	6.281	16	.7739	.1935

Next is the table showing the correlation. (It is useful, as we saw, to know about the effectiveness of the repeated measures design, though it usually isn't reported.)

Paired Samples Correlations

		N	Correlation	Sig.
Pair 1	temper.helm & temper.nohlem	16	.329	.213

Finally, we have the table we are actually interested in – it's the results of the *t*-test.

Paired Samples Test

		Paired Differences					t	df	Sig. (2-tailed)
		Mean	Std. Deviation	Std. Error Mean	95% Confidence Interval of the Difference				
					Lower	Upper			
Pair 1	temper.helm - temper.nohlem	-.0313	.8845	.2211	-.5026	.4401	-.141	15	.889

The Wilcoxon test in SPSS is very similar to the *t*-test. Select **Analyze Nonparametric Tests ⇒ 2 Related Samples**.

As before, choose your two variables. However, this time, in order to click on the second variable, you need to hold down the Control key. Use the arrow button to put them into the box on the right, and press **OK**. (You'll notice that there are a selection of possible tests; however, the Wilcoxon test is the one that is selected by default.)

The first part of the output gives the number of positive and negative ranks, their means and totals.

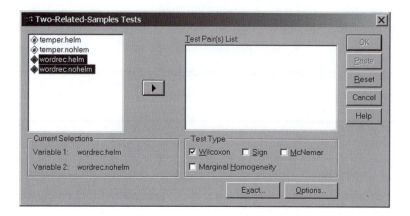

Ranks

		N	Mean Rank	Sum of Ranks
wordrec.nohelm - wordrec.helm	Negative Ranks	4[a]	7.13	28.50
	Positive Ranks	12[b]	8.96	107.50
	Ties	0[c]		
	Total	16		

a. wordrec.nohelm del word rec1 < wordrec.helm del word rec1
b. wordrec.nohelm del word rec1 > wordrec.helm del word rec1
c. wordrec.nohelm del word rec1 = wordrec.helm del word rec1

The second part gives z and the significance. It doesn't explicitly give you the Wilcoxon T, but we know that it is the smaller of the two sums of ranks.

Test Statistics[b]

	wordrec.nohel m del word rec1 - wordrec.helm del word rec1
Z	-2.052[a]
Asymp. Sig. (2-tailed)	.040

a. Based on negative ranks
b. Wilcoxon Signed Ranks Test

The procedure for the sign test is almost exactly the same as the Wilcoxon test. Select **Analyze ⇒ Nonparametric Tests ⇒ 2 Related Samples**. Choose your two variables (remembering that you need to hold down Control to select two variables). Change the **Test Type** from Wilcoxon to Sign. Click **OK**.

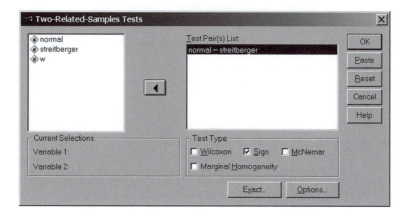

The first part of the output reports the number of positive differences, negative differences and ties.

Frequencies

		N
streitberger - normal	Negative Differences[a]	19
	Positive Differences[b]	14
	Ties[c]	3
	Total	36

a. streitberger < normal
b. streitberger > normal
c. streitberger = normal

The second part gives z and the p-value. (We didn't look at the calculation of z, because it's easier to either use a table, or use the binomial distribution). Note that, as with the Wilcoxon test, the test statistic is not given.

Test Statistics [a]

	streitberger - normal
Z	-.696
Asymp. Sig. (2-tailed)	.486

a. Sign Test

6

Analysing data from independent groups: continuous and ordinal measures

KEY TERMS

box and whisker plot
chi-square test
Cohen's *d*
confidence interval
continuous (interval) scale
control group
effect size
experimental design

homogeneity of variance
independent groups design
independent groups *t*-test
Mann–Whitney test
non-parametric test
normal distribution
pooled variance *t*-test
power

quasi-experimental design   unpooled variance *t*-test
standard deviations   variance
standard error   *z*-score
type I error rate

INTRODUCTION

This chapter tells you how to analyse data from experiments that use an independent groups (or between-subjects) design. It tells you how to get from charts and data to probability statements. You should be warned that when you turn the pages you will find equations with terrifying sequences of numbers and Greek symbols. They look much worse than they really are and you will not need to use anything more sophisticated than the calculator on your mobile phone. As with the previous chapter, the statistical tests we are presenting here use the concepts we covered in earlier chapters: the standard deviation, standard error and confidence intervals. Enjoy.

INDEPENDENT GROUPS DESIGNS

The most common **experimental design** in psychological research is the **independent groups design**. It is used for comparing two (or more) groups which are independent of one another – meaning there are different people in each group.

We can use this to design the sort of experiment (sometimes called a 'true experiment') in which we randomly assign people to one of two conditions – for example, a treatment and **control group** – and then take a measurement.

We can also use it for a non-experimental or **quasi-experimental design**. In this case we do not assign people to conditions, as they already belong to different groups. For example, we can compare the scores of males and females, to see if there is a sex difference in a measure. For example, Furnham and Gasson (1998) asked parents to estimate the intelligence of their children. They wanted to see if the parents rated the male and female children differently, and not surprisingly, they rated their boys higher than their girls. Clearly we cannot carry out a pure experiment on this issue because we can't take a pool of participants and say to one lot 'you be boys'. Another example is provided by Rutherford, Baron-Cohen and Wheelwright (2002) who compared people with Asperger's syndrome, high functioning autism and normal adults on their ability to do an auditory theory of mind task. They found that people with Asperger's and high functioning autism performed less well on the task.

We can use three different kinds of dependent variable with this type of study: continuous outcomes, ordinal outcomes and categorical outcomes. However, because there are a few complications with these types of analysis, we have split this into two chapters. This chapter will deal with continuous outcomes and ordinal outcomes; Chapter 7 will deal with categorical outcomes.

Advantages and disadvantages of independent groups designs

The main advantage of the independent groups design is simply that it avoids the problems that are inherent in the repeated measures design (see Chapter 5); that is, there are no practice effects, sensitisation or carry-over effects. For a large number of studies, repeated measures designs are out of the question and we have to use an independent groups design. This might be because the nature of the study is 'one shot', that is, you cannot ask someone to take part in the study twice – the second time it will not work.

The main disadvantage of the independent groups design is the exact opposite of the repeated measures design. You need more people.

STATISTICAL TESTS FOR INDEPENDENT GROUPS DATA

In this text we are going to cover three statistical tests available for independent groups designs:

1. the independent groups *t*-test;
2. the Mann–Whitney test (also called the Wilcoxon–Mann–Whitney test, equivalent to the Wilcoxon rank-sum test which we mentioned in Chapter 5);
3. the chi-square test (which we will deal with in Chapter 7).

The test you choose depends on the data you are testing. The **independent groups *t*-test** is (usually) the most powerful and is the test most likely to spot significant differences in your data. However, you cannot use it with all independent groups data, and you have to be sure that your data satisfy some conditions before you choose this test. The next choice is commonly the **Mann–Whitney test** which deals with all data that can be ordered (ordinal data). The **chi-square test** deals with data in the form of categories (nominal data).

THE INDEPENDENT GROUPS *T*-TEST

The first test we will examine is the independent groups *t*-test, also known as the between subjects *t*-test or the two-samples *t*-test. To use an independent samples *t*-test, we have to make two (or three) assumptions about our data:

1. The data are measured on a **continuous (interval) scale**. This assumption is (relatively) easy. We should know if our data are measured on a continuous scale. However, we get the problem that we always get – almost no data in psychology are *really* measured on a *truly* continuous scale. We would say that as long as your scale has at least seven points, then you can treat it as if it were normal. (This is common practice in psychological research.)

2. The data within each group are *normally distributed*: We need to make sure that the data are approximately normally distributed, *within each group*.

3. The **standard deviations** of the two groups are equal. Actually, although you might read this in many statistics books, it isn't true that the standard deviations need to be equal. (There are actually two kinds of *t*-test, one makes this assumption, and one doesn't. It's just that the one which makes this asumption is easier. We'll explain this below in the common mistake box but if you don't want to know about that then just miss out that box.)

Common Mistake: Normal distribution and the independent samples *t*-test

It is a common mistake to look at the overall distribution of the data to determine whether the data are appropriate for an independent samples *t*-test. This is not the assumption that is made. For example, look at the histogram shown in Figure 6.1. It appears that the distribution is positively skewed. We might conclude, given these data, that the independent samples *t*-test is inappropriate.

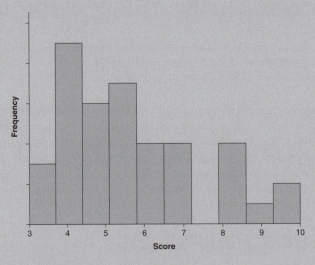

Figure 6.1   Histogram of two groups combined

(Continued)

(Continued)

However, this is made up of two groups – one has 30 individuals in it, the other one has 10 individuals in it. When we plot separate histograms – Figure 6.2 – we can see that the distributions in both groups are approximately normal. There is no problem here.

(a)

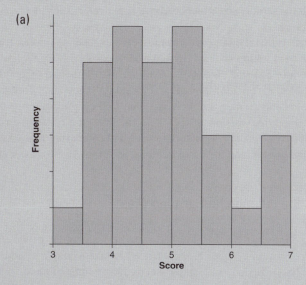

(b)

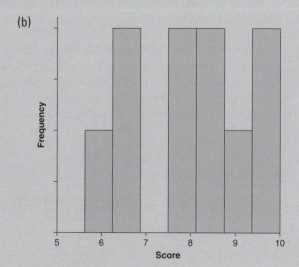

Figure 6.2   Histogram of (a) group 1 ($N = 30$) and (b) group 2 ($N = 10$)

Dispelling myths

There are a couple of myths around the *t*-tests and sample sizes that we want to dispel. We don't know where these myths come from, and in fact we have never read them in a book, but we have heard them said.

The first is that the sample size must be above some value, such as 6, for the *t*-test to be valid. This is not true.

The second myth is that the sample sizes must be balanced, or similar. It is easy to show that this is untrue by thinking about it. Imagine we measure 1,000,000 adult humans, and find that they are all between 3 feet tall and 8 feet tall. Somebody then claims that they have (randomly selected) an adult human and found that they are 1 foot tall. We can say that this is possible but extremely unlikely, and that's all a significance test does. We need to use a slightly modified version of the *t*-test for this type of very small sample, and Crawford and Howell (1998) present an approach for comparing two groups, where one group contains one person, and the other contains as few as five (or as many as 50).

Calculation of the independent groups *t*-test

In this section and the next we'll follow the same series of steps as we followed for the repeated measures *t*-test in Chapter 5, but we need to take a couple of additional steps.

Wright et al. (2005) carried out a study where they compared the effectiveness of two different treatments for chronic fatigue syndrome in children. The first treatment, known as pacing, encourages the child to exercise to the point of tolerance but to avoid over-exertion, and resting when necessary but trying to avoid total rest. The second treatment was similar to the pacing program but also included cognitive behavioural therapy to try to change the child's attributions about their condition and to help them with active coping strategies (it is referred to as an active rehabilitation programme). One of the variables assessed was depression, measured using the Birleson Depression Questionnaire (Birleson, 1981). The results of the two groups are shown in Table 6.1.

Table 6.1   *Depression data from Wright et al. (2005) study of pacing and active rehabilitation in CFS*

	Group A: Pacing	Group B: Active rehabilitation
	14	11
	16	11
	9	9
	18	18
	13	3
Mean	14.0	10.4

We first need to check the **normal distribution** assumption, remembering that it is the distribution of each group that we are interested in, and not the overall distribution. One way to do this would be to present a separate histogram for each group. This would be fine, but it does take up rather a lot of space. Taking up a lot of space is a bad thing, for two reasons. When you are a student, it means that your report becomes rather thick, and therefore heavy. This makes it really hard for your lecturers to carry, and this makes them sad. Second, when you are a professional researcher, it means that your report is longer. Journals and publishers don't like long reports, because that means that they use more paper, and if they use more paper, they cost more, and that makes the publishers sad.[1]

Much more space-conscious is a **box and whisker plot** – you can show the distribution of two (or more) groups for the same amount of space (and space, remember, means money). In other words, two distributions for the price of one.

Figure 6.3 shows the distribution of these two groups. They both appear to be reasonably normal, and it appears that the pacing group has a higher depression score than the active rehabilitation group. What we have to find out now is whether this visual difference will turn out to be a statistically significant difference.

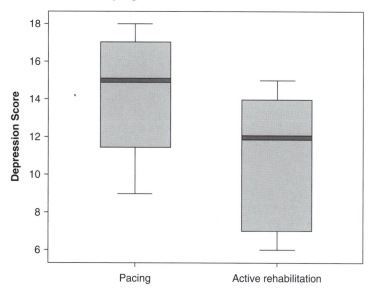

Figure 6.3   Box and whisker plots showing the distributions of the two groups

---

[1] In a similar vein, when people like us write a book, the publishers want to ensure that we don't make it too long because if we make it too long, it costs more for them to print. If it costs more for them to print, they don't make as much money when you buy the book, and this makes them sad. Alternatively, they have to put the price up, then you don't buy it, and this means that they don't make any money at all, and this makes them even sadder. As all this sadness is taking up a lot of paper, we'd better stop.

Because we have approximately equal sample sizes, we can calculate the pooled variance t-test. If you want an example of the unpooled variance t-test (Welch's test) you can jump to page 149.

Step 1: Calculate the standard deviation (σ) of each group.
The standard deviation formula (just in case you've forgotten it) is:

$$\sigma = \sqrt{\frac{\sum(x - \bar{x})^2}{N - 1}}$$

Table 6.2 shows the calculation of the standard deviation. We've done it briefly, but if you want more explanation, see page 40.

Table 6.2 *Calculation of the standard deviation for both groups*

Group A: Pacing   Group B: Active rehabilitation

Score x	Mean $\bar{x}_a$	$(x - \bar{x}_a)^2$	Score x	Mean $\bar{x}_b$	$(x - \bar{x}_b)^2$
14	14	0	11	10.4	0.36
16		4	11		0.36
9		25	9		1.96
18		16	18		57.76
13		1	3		54.76

$$\sum(x - \bar{x}_a)^2 = 46 \qquad\qquad \sum(x - \bar{x}_b)^2 = 115.2$$

$$\frac{\sum(x - \bar{x}_a)^2}{N - 1} = 11.5 \qquad\qquad \frac{\sum(x - \bar{x}_b)^2}{N - 1} = 28.8$$

$$\sigma_a = \sqrt{\frac{\sum(x - \bar{x}_a)^2}{N - 1}} = 3.39 \qquad\qquad \sigma_b = \sqrt{\frac{\sum(x - \bar{x}_b)^2}{N - 1}} = 5.36$$

Step 2: Calculate the standard deviation of the difference.
We have the standard deviation of our two groups, σ_a for group A, and σ_b for group B. The standard deviation of the difference is almost, but not quite, the average of the standard deviations. The formula for the standard deviation of the difference is given by

$$\sigma_{\text{diff}} = \frac{\sigma_a^2(n_a - 1) + \sigma_b^2(n_b - 1)}{n_a + n_b - 2}$$

where n_a means the number of people in group A and n_b is the number of people in group B. We can plug our numbers into the equation:

$$\sigma_{diff} = \frac{\sigma_a^2(n_a - 1) + \sigma_b^2(n_b - 1)}{n_a + n_b - 2}$$

$$= \frac{3.39^2(5 - 1) + 5.36^2(5 - 1)}{5 + 5 - 2}$$

$$= \frac{46.00 + 115.20}{8}$$

$$= 20.15$$

Tip: Short cut (step 2)

If you were something of a whiz at maths when you were at school, you will have realised that if the sample sizes are equal (as ours are), then the formula simplifies to:

$$\sigma_{diff} = \frac{\sigma_a^2 + \sigma_b^2}{2}$$

and because the groups in our sample data are the same size we can use this formula:

$$\sigma_{diff} = \frac{\sigma_a^2 + \sigma_b^2}{2} = \frac{3.39^2 + 5.37^2}{2} = \frac{11.50 + 28.8}{2} = 20.15$$

Now we have the standard deviation of the difference, we can calculate the standard error of the difference.

Step 3: Calculate the standard error of difference.
This is given by:

$$se_{diff} = \sqrt{\frac{\sigma_{diff}}{n_a} + \frac{\sigma_{diff}}{n_b}}$$

We put the values into our equation:

$$se_{diff} = \sqrt{\frac{\sigma_{diff}}{n_a} + \frac{\sigma_{diff}}{n_b}} = \sqrt{\frac{20.15}{5} + \frac{20.15}{5}} = \sqrt{8.06} = 2.84$$

Tip: The short cut continues (step 3)

Once again, we can simplify this if the two sample sizes are equal:

$$se_{\text{diff}} = \sqrt{\frac{\sigma_{\text{diff}}}{N \times 0.5}}$$

where N is the total sample size.
Because these sample sizes are the same we can use this formula.

$$se_{\text{diff}} = \sqrt{\frac{\sigma_{\text{diff}}}{N \times 0.5}} = \sqrt{\frac{20.15}{10 \times 0.5}} = \sqrt{8.06} = 2.84$$

Step 4: Calculate the confidence intervals.
We can now calculate the confidence intervals around the difference between our means. The means were 10.4 for the pacing group (A) and 14.0 for the active rehabilitation group (B). Therefore, the difference between the means is 14.0 – 10.4 = 3.6. The confidence intervals are given by:

$$\text{CI} = d \pm t_\alpha \times se$$

We want to use 95% confidence intervals, and so α (alpha) is 0.05. We need to look up the critical value for t, at the 0.05 level. To do this, we need to know the degrees of freedom (df).[2] For the pooled variance t-test, degrees of freedom are very easy because they are given by:

$$N_1 + N_2 - 2$$

The df are therefore:

$$5 + 5 - 2 = 8$$

If we consult the table in the Appendix (or a computer) we find that the value is 2.31.
We can put this into our equation and calculate the confidence intervals

$$\text{Lower 95\% CL} = 3.6 - 2.31 \times 2.84 = -2.95$$

and an upper 95% confidence limit (UCL) of

$$\text{Upper 95\% CL} = 3.6 + 2.31 \times 2.84 = 10.15$$

---

[2]To brush up on degrees of freedom go to page 91 in Chapter 4.

The equal standard deviations assumption

OK, we need to take a little break here and consider the equal standard deviations assumption which is also known as the **homgeneity of variance** assumption (homogeneity meaning similarity, and **variance**,[3] you will remember, refers to the spread of the data). We're afraid that this assumption is a bit tricky, and it's tricky for two reasons. The first is that there are two versions of the *t*-test: the **pooled variance *t*-test**, which *does not* make this assumption, and the **unpooled variance *t*-test**, which *does* not make this assumption.

Some writers like to leave the surprise to the end, leaving you, the reader, to wait, with bated breath, to see what will happen. This just causes stress, so in the interests of a stress-free life the following will now be revealed:

- If you have (approximately) equal sample sizes in your two groups, use the pooled variance *t*-test.
- If you don't have (approximately) equal sample sizes in the two groups, use the unpooled variance *t*-test.

There, now you can ignore the optional extra box if your want, though it does discuss the second reason why the homogeneity of variance assumption is a bit tricky – would you really want to miss that?

Optional Extra: Testing variances

There are a number of different ways to decide if your variances (or standard deviations) are the same. One of the most common is Levene's test. If Levene's test gives a statistically significant result, this means that your variances are different from one another and you should use the unpooled variance *t*-test, which does not assume homogeneity of variance. If Levene's test is not statistically significant, you have no evidence that your variances are different, in which case you may be able to use the pooled variance *t*-test (that's the *t*-test); see Figure 6.4.

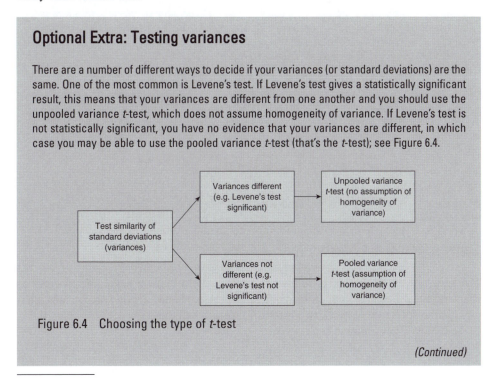

Figure 6.4   Choosing the type of *t*-test

(Continued)

---

[3] The variance is the square of the standard deviation.

(Continued)

OK, now that's clear, we can tell you the second reason why the homogeneity variances assumption is a bit tricky. The problem is that a non-significant result does not mean that the variances are the same. It just means that we haven't found that the variances are different. And the problem with the tests, such as the Levene's test, is that they are dependent on the sample size, so when the sample size is small, Levene's test is not very good at detecting differences in the variances. When the sample size is large, the Levene's test is very good at detecting differences in the variances.

OK, when do you think that it matters most that the variances are the same? Yep, that's right: when the sample size is small. So, when Levene's test is good at telling us when the variances are different precisely when we don't really care. And when Levene's test is not very good is precisely when we do care. It's a bit like having a solar powered torch – it only works when the sun is shining. (We've nearly finished, and if you didn't quite understand the last part, you are really going to like the next part.)

It turns out that homogeneity of variance doesn't really matter when the sample sizes are about equal. So if we have equal (or approximately equal) sample sizes we can ignore the assumption of homogeneity of variance, and use the pooled variances *t*-test.

When the sample sizes are unequal, homogeneity of variance matters a lot more. Given that we only have tests of homogeneity of variance that can tell us if we definitely have it, not if we definitely don't have it, we should not rely on these, and if the sample sizes are unequal, we should use the unpooled variance *t*-test. (If you are really gripped by this, there is an excellent article by Zimmerman (2004) that you should read.)

Anyway, our modified version of Figure 6.4 is shown in Figure 6.5.

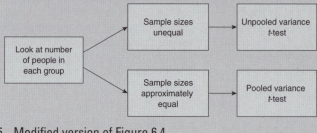

Figure 6.5   Modified version of Figure 6.4

General form of the *t*-tests

The general form of the *t*-tests follows a similar pattern that we have seen in previous chapters. The difference is that instead of being interested in mean scores we are now interested in the difference between two means, so we will call this *d*.

We calculate *t* as follows:

$$t = \frac{d}{se}$$

And the **confidence interval** is given by:

$$\text{CI} = d \pm t_\alpha \times se$$

The part that presents more of a challenge in this situation is the **standard error**. We know the standard error for each variable, but we need to combine those into an average standard error.

Optional Extra: Why not just calculate two sets of CIs and see if they overlap?

Instead of going to all the trouble to calculate the standard error of the difference, why don't we just calculate the 95% CIs of each group, and see if they overlap.

For example, imagine that for groups A we have

Mean = 25, 95% CI = 20, 30

and for group B

Mean = 35, 95% CI = 31, 39

In this case the upper limit of group A is lower than the lower limit of group B, so we can say that the differences are statistically significant.

We could do this. But we would be wrong. There are two problems with this approach. First, imagine the following: for group A we have

Mean = 25, 95% CI = 19, 31

and for group B

Mean = 35, 95% CI = 31, 39

The confidence intervals touch; the upper limit of group A is equal to the lower limit of group B. Therefore they are not statistically significant. Sorry, but this is wrong. It is wrong for two reasons.

First, let's look at group A: in 95% of studies, the CI will include the population mean, so in 5% of studies, the mean will be outside these boundaries. In group B similarly, half of the time the study will find the mean to be too low, and half of the time it will be too high. If the CIs touch, then in 5% of studies the group A mean will be that high, and in 5% of studies the group B mean could be that low. The probability associated with the null hypothesis is not therefore 5%, rather it is closer to 5% of 5%, which is 0.25% – rather than using 1 in 20 as a cut-off, we would be using 1 in 400 as a cut-off, which is a little different.

(Continued)

(Continued)

But there's even another reason why this would be wrong. We aren't really interested in each group separately, we are interested in the difference between the groups. Remember that the standard error is calculated by:

$$se = \frac{\sigma}{\sqrt{N}}$$

So the larger the sample size, the smaller the standard error. If we estimate the standard error of each group separately, we will calculate the standard error with a smaller sample size, so the standard error will be too big. When we calculate the standard error of the difference, we use the whole sample size, and so we have a smaller standard error.

It is quite possible for the confidence intervals to overlap, and still to have a statistically significant difference (although this does not stop journal articles from reporting the confidence intervals for each group separately).

Test yourself 1: True or false?

True or false: There is a 95% chance that the true population mean is between −2.95 and 10.50.

Answer is given at the end of the chapter.

Note that there is quite a lot of uncertainty in the confidence intervals. There is a wide range, which was caused by our small sample. Also note that the confidence intervals includes zero, which means that pacing may not be as good as active rehabilitation or that it may be that pacing is, better. It is more likely that pacing is not as good, but our results do not allow us to know. We would report the confidence intervals by writing: 'The mean score for pacing was 10.4, and the mean score for active rehabilitation was 14, thus poeple in the active rehabilitation group scored 3.6 points higher (95% CIs − 2.95, 10.15).

Step 5: Calculate t.
This will give us the probability associated with the null hypothesis:

$$t = \frac{d}{se} = \frac{\bar{x}_a - \bar{x}_b}{se} - \frac{14 - 10.4}{2.84} = 1.27$$

Again, we look up the value for *t*, and find the probability of getting a value of *t* at least this large (in other words an effect at least this large) if the null hypothesis is true.

The degrees of freedom are still given by:

$$N_1 + N_2 - 2 = 5 + 5 - 2 = 8$$

Test yourself 2: True or false?

True or false: We can say that we have found that the two treatments were equal.

Answer is given at the end of the chapter.

Using a computer, we find that p is equal to 0.24. As this value is greater than 0.05, we cannot reject the null hypothesis that the two approaches are equally beneficial.

Step 6: Report the results.

We can say something like: 'The active rehabilitation group had a mean score of 10.4 (standard deviation 5.36), the pacing group had a mean score of 14 (standard deviation 3.39). The difference between the scores was 3.6, with 95% confidence intervals of −2.95, 10.15; the difference was not statistically significant($t = 1.27$, df = 8, $p = 0.24$).'

Unpooled variance *t*-test

The unpooled variance *t*-test is a modification of the *t*-test, which does not make the assumption of equal variances. It is sometimes known as Welch's test, because (and you'll be surprised by this) it was developed by Welch (1938).

As we said earlier, it turns out that the assumption of homogeneity of variance doesn't really matter, unless you have unequal sample sizes, in which case it matters so much that you should always use it. There is an optional extra box below describing how we know this. For now you can take our word for it. And yes, we know that you will probably want to take our word for it, rather than read the optional extra. That's why we call them *optional* extras.

Optional Extra: How much does it matter whether I use the pooled or the unpooled variances *t*-test?

One way to find out is to calculate the **type I error rate**, under different conditions of different standard deviation and different sample sizes. We would expect the type I error rate to be 0.05 – if it deviates from this value, this is a bad thing. Figure 6.6 shows the type I error rate for different values of the standard deviation, and different sample sizes in each group. Each line represents a different ratio of sample sizes in the two groups; along the *x*-axis is the ratio of the standard deviations. You can see that if the allocation to groups is 50:50, the effect of differences in the standard deviations is very small. If the difference in the samples is 60:40, or 40:60, then increasing the difference in the standard deviations affects the type I error rate. Even at 60:40 – not dreadfully far from 50:50, when one standard deviation is twice the other, the type I error rate rises to 0.08 – in other words, if we think our *p*-value is really 0.05, it is not, it is actually 0.08.

(Continued)

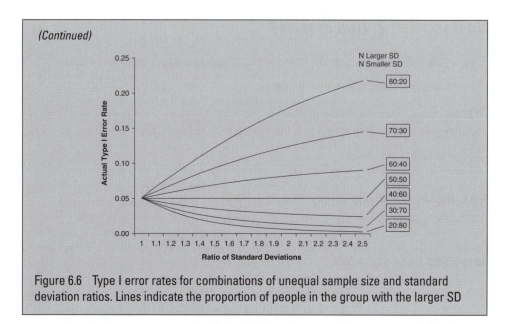

Figure 6.6   Type I error rates for combinations of unequal sample size and standard deviation ratios. Lines indicate the proportion of people in the group with the larger SD

First, let's think about why we might have unequal sample sizes. It's always better, if possible, to have equal sample sizes because this gives you the best chance of getting a statistically significant result, and the narrowest confidence intervals. But there are three main occasions when we might use unequal sample sizes.

1. If we are comparing two naturally occurring groups, and they are different sizes. If we wanted to compare male and female psychology students, in most universities there are more females than males, so we will end up with an unbalanced sample. If we want to compare people with a specific type of brain injury with people who do not have such an injury, again, we will find that we have unequal sample sizes.

2. It may be very difficult or expensive for one of the interventions. For example, if we want to examine the effects of a very large audience on people's behaviour, we will have two groups: no audience and large audience. The no-audience group is cheap and easy to run. The large-audience group is expensive and difficult to run, so we might have more people in the no-audience group than in the large-audience group.

3. There may be an ethical or a recruitment issue. If we believe that one treatment works better than another but no study has been carried out to investigate this, then we really need to do an experiment to confirm it. However, if we think that a treatment works, should we give it to only half of the people? How would you feel if you were ill and were allocated to a control group that is given no treatment? It might be better to give it to as many people as possible. Similarly, if people are likely to want to be in one group more than another, it might increase the number of people willing to take part in the study if they realise that there is a better than 50:50 chance that they will get to be in the group they want to be in. Goodwin, et al. (2001) used this approach. They wanted to investigate the effects of supportive-expressive group therapy on women who had been diagnosed with breast cancer. Women wanted to be in the treatment group, rather than the control group, so the authors used a 2:1 allocation ratio, to improve their recruitment.[4]

---

[4]For a review, and more discussion, of the reasons for unequal allocation, see Dumville, Miles, Hahn and Torgerson (2006).

Table 6.3   *Tension-Anxiety results from Goodwin et al. (2001)
study of group therapy in breast cancer patients*

	Change in Tension-Anxiety		
Group	Mean	SD (σ)	N
Control (A)	+1.9	5.7	45
Therapy (B)	−1.5	6.9	102

Calculation of the unpooled variance *t*-test

You will have noticed that one of the nice things about the unrelated *t*-test is that we don't need any more information than the means and standard deviations of each group to calculate it.

In the study by Goodwin et al. (2001), they ended up with 45 people in the control group, and 102 in the intervention group. One of the outcomes they measured was change in the level of Tension-Anxiety. They measured this for each person before the treatment started, and again afterwards. For each person, they calculated the change in the level of Tension-Anxiety. The means and standard deviations are shown in Table 6.3. The control group had an increase in their level of Tension-Anxiety, and the therapy group had a decrease. We want to know whether this result is statistically significant.

Step 1: Calculate the standard deviations.
We've done this, and it's in Table 6.3.

Step 2: Calculate the standard error of difference.
The procedure is the same as for the pooled variance *t*-test. We first need to find the standard error of the difference. This is a whole lot easier than with the pooled variance *t*-test:

$$se_{\text{diff}} = \sqrt{\frac{\sigma_a^2}{n_a} + \frac{\sigma_b^2}{n_b}}$$

Really, that's all there is to it. So

$$se_{\text{diff}} = \sqrt{\frac{\sigma_a^2}{n_a} + \frac{\sigma_b^2}{n_b}} = \sqrt{\frac{5.7^2}{45} + \frac{6.9^2}{102}} = \sqrt{1.19} = 1.09$$

Step 3: Calculate the degrees of freedom.
In case you thought you had got off lightly with the unpooled variance *t*-test, the calculation of the degrees of freedom makes up for it. The degrees of freedom are calculated using:

$$df = \frac{(\sigma_a^2/n_a + \sigma_b^2/n_b)^2}{(\sigma_a^2/n_a)^2/(n_a - 1) + (\sigma_b^2/n_b)^2/(n_b - 1)}$$

If we substitute the numbers into this equation, and work it out:

$$df = \frac{(\sigma_a^2/n_a + \sigma_b^2/n_b)^2}{(\sigma_a^2/n_a)^2/(n_a - 1) + (\sigma_b^2/n_b)^2/(n_b - 1)}$$

$$= \frac{(5.7^2/45 + 6.9^2/102)^2}{(5.7^2/45)^2/(45 - 1) + (6.9^2/102)^2/(102 - 1)}$$

$$= \frac{(0.72 + 0.47)^2}{0.72^2/44 + 0.47^2/101}$$

$$= 1.19^2/(0.012 + 0.0022)$$

$$= 1.41/0.014 = 100.91$$

Optional Extra: Freedom and power

Remember that the degrees of freedom are usually related to the sample size? Because we haven't been able to pool the variances, the df have been lowered. Effectively this means that our sample size has been lowered. Given that a larger sample gives a smaller standard error, and therefore a better chance of a significant result, using this version of the t-test can reduce the chance of getting a statistically significant result (the chance of getting a significant result is called **power**, and we will look at it in Chapter 11) particularly if the larger group has a smaller variance. If this is the case, you might be better off using a non-parametric test, such as the Mann–Whitney U test, which, conveniently, is next.

Optional Extra: A test too far

There's another method that we can use when we have unequal variances called Satterthwaite's method. Even though you are the kind of person who reads these optional extra sections, we think you've probably had enough. We are just warning you in case you do come across it at some point. (Some computer programs use it.)

The df are therefore 100.91. (It's a bit curious to have df that are not whole numbers, but mathematically it is possible. When the tables only have whole numbers, use the next whole number below.)

Now we know the df, we are back to the formulae that we have come to know and love.

Step 4: Calculate the confidence intervals.

The formula is the same as for the pooled variance *t*-test:

$$CI = d \pm t_{\alpha/2} \times se$$

We need to know the critical value for *t* with 100.91 df – using any of the approaches described on pages 94–5, we can find that this is 1.98.

Therefore the 95% confidence intervals are given by:

Lower 95% CI = 3.4 − 1.98 × 1.09 = 1.24
Upper 95% CI = 3.4 + 1.98 × 1.09 = 5.56

Step 5: Calculate the value of t.

Again we use the same formula as for the pooled variance *t*-test, including the new standard error:

$$t = \frac{d}{se} = \frac{\bar{x}_a - \bar{x}_b}{se}$$
$$= \frac{1.9 - (-1.5)}{1.09}$$
$$= \frac{3.4}{1.09} = 3.12$$

We now find the probability associated with a value of *t* – with 101.9 df – the *p*-value is 0.002.

Step 6: Report the results.

We would report the results in the following way: 'The control group had an increase in the mean anxiety-tension score of 1.5 (standard deviation 5.7), the group therapy group had a decrease in their anxiety-tension score of 1.9 (standard deviation 6.9). The difference between the means is 3.4 (95% CI 1.24, 5.56; $t = 3.12$, df = 100.9, $p = 0.002$).

Effect size for independent groups *t*-test

We can often describe the difference between two samples by stating the difference between the two means, for example 'The mean male height was 4 inches higher than the mean female height' or 'Children given the intervention ate a mean of 1.1 more portions of fruit and vegetables per day'.

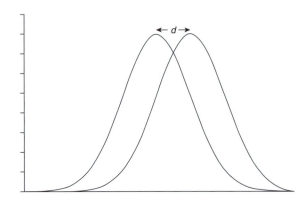

Figure 6.7 Two overlapping normal distributions, with *d* shown

However, often the scale that is used is not one that actually makes any sense (unless you are very familiar with the scale). For example, 'The mean score of the group that underwent psychotherapy was 2 points lower than the mean score of the control group'. Is that good or bad? It depends on what the scale is likely to score. If the scale goes from 0 to 100, that sounds bad. If it goes from 0 to 4, it sounds pretty good.

The way around this is to use a measure of **effect size**, and in the case of the independent groups *t*-test an appropriate measure of effect size is called Cohen's *d*.

Cohen's *d* is a measure of how far apart the means of the two samples are, in standard deviation units. It doesn't matter what the range of possible scores is – we are interpreting it in terms of the standard deviation. Figure 6.7 shows two normal distributions – the value of *d* is the difference between the means, divided by the (pooled) standard deviation.

We could write this as:

$$d = \frac{\bar{x}_1 - \bar{x}_2}{\sigma_{\text{within}}}$$

where σ_{within} is the pooled standard deviation estimate – however, that's a bit tricky to work out, and there's a much easier formula:

$$d = \frac{2t}{\sqrt{\text{df}}}$$

where *t* is the result of the *t*-test, which we have already worked out, and df is the degrees of freedom, which is $N_1 + N_2 - 2$.

Substituting these values into the equation:

$$d = \frac{2 \times 1.27}{\sqrt{8}} = \frac{2.54}{2.82} = 0.89$$

Cohen's d is often interpreted according to the following rules:

- large effect size: $d = 0.8$
- medium effect size: $d = 0.5$
- small effect size: $d = 0.3$

It can be as low as 0 (it cannot be negative) and, unlike a correlation (which cannot be higher than 1), it has no upper limit, although values above 1 are rare.

THE MANN–WHITNEY U TEST

The final test that we will examine in this chapter is the Mann–Whitney U test. This test compares two unrelated groups and is used when the independent samples t-test cannot be used. It is a **non-parametric test**, and therefore does not make the assumptions that the t-test makes of normal distribution and interval data.

Optional Extra: Mann and Whitney

The Mann–Whitney U test was developed (you'll be surprised to hear) by Mann and Whitney (1947). It is equivalent to the Wilcoxon rank-sum test, which was developed about the same time, but is actually a little easier to work out. It's often called the Wilcoxon–Mann–Whitney test for this reason. But we think that's a bit confusing.

The two sets of authors did not know about each others' work, and so developed the test independently.

Bender, Azeem and Morrice (2000) wanted to compare birth order of people with schizophrenia and other conditions in Pakistan. They wanted to see if people with schizophrenia had fewer older siblings than people suffering from other conditions. Some of their data are shown in Table 6.4, which shows the number of elder siblings that people diagnosed with schizophrenia and bipolar disorder had.

Figure 6.8 shows the percentage of people in each of the two diagnostic categories who had each number of older siblings. Both of the distributions are positively skewed, with the schizophrenia group showing more positive skew than the bipolar group.

Table 6.4   *Results of Bender et al. (2000)*

Number of elder siblings	Number of patients with mental disorder	
	Schizophrenia	Bipolar disorder
0	10	9
1	2	5
2	2	2
3	1	3
4	1	2
5	0	2
6	0	0
7	0	1

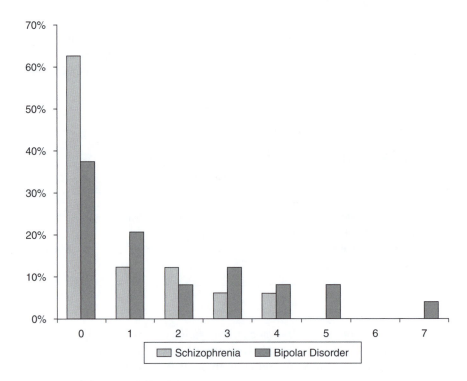

Figure 6.8   Bar chart showing the number of older siblings of people diagnosed with bipolar disorder and schizophrenia

Tip

For this chart, why did we choose to use percentages, rather than numbers, as we always have before?

Because there were different numbers of people in each group. Comparing the distributions is difficult when the bars are different heights because of the different numbers of people in each group. Figure 6.9 shows the histogram with the frequency, rather than the percentage. The heights of the first bar are very similar to one another, but this is deceptive. The bipolar bar is higher, because there are more people in that group.

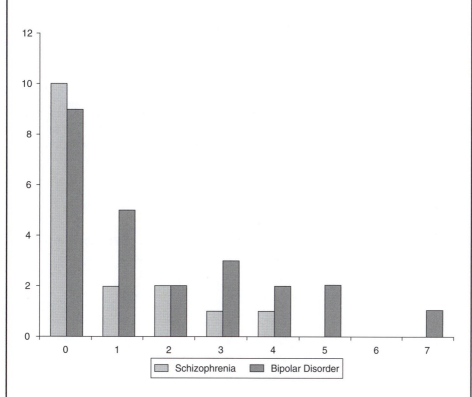

Figure 6.9   Figure 6.8, using frequency

Tip: Watch the data

Don't let the numbers and symbols baffle you. Follow the logic of the test. If there is a very clear difference between the two conditions then all the low ranks will be in one condition and all the high ranks will be in the other. The more they are mixed up the less clear is the difference between them. Therefore the sum of the ranks for the two conditions should be very different if there is a clear effect and quite similar if there is not.

Just by looking at the data you can estimate whether there will be a significant effect.

Calculating the Mann–Whitney test

Step 1: Ranking.

The first stage in the Mann–Whitney test is to *rank the data*, as if they were in one group. For a reminder of how to rank, see page 122. Table 6.5 shows the number of older siblings for each person diagnosed with schizophrenia or bipolar disorder. In the column titled 'Rank' we have entered the rank of each of the scores.

Step 2: Calculate U_1.

We separate out the two groups. We put the ranks of the people diagnosed with schizophrenia in one column, and the ranks of the people diagnosed with bipolar disorder in the other column. We then find the total of each of the columns, calling one of them group A (schizophrenia) and one of them group B (bipolar). The formula that we use is:

$$U_1 = N_a \times N_b + \frac{N_a \times (N_a + 1)}{2} - \sum R_a$$

Where N_a is the sample size in group A, which is 16; N_b is the sample size for group B which is 24; and ΣR_a = the sum of the ranks in group A, which is 271.5. So

$$U_1 = 16 \times 24 + \frac{16 \times (16 + 1)}{2} - 271.5$$

$$= 284 + \frac{272}{2} - 271.5$$

$$= 284 + 136 - 271.5$$

$$= 248.5$$

Step 3: Calculate U_2.

There are two ways to do this. The hard way is to swap the groups, calling schizophrenia group B, and depression group A, and recalculate U_1. The easy way is to use the formula

$$U_2 = N_a \times N_b - U_1$$

Table 6.5   *Calculation of the Mann–Whitney test*

Number	Group	No. of elder sibs	Rank	Schizophrenia rank (A)	Bipolar rank (B)
1	S	0	10	10	
2	S	0	10	10	
3	S	0	10	10	
4	S	0	10	10	
5	S	0	10	10	
6	S	0	10	10	
7	S	0	10	10	
8	S	0	10	10	
9	S	0	10	10	
10	S	0	10	10	
11	B	0	10		10
12	B	0	10		10
13	B	0	10		10
14	B	0	10		10
15	B	0	10		10
16	B	0	10		10
17	B	0	10		10
18	B	0	10		10
19	B	0	10		10
20	S	1	23	23	
21	S	1	23	23	
22	B	1	23		23
23	B	1	23		23
24	B	1	23		23
25	B	1	23		23
26	B	1	23		23
27	S	2	28.5	28.5	
28	S	2	28.5	28.5	
29	B	2	28.5		28.5
30	B	2	28.5		28.5
31	S	3	32.5	32.5	
32	B	3	32.5		32.5
33	B	3	32.5		32.5
34	B	3	32.5		32.5
35	S	4	36	36	
36	B	4	36		36
37	B	4	36		36
38	B	5	38.5		38.5
39	B	5	38.5		38.5
40	B	7	40		40
Sum			820	271.5	548.5

Putting the numbers in gives us:

$$U_2 = 16 \times 24 - 271.5$$
$$= 384 - 271.5$$
$$= 384 - 248.5 = 135.5$$

Step 4: Find U.
U is the smaller of U_1 and U_2. We have

$$U_1 = 248.5$$
$$U_2 = 135.5$$

So $U = 135.5$.

Step 5: Find the p-value.
To find the statistical significance associated with the Mann–Whitney U, you can use tables, such as those provided in Appendix 2. If you look in that table, you will find that the critical value of U, with 16 participants in one group and 24 in the other group, is 120. Because our value for U is above this, the result is not statistically significant at the 0.05 level.

Step 5a: Calculate the p-value in larger samples.
The problem with tables of U is they have to get very large to cope with all of the variations in sample sizes that exist. The alternative, if you are feeling brave, is to convert the U-score to a z-score, which can then be used to get the correct p-value. We use the formula:

$$z = \frac{U - n_1 n_2/2}{\sqrt{n_1 n_2 (n_1 + n_2 + 1)/12}}$$

where U is the value we just calculated, n_1 is the number of people in the group with the larger ranked column total, and n_2 is the number of people in the group with the smaller ranked column total.

	Tip
	Don't panic! Although the formula looks intimidating you just have to substitute the values and all of a sudden it doesn't look so bad. While you do it you might try thinking of your favourite things. That should help as well.

For our data $n_1 = N_b = 24$ and $n_2 = N_a = 16$, so we have

$$z = \frac{U - n_1 n_2/2}{\sqrt{n_1 n_2 (n_1 + n_2 + 1)/12}}$$

$$= \frac{135.5 - 24 \times 16/2}{\sqrt{24 \times 16 \times (24 + 16 + 1)/12}} = \frac{135.5 - 192}{\sqrt{384 \times 41/12}} = \frac{-56.5}{\sqrt{1312}} = -1.56$$

We can look this up in a z-table, or use a computer, and find the probability associated with a z of 1.56 is 0.059. This gives the one-tailed significance so we need to multiply this value by 2 to get the two-tailed significance (which is what we usually use), which is 0.118. We do not have sufficient evidence to reject the null hypothesis.

Optional Extra

Actually, we have slightly simplified that – if there are ties in the data, that is, two or more people with the same score, the z calculation is made more complicated. We have a lot of ties, and if we correct for the ties, the p-value is 0.097, which will have made little difference.

Mann–Whitney test and distributional assumptions

The t-test compares the means of two groups and tells us whether the difference in the means is statistically significant. The Mann–Whitney test doesn't compare the means so it might be tempting (and it is common) to say that it compares the medians. Unfortunately, it doesn't (necessarily).

Let's have a look at an example. Three studies were carried out, and the results are shown in Table 6.6.

Table 6.6   *Results of three studies, analysed using Mann–Whitney test*

	Study 1		Study 2		Study 3	
	A	B	A	B	A	B
1	10	0	13	1	9	0
2	10	1	13	2	9	1
3	10	2	13	3	9	2
4	10	3	13	4	9	3
5	10	4	13	5	9	4
6	10	5	13	6	9	5
7	10	6	13	7	9	6
8	10	10	13	8	9	10
9	11	10	13	9	11	10
10	12	10	13	10	12	10
11	13	10	13	11	13	10
12	14	10	13	12	14	10
13	15	10	13	13	15	10
14	16	10	13	14	16	10
15	17	10	13	90	17	10
Sum of ranks	313	152	307.5	157.5	281	184
Median	10	10	13	8	9	10
Mean	11.87	6.73	13	13	13	9.5
U			32	37.5	64	
p			<0.001	0.001	0.045	

For study 1, there is a statistically significant difference between the groups. The sum of the ranks shows that group 1 is ranked, on average, higher than group 2. The medians are *the same*. The Mann–Whitney test is not comparing the medians. So maybe it's comparing the means.

Look at study 2. The sum of ranks is again higher for group 1, so that group is ranked higher, and the result is statistically significant. However, the mean scores for the two groups are the same – so the test is not comparing means either.

And just to show how weird this can get, in study 3, group 1 has a higher sum of ranks, so they are ranked higher, and this result is statistically significant. However, look at the medians. The median for group 1 is *lower* than for group 2.

In conclusion, the Mann–Whitney test does not compare medians, and it doesn't compare means. So what does it compare? It compares ranks.

However, if we can make the assumption that the shape of the distributions in the two groups is the same, we can say that the Mann–Whitney test compares the medians. (Sometimes non-parametric tests are described as 'distribution-free' tests; however, as we have just shown, the Mann–Whitney U test is not distribution-free, which demonstrates that distribution-free isn't a very good name.

Effect size for the Mann–Whitney test

We have just seen that we can't use the medians to describe the difference between the two groups when we have used a Mann–Whitney test. And we can't use the mean either. So, what do we do?

What we do is use a value called θ, which is the Greek letter theta. This asks, if we randomly choose a person from each group, what is the probability that the group B person's score will be higher than, or equal to, the person in group A that we choose. If we wanted to be technical, we could write that as:

$$\theta = \text{Prob}(B > A) + 0.5 \times \text{Prob}(B = A)$$

The bad news is that most programs won't work this out for us. The good news is that it's very easy to work out:

For study 1

$$\theta = U/N_A N_B = \frac{32}{15 \times 15} = \frac{32}{225} = 0.142$$

For study 2

$$\theta = U/N_A N_B = \frac{37.5}{225} = 0.167$$

For study 3

$$\theta = U/N_A N_B = \frac{64}{225} = 0.284$$

In each case, the result shows that it is likely that the person in group A will have the higher score – this is consistent with the sums of rank that we see in Table 6.6.

SUMMARY

We have looked at three ways to analyse independent groups designs data. As ever, the selection of the test depends on the characteristics of the data. Was it a continuous variable? Were the data normally distributed? Were the groups of equal size? If you don't know why these questions are important, then you haven't read the chapter. We'll give you the same health warning that we gave at the end of the previous chapter in that we have only looked at simple designs with one independent variable with only two levels of that variable. Although it gets more complicated than this the principles stay the same. Keep the faith.

Test yourself answers

Test yourself 1

False. In 95% of studies, the confidence intervals will include the population mean. This is not quite the same thing. See page 97.

Test yourself 2

False, for two reasons. First, we didn't find them to be equal, we found that pacing had a mean depression score of 10.4, whereas active rehabilitation had a mean depression score of 14.

Second, we weren't testing to see if the two groups were equal. We were testing to see if the groups were different. We didn't find a difference (in the population), but that doesn't mean that such a difference is not there to be found.

USING SPSS

To carry out the tests that we have described in this chapter, you need your data in two columns. One column, the grouping variable, should be the group the person is in, and this should use something like a 1 to indicate one group, and a 0 to indicate the other group. The other column will have the scores on the outcome (dependent) variable.

To carry out an *independent samples t-test,* select **Analyze, Compare Means, Independent-Samples T Test**. The following window appears:

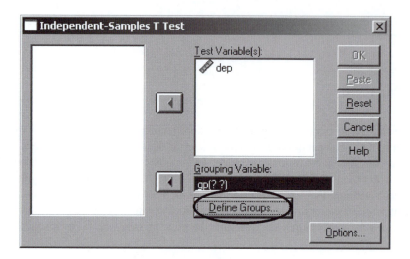

Put the outcome into the **Test Variables** box, and the group variable into the **Grouping Variable** box. Click on the **Define Groups** button. You need to enter the values that define the two groups (these can be numbers or text). If you're anything like us, you've forgotten, so click **Cancel** and go and check.

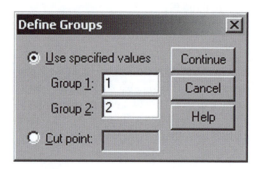

Click Continue , and then OK .

The first part of the output is a set of descriptive statistics – this shows the sample size, mean, standard deviation and standard error.

Group Statistics

	gp	N	Mean	Std. Deviation	Std. Error Mean
dep	1.00	5	14.0000	3.39116	1.51658
	2.00	5	10.4000	5.36656	2.40000

It's worth checking this closely to make sure that there are no surprises. Are the sample sizes what you expected?

The next part of the output is a bit confusing. It's one long table, which looks like this:

Independent Samples Test

	Levene's Test for Equality of Variances		t-test for Equality of Means					95% Confidence Interval of the Difference	
	F	Sig.	t	df	Sig. (2-tailed)	Mean Difference	Std. Error Difference	Lower	Upper
Equal variances assumed	.356	.567	1.268	8	.240	3.6000	2.839	-2.9468	10.1467
Equal variances not assumed			1.268	6.755	.247	3.6000	2.839	-3.1628	10.3628

What has happened is that SPSS has done two *t*-tests. The first row shows the results of the standard *t*-test, where equal variances are assumed. The second row has done the corrected *t*-test, where equal variances are not assumed.

However, in the first row it has also done Levene's test – this is testing the homogeneity of variance assumption (although see pages 140–1).

Common Mistake: Reporting the wrong *p*

The first *p*-value that you encounter in the *t*-test output *isn't* the *p*-value for the *t*-test. The *p*-value is referred to as Sig. (2-tailed) by SPSS.

To carry out a Mann–Whitney *U* test, select Analyze⇒Nonparametric Tests⇒2 Independent Samples. Put the outcome variable into the **Test Variable List** box. Put the predictor variable into the **Grouping Variable** box. Click on **Define Groups**.

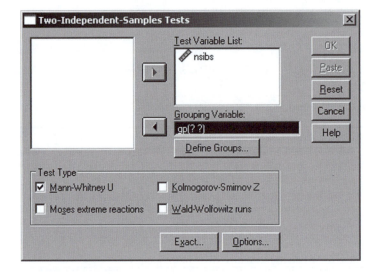

Enter the two numbers that define the groups. (When we looked at the *t*-test dialog on page 164, you could enter text or numbers. Although this looks the same, you can only enter numbers, not text.)

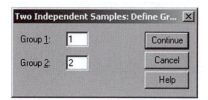

Click Continue , and then OK .

The first part of the output contains the number of people in each group, and the mean rank and sum of ranks. Use the mean rank to find which group is scoring higher.

Rank

	gp	N	Mean Rank	Sum of Ranks
nsibs	1 B	24	22.85	548.50
	2 S	16	16.97	271.50
	Total	40		

The second part of the output is the test statistics. You are given the value for *U* from the Mann–Whitney test, the value for *W* from the Wilcoxon test (we didn't cover that), *z* and two different significance values. The first is the asymptotic significance, which is the one you should look at. The second is the exact significance, which is not corrected for ties. (If there are no ties, the exact significance does not appear.)

Test statistics[b]

	nsibs
Mann–Whitney U	135.500
Wilcoxon W	271.500
Z	-1.658
Asymp. Sig. (2-tailed)	.097
Exact Sig. [2*(1-tailed Sig.)]	.120[a]

a. Not corrected for ties
b. Grouping variable: gp

7

Analysing data from independent groups: categorical measures

> **What's in this chapter?**
>
> - Categorical data
> - Odds
> - Confidence intervals and *p*-values
> - Chi-square
> - Fisher's exact test
> - Using SPSS

KEY TERMS

2-4-6 problem	normal distribution
absolute difference	number needed to harm
categorical data	number needed to treat
chi-square (χ^2) test	odds ratio
confidence intervals	percentage
continuity correction	proportion
degrees of freedom	psychokinesis
Fisher's exact test	relative risk decrease
nominal data	Yates' correction

INTRODUCTION

This chapter tells you how to analyse independent data that are in the form of categories. We often want to know whether something works or not, whether it is right or wrong and whether someone is hip or minging. There are no half measures; it is one or the other. When we get data of this kind we can ask the same questions we asked in earlier chapters and so estimate the probability of arriving at our results by chance. There are three more tests to look at here, though we will concentrate on the chi-square test.

CATEGORICAL DATA

Sometimes the variable that we are interested in measuring is **categorical** or **nominal**. That is, it can only take on one of a limited number of values, often simply yes or no. For example:

- Wiseman and Greening (2005) were interested in examining the effects of suggestion on perception. They showed people a film of someone using **psychokinesis** (the ability to move objects by mental effort, to bend a metal key. When the 'psychic' (who was actually a magician) put the key down, one group heard them say 'It's still bending', the other group heard nothing. The researchers were interested in whether people believed the key really did continue to bend after it had been placed on the table. The outcome had only two categories, either they thought it was still bending, or they thought it was not still bending: *yes or no.*
- MacFarlane et al. (2002) wanted to look at the effect of a patient information leaflet on the likelihood that a person would take antibiotics or not. The outcome had two categories: the person either took the antibiotics or they didn't: *yes or no.*
- Gale and Ball (2006) examined the ability of people to solve the **2-4-6 problem**. People are given the series of numbers 2-4-6, and they are asked to generate more sequences of three numbers using the same rule that generated 2-4-6. The experimenter tells them if the numbers match the rule or not. When they think they know the rule they can say the answer. The rule is actually 'three ascending numbers'. People don't find this out because they think the rule is 'Add 2 each time' or something similar. They do not try to *test* their beliefs. Introducing a second goal to solve a second problem at the same time as the first task is being carried out increases the proportion of the time that the participant gets the 2-4-6 task correct. Gale and Ball divided people into two groups; one group was given the single goal (SG), and one group was given the dual goal (DG). People either solved the 2-4-6 problem or they didn't: *yes or no.*

Optional Extra: The 2-4-6 problem

It may not seem obvious, but the issue of the 2-4-6 rule is linked to issues of statistical significance and scientific research. People are bad at the 2-4-6 rule problem,

(Continued)

(Continued)

because they generate a hypothesis, and then they don't try to prove themselves wrong. In the same way, when we do statistical hypothesis tests, what we are trying to do is find evidence against the null hypothesis. What we think we are doing is trying to prove that we are correct. The 2-4-6 rule is much harder than it should be because our brains are just not designed to work that way. In the same way, understanding the logic of statistical hypothesis testing is much harder than it should be.

SUMMARISING CATEGORICAL DATA

When we have continuous data, we usually take the mean as a measure of average. When we have ordinal data, we usually use the median as a measure of average. So you might think that when we have categorical data, we should use the mode as a measure of average. You would be wrong. The mode is very rarely an appropriate measure simply because it doesn't tell us very much. For example, in the studies that we described above here are the modal responses for each group:

- Wiseman and Greening (2005). For the suggestion group, the mode was no; for the no-suggestion group, the mode was *no.*
- MacFarlane et al. (2002). For the leaflet group, the mode was no; for the no-leaflet group, the mode was *yes.*
- Gale and Ball (2006). For the SG group, the mode was no; for the DG group, the mode was *yes.*

We can provide much more and more useful, information very easily. Instead of just giving the mode, we could give the proportion of people in each group for whom the answer is yes:

- Wiseman and Greening (2005). Suggestion group, 9/23 (39%); No-suggestion group, 1/23 (4%).
- MacFarlane *et al.* (2002). Leaflet group, 49/104 (47%); No-leaflet group, 63/102 (63%).
- Gale and Ball (2006). SG group, 6/30 (20%); DG group, 23/30 (77%).

This way of presenting the information gives a lot more information about the size of the difference. In the Wiseman and Greening study, the difference is very large, from very few people, to almost half. In the MacFarlane study, even though the modes were different the actual difference was not very large. Finally, in the Gale and Ball study, the modes were different just as in MacFarlane et al., but the size of the difference was much larger.

DESCRIPTIVE STATISTICS FOR PROPORTIONS

Summary Statistics

When it comes to describing the results of these studies we can get into a bit of a tangle if we don't think about what we are doing. We want to describe the percentage of people in each group and the differences between them (and later on we will get on to the 95% confidence intervals – something to look forward to there). If we are dealing with the mean to describe the differences we just display the mean values. With the *proportion* or *percentage*, life is not quite so easy though.

The first problem is *what percentage*? This seems like a curious question because it's obvious, isn't it? Well, yes it is, until you use a computer and it asks you what percentage, and it's a very common mistake to give the wrong one. Alternatively, if students don't know which the right one is, they give more than one. Table 7.1 shows the results from the study by Gale and Ball.

First we have the number of people. In the SG task, 24 people were incorrect and 6 were correct, a total of 30. In the DG task, 7 were incorrect, 23 were correct, a total of 30. Next, we have the row percentages. These are sensible. They tell us that 20.0% of the SG group solved the task and that 76.7% of the DG group solved the task.

Next we have the column percentages. These tell us that, of the people who got the task correct, 22.6% were in the DG group. The first problem with this percentage is that it is dependent not just on the number who solved the task, but also on the number of people in each group. If I tell you that 10% of the people who solved the task were women, that doesn't sound good. But if I tell you that 10% of the sample were women, that makes

Table 7.1   *Results from Gale and Ball (2006), with totals and three kinds of percentage*

			Correct?		Total
			No	Yes	
		N	24	6	30
		% within Task	80.0%	20.0%	100.0%
	Single Goal	% within Correct?	77.4%	20.7%	50.0%
	(SG)	% of Total	40.0%	10.0%	50.0%
Task		*N*	7	23	30
		% within Task	23.3%	76.7%	100.0%
	Dual Goal	% within Correct?	22.6%	79.3%	50.0%
	(DG)	% of Total	11.7%	38.3%	50.0%

things rather different. The second problem with this figure is that it just doesn't tell us what we want to know.

Finally, we have the total percentage. This tells us that 40% of the total sample was in the SG task group, and did not solve the task correctly. Again, this doesn't tell us what we want to know. So it's not such a silly question to ask *what percentage?*

Test yourself 1

The following is part of a table that appeared in *The Times* on 11 November 2004. It shows the responses to the question 'How often do you go to church?'

	UK				USA	
	All voters	Labour voters	Tory voters	Lib. Dem. voters	Bush voters	Kerry voters
More than weekly	2%	2%	3%	1%	63%	35%
Weekly	10%	10%	13%	7%	58%	41%
Monthly	5%	6%	4%	6%	50%	50%
A few times a year	36%	36%	38%	40%	44%	55%
Never	47%	46%	43%	44%	34%	64%

What is wrong with this table?

Answer is given at the end of the chapter.

DIFFERENCES BETWEEN GROUPS

Absolute and relative change

When we wanted to express the difference between the mean of two groups, it was easy. We said that if the mean of group A was 10 and the mean of group B was 12, then the difference in the means was 2. We then put a confidence interval around that difference. When it comes to the difference between two proportions, life's a little harder. There are three main ways of showing what the difference is (and a fourth one as well). And they can all look very similar to each other and it's often not clear which one people are talking about. (Though not people like you, because after you have read this section you will always make it very clear.)

Let's look at the ways to represent the difference using the MacFarlane et al. data. They found that 49 people out of 104 in the leaflet group took the antibiotics (47%), and that 63 people out of 101 in the control group took the antibiotics (62%). So, how much reduction in tablet taking did the leaflet cause?

The first way to look at the data is to use the **absolute difference**:

$$62\% - 47\% = 15\%$$

The absolute reduction in the percentage of people who took the antibiotic is 15%. However, we could also ask what the reduction in antibiotic use was *as a proportion of those in the leaflet group:*

$$\frac{62\% - 47\%}{62\%} = 0.24 = 24\%$$

So giving people a leaflet reduces the chances that the person will take antibiotics by 24%. This is the *relative risk decrease.*

We can also present this as the relative probability of taking the medicine, as *a proportion of those who would have taken the medicine:*

$$\frac{62\% - 47\%}{47\%} = 0.32 = 32\%$$

Optional Extra: Relative and absolute differences

The problem is, it's not just you (the reader) and we (the authors) who are confused. We are (we like to think) relatively intelligent, and we are reading (writing) a book on this. How do others cope? (Sometimes these people are talked about as consumers of research. They are the ones that act on what research finds.)

The answer is, they don't. Here are three recent news stories:

'The researchers found it reduced the likelihood of death from all causes by up to 36%.' (BBC News, 19 May 2004)

'23% of students in private rented accommodation share their digs with a variety of vermin and pests, including mice, bed bugs, rats and slugs – a jump of seven percentage points on a 2001 NUS survey.' (*Guardian*, 13 May 2004)

'Deputy Prime Minister John Prescott told the House of Commons on Wednesday that turnout in the region had increased by 7.3%.' (BBC News, 9 June 2004)

(Continued)

(Continued)

Were they talking about relative or absolute differences? We don't know, and they probably don't know either, because they haven't read this (or something which makes the same point); but it does make rather a lot of difference.

If the probability of dying has dropped by 36%, does that mean it has gone from 40% to 4% – if so, that's quite impressive. Or does it mean it has gone from 40% to 25.6% – not to be sniffed at, but a lot less impressive.

We'll come back to journalists and figures in a minute. First, we've got to add a new complication.

So hang on, let's get this straight. You can say: '*Giving someone a leaflet reduces the chances of her taking antibiotics by 15%.*' Phil can say: '*Giving someone a leaflet reduces the chances of her taking antibiotics by 24%*'.

Jeremy can say: 'Not giving someone a leaflet increases the chances of someone taking antibiotics by 32%'.

Are we all telling the truth? Well yes, we are. It's a bit confusing. The data are all correct but they give a different impression about the amount of change. It's very easy to create this confusion accidentally, but it's fair to say that some people create it on purpose. Any discussion about health with politicians from different parties involves them quoting from an array of statistics. Even if we accept the numbers are correct (*you're not implying that our politicians sometimes don't tell the truth are you? – Ed*), they are able to argue for hours trading numbers that give a very different impression about the state of the NHS.

Odds ratio

We need to consider a third way to show the difference between two proportions. It's a bit trickier but it's the most common way to do it. The method is called the **odds ratio**. Odds are a bit trickier than percentages or proportions (unless you hang out in places like Ladbrokes, in which case this will all be familiar to you). We'll start with a question. What are the odds of throwing a 6 on a die?

If you said '1 in 6', you are an honourable and noble person who has not thrown every last penny into the hands of the betting shops. Unfortunately, you are also wrong because this is not how odds are calculated.

The odds are 5 to 1, or 5: 1. The event will not happen 5 times for each time that it does happen.

Similarly, what are the odds of a coin coming up heads when it is tossed?

The odds are 1: 1, or evens. It will happen one time, for each time it does not happen.

And, what are the odds of picking a jack, queen or king from a pack of cards?

The odds are 10: 3. There are 13 kinds of card, three are jack, queen or king, 10 are not. It will happen (on average) 3 times for every 10 times it does not happen.

Statisticians present their odds differently from betting shops. Odds are always presented as 'something to one'. If you go to the bookies then you might find odds being offered on Lucky Boy at 9 to 5, or 13 to 8. A statistician, however, would not say that the odds were 9: 5, they would say that they were 1.8: 1. However, because statisticians *always* present odds as 'something to one', they can miss out the 'to one' bit. The odds would therefore be 1.8.

 Tip

In everyday life we like percentages because we seem to be able to understand them. A percentage is a proportion of 100. So if your football team wins 7 out of 10 matches we say it wins 70% of the time. A statistician does not like percentages and instead expresses this as a proportion of 1 (rather than 100). The statistician says that the probability of your team winning is 0.70. (*Though if they are talking about Phil's team they say the probability of winning is 0.1, in a good year – Ed.*)

If you know the probability, p, you can calculate the odds using the following formula:

$$\text{odds} = \frac{p}{1-p}$$

For example, in the MacFarlane study, the probability of a person in the leaflet group taking their antibiotics is 47% which is 0.47. So to calculate the odds:

$$\text{odds} = \frac{p}{1-p} = \frac{0.47}{1-0.47} = 0.89$$

Similarly, we can calculate the odds for the control group:

$$\text{odds} = \frac{p}{1-p} = \frac{0.62}{1-0.62} = 1.63$$

We then express the change in the odds using the *odds ratio,* OR.

$$OR = \frac{0.89}{1.63} = 0.54$$

Alternatively, we can also express the odds in the opposite direction:

$$OR = \frac{1.63}{0.89} = 1.83$$

Notice that $1/1.83 = 0.54$.

Optional Extra: Calculating the odds ratio

There's an easier way of calculating the odds ratio.

If we put our data into a table and we call the cells in the table A, B, C, D, as shown in Table 7.2, then the odds ratio is given by the formula:

$$OR = \frac{AD}{BC}$$

If we put our numbers in:

$$OR = \frac{AD}{BC} = \frac{49 \times 39}{55 \times 63} = \frac{1911}{3465} = 0.54$$

Table 7.2   *MacFarlane et al. results*

		Given leaflet			
		Yes		No	
Antibiotic	Yes	A	49	B	63
	No	C	55	D	39

So we now have another way of expressing our data: the odds ratio, which is 1.83. The odds of taking the antibiotics are 1.83 times higher, if people are not given a leaflet.

So, let's get this straight, we can say any one of five things to describe the effect of the leaflet:

- Giving someone a leaflet reduces the chances of their taking antibiotics by 15%.
- Giving someone a leaflet reduces the chances of their taking antibiotics by 24%.
- Not giving someone a leaflet increases the chances of someone taking antibiotics by 32%.
- Giving someone a leaflet means the odds of them taking antibiotics are 0.54 times lower.
- Not giving someone a leaflet means the odds of them taking antibiotics are 1.83 times higher.

Now, you might ask, this all seems a little complex, and does it really matter? And we say yes. If it didn't matter we wouldn't say it. You yawn and put the book down. But hold on before you do that, because this is one of the most important things that we mention in this book.

It is important because a lot of information is presented to us by the media about health, and health outcomes are often dichotomous and use things like relative risk and odds ratios to present the information. One of the most famous cases was the 1995 'pill scare'. A very large international study (with 24 authors) was published in *The Lancet* (a highly regarded medical journal) which suggested that taking a certain type of contraceptive pill might lead to a fatal embolism. The authors presented the results in terms of odds ratios. The odds ratio if you were taking the pill was between 3 and 4 for different countries, and different types of thrombosis. The odds of dying of thrombosis was between 3 and 4 times higher, if you were taking the contraceptive pill than if you were not. This sounds pretty serious.

At this point in the story we need to digress, to explain why the story had even more impact than it might have done. Both *The Lancet* and the *British Medical Journal* (the other highly regarded UK-based journal to cover medicine) come out on Friday. Journalists read this and report it, and most people will hear about it on the news that night. The problem is that if the story is not reported very well (as we will see, this one wasn't), then the first time that anyone can talk to their doctor about it, or that someone from the health service can go on the news to explain, is often Monday. By this time people have had a whole weekend to think about it and act on it.

Tip
If you are interested in seeing evaluations of the way that health stories are reported in newspapers, the National Health Service in the UK has a service called *Hitting the Headlines* that evaluates health stories, and compares what was written in the newspaper with the public information available. It is on the web at http:// www. nelh.nhs.uk/hth/

Anyway, back to the story. What the reporters might have said is that the risk of a woman having an embolism is around about 0.003%. This increases if the woman is taking the pill to around 0.009%, a change of 0.006% (compare that with around 0.06% who are likely to have an embolism while pregnant, or with 0.17% who will die from smoking related diseases, or 0.008% who will die in road accidents).

There are two problems relating to how this type of news is reported. The first is that the journalists' job is not to tell the truth, but to sell newspapers. Which of the following will sell more papers?

- Pill increases risk of embolism by 0.006%.
- Pill increases risk of embolism by 300%.

The second is, to quote Adams (1997):[1] 'Reporters are faced with the daily choice of painstakingly researching stories or writing whatever people tell them. Both approaches pay the same.'

Number needed to treat (NNT)

Before we finish, we want to mention one more method of presenting the effect of an intervention which is commonly used in medicine, though much less commonly used in psychology. It's called the **number needed to treat (NNT)** or **number needed to harm (NNH)**.

The NNT asks '*How many people do I have to treat with X, rather than Y, in order that I can expect that one person does Z?*'. Let's look at the MacFarlane study again. *How many people do we have to treat with a leaflet (X), rather than no leaflet (Y), in order that we could expect that one person does not take the antibiotic (Z).* This is the number needed to treat. The number needed to harm asks '*How many people have to do something, before we would expect that one of them would come to harm as a result?*'. For example, for smoking the number is somewhere between 2 and 3. If two people started to smoke we would expect one of them to come to some serious harm from some condition (ok, no euphemisms, we mean die because of their smoking), who would not have otherwise done so had they not smoked.

Optional Extra: Mortality data

Of course, everyone is going to die sometime. It's a question of whether you died before you would have done, had you not smoked – this gets a bit confusing because we are tempted to say things like 'People who ate 5 fruit and vegetables a day were less likely to die than people who didn't'. But of course, everyone is likely to die – more than likely, certain. What they should say is '… were less likely to die in any given period of time'.

When medical researchers look at either the potential harm of something, like smoking, or the good of something, like attending screening for cancer, they don't care how anyone died, they just care if someone did die or not – this is called *all-cause mortality*. If you died crossing the road to buy a pack of cigarettes, you would count as a death against smoking. If you died because you left the pub because it was too smoky, and fell down the stairs, this would count as a death against not-smoking. Some studies that were carried out to evaluate the effects of breast screening programmes found that the programme reduced the chance of a woman dying of breast cancer (in any given time period, of course), but did not reduce the chances of a woman dying (full stop). This was rather a curious result, and seems to have been due to differences in the groups (Alexander et al., 1999).

---

[1]Adams isn't a famous psychologist, he's the person who writes the Dilbert cartoon strip.

The NNT is very easy to calculate.[2] It is simply

$$\text{NNT} = \frac{1}{\text{Absolute risk difference}}.$$

So, for MacFarlane et al.,

$$\text{NNT} = \frac{1}{0.15} = 6.67$$

Some people suggest that NNT should be rounded up to the next whole number. In which case we can say if we give seven people a leaflet we expect one person will not take their antibiotics who would have done with no leaflet.

CONFIDENCE INTERVALS AND *P*-VALUES

Confidence intervals

You will be pleased to hear that we are not going to calculate **confidence intervals** for all of the descriptive statistics that we calculated. Although it is possible, most of them are rarely used so the only one we are going to concentrate on is the odds ratio. We will use the data from the Gale and Ball study. It can help to put the data into a table, as before.

The first step is to calculate the odds ratio. We'll use the easy way. For the Gale and Bell data (Table 7.3) we have

Table 7.3 *Results from Gale and Ball*

			No		Yes	
			\multicolumn{4}{c}{Correct?}
Task	Single Goal	N	A	24	B	6
	Dual Goal	N	C	7	D	23

$$OR = \frac{AD}{BC} = \frac{24 \times 23}{6 \times 7} = \frac{552}{42} = 13.1$$

---

[2] The NNH is calculated in exactly the same way.

So, the odds of getting the correct solution to the problem are 13.1 times higher if a person is in the DG group than if they are in the SG group. However, this is a sample estimate, and we want to calculate the confidence intervals around that to give some idea of the level of uncertainty.

Calculate ν

Next we have to calculate a statistic called ν, which might look to you a bit like a *v*, but it's actually the lower case Greek letter nu, which is pronounced 'new' (or 'noo', it's a matter of taste). ν is a bit like the standard error of the odds ratio, as we'll see in a minute or two. It is given by

$$\nu = \sqrt{\frac{1}{A} + \frac{1}{B} + \frac{1}{C} + \frac{1}{D}}$$

If we put our numbers into the equation:

$$\nu = \sqrt{\frac{1}{A} + \frac{1}{B} + \frac{1}{C} + \frac{1}{D}}$$

$$= \sqrt{\frac{1}{24} + \frac{1}{6} + \frac{1}{7} + \frac{1}{23}}$$

$$= \sqrt{0.042 + 0.167 + 0.143 + 0.043}$$

$$= 0.63$$

You might not be surprised to hear that it's all related to the **normal distribution** so we need the value of the normal distribution associated with the cut-offs that we want to use. We want to use a 95% confidence interval so we can either use a computer or check the relevant table (or simply remember because it's always the same number) that the value we want is 1.96. We can write this as $z_{\alpha/2}$. (The /2 bit is needed, because it is two-tailed.)

The confidence intervals of the odds ratio are given by:

$$\text{Lower CL} = OR \times \exp(-1 \times z_{\alpha/2} \times \nu)$$

and the upper confidence limit (UCL) is

$$\text{Upper CL} = OR \times \exp(z_{\alpha/2} \times \nu)$$

Optional Extra: What's the exp?

You probably came across exp at school, but you might have forgotten. Exp is short for the exponential. If you have a scientific calculator, it will have a button that can calculate the exponential. It might be labelled $\boxed{e^n}$, or you might need to press inverse,

(Continued)

(Continued)

and then the button labelled $\boxed{In}$. In spreadsheet packages, like Excel, the function is called $\boxed{exp}$.

If you aren't sure, then calculate $\boxed{exp(1)}$. This should give you a number that starts 2.71828. (We've put some more on this on the website.)

Putting the numbers in, we have

Lower CI = $13.1 \times exp(-1 \times z_{\alpha/2} \times v)$
Lower CI = $13.1 \times exp(-1.96 \times 0.63)$
Lower CI = $13.1 \times exp(-1.23)$
Lower CI = 13.1×0.29
Lower CI = 3.84

and

Upper CI = $13.1 \times exp(z_{\alpha/2} \times v)$
Upper CI = $13.1 \times exp(1.96 \times 0.63)$
Upper CI = $13.1 \times exp(1.23)$
Upper CI = 13.1×3.42
Upper CI = 45.0

Reporting the result

The results are reported very similarly to the results of a test of a difference between means. We would say: '*6 out of 30 people in the single goal group successfully completed the task, whereas 23 out of 30 people in the dual goal group successfully completed the task, OR = 13.1, 95% CI = 3.84, 45.0*'.

A couple of things to note. First, when we had confidence intervals of a mean, the intervals were symmetrical, so the lower CL was the same amount below the mean as the upper CL was above it. This is not the case for the odds ratio because in our example the lower CL is (about) 10 below the odds ratio, while the upper CL is (about) 30 above it. Second, the confidence intervals do seem to be very wide. That's just the way they are and upper CLs can stretch into hundreds, with small sample sizes. If we want more certainty, we must have a bigger sample.

Calculating *p*-values

Given the plethora of ways of displaying the difference between two proportions, you will probably be pleased to hear that there is only one way to calculate the probability value, well, sort of only one way. The test we need is called the chi-square test.

Tip
Chi is the Greek letter χ, and it is pronounced 'ky', like sky without an s. It's not pronounced chye, like child, without the 'ld' (although you frequently hear people say chi(ld)). They are wrong. Be sure to tell them. Especially if they are your lecturer.

CHI-SQUARE χ^2

The **chi-square test** was developed by Pearson, and hence it is sometimes known as the Pearson χ^2 test.

The first stage in the χ^2 test is to put the values into a table like Table 7.3, but add totals to it (Table 7.4). Notice that we are still calling the cells A, B, C and D.

Table 7.4   *Table 7.3 with totals for rows and columns*

		Correct?		Total
		No	Yes	
Task	Single Goal	A 24	B 6	30
	Dual Goal	C 7	D 23	30
Total		31	29	60

You now have to calculate the expected values for each cell, which are referred to as E. The expected values are the values that we would expect if the null hypothesis were true; the null hypothesis in this case being that the task type had no effect.

Optional Extra: You say 'chi-square', I say 'chi-squared'

Chi-square or chi-squared? SPSS and Mplus refer to chi-square, Excel, Stata and Mathematica to chi-squared. The Cochrane Style Guide says chi square *or* chi squared. We typed both "square" and "squared" versions into Google to see which was more popular. Google says that there are 206,000 pages with 'chi-squared' (or 'chi squared' – Google can't tell the difference) on them, and 952,000 with 'chi-square'.

(Continued)

(Continued)

The chi-square test was developed by Karl Pearson, and we spent some time trying to find out which version he used. Pearson was the editor of the journal *Biometrika* for over 30 years, so we looked through that too (not all of it), to see if we could find a reference to chi-square or chi-squared, but all we ever found was χ^2.

 Tip

The chi-square test carries out a lot of simple mathematical calculations. It repeats the same calculation for each box in your table. In this case that means doing the calculations 4 times. This makes the workings look very messy but keep in mind that we are just doing the same calculation for each and it should make sense.

The expected values are given by

$$E = \frac{R \times C}{T}$$

Where R refers to the total for a given row, C the total for a given column, and T the grand total.

$$\text{Cell } A: E = \frac{30 \times 31}{60} = 15.5 \quad \text{Cell } B: E = \frac{30 \times 29}{60} = 14.5$$

$$\text{Cell } C: E = \frac{30 \times 31}{60} = 15.5 \quad \text{Cell } D: E = \frac{30 \times 29}{60} = 14.5$$

Table 7.5 *Expected and observed values added*

		Correct?		
		No	Yes	Total
Task	Single Goal	O 24 A E 15.5	O 6 B E 14.5	30
	Dual Goal	O 7 C E 15.5	O 23 D E 14.5	30
Total		31	29	60

We now have two values for each cell; the observed value (which we can call O), and the expected value (E); see Table 7.5. Now all we need to know is the distance between the observed value and the expected value so we can take the differences and add them up. Almost, but not quite. The difference needs to take account of the sample size. If the difference between the observed and expected values is 6, and the expected value is also 6, we are out by a long way. On the other hand, if the expected value is 1,000,000, then that is pretty close.

The formula for the test statistic, χ^2, is given by

$$\chi^2 = \sum \frac{(O - E)^2}{E}$$

The Σ symbol means 'find the sum of'. This means, calculate this value for each cell and then add them to get the total:

Cell A: $\dfrac{(24 - 15.5)^2}{15.5} = \dfrac{72.25}{15.5} = 4.66$ Cell B: $\dfrac{(7 - 15.5)^2}{14.5} = \dfrac{72.25}{14.5} = 4.98$

Cell C: $\dfrac{(24 - 15.5)^2}{15.5} = \dfrac{72.25}{15.5} = 4.66$ Cell D: $\dfrac{(7 - 15.5)^2}{14.5} = \dfrac{72.25}{14.5} = 4.98$

We then add up each of these values to get χ^2.

$$\chi^2 = 4.66 + 4.98 + 4.66 + 4.98 = 19.29$$

Before we can look up the value of χ^2, either by using the tables which you can find in Appendix 7a, or by using a computer (which, as always, is better) we need to know the value for the **degrees of freedom** (df), which is given by

$$df = (\text{Number of rows} - 1) \times (\text{Number of columns} - 1)$$

There are two rows, and two columns, so

$$df = (2 - 1) \times (2 - 1) = 1 \times 1 = 1$$

So if we check the probability of finding a value of χ^2 as high (or higher) than 19.29, with 1 df either using a table or computer we find the value is less than 0.001.

 Tip: How to calculate the *p*-value in Excel

If you want to use Excel to calculate the *p*-value, given a value for χ^2, then type

=chidist(chi-square, df)

We type   =chidist(19.29, 1)

and Excel says   0.000011

which we will call $p < 0.001$.

Issues with χ^2

Before we move on, there are a couple of complications that we need to alert you to.

One of them is an assumption made by the χ^2 test which is that all of the expected values (in a 2×2 table) must be greater than 5. If the table is larger than 2×2, then 80% of the expected values need to be above 5. Even if you do the test on a computer, the program may not warn you that this is the case. If your data do not satisfy this assumption you can use Fisher's exact test instead, and we will look at that below.

The second thing we need to warn you about is that when we have a 2×2 table the χ^2 test is a little bit liberal, and statisticians don't like a liberal test. A liberal test is slightly more prone to say that a result is statistically significant than it should be, so the type I error rate is not 0.05 but a bit higher than that (see a description of type I errors on page 88). One approach to dealing with this is to use **Yates' correction** for continuity which is sometimes just called the **continuity correction**. To use the correction we subtract 0.5 from the top of the formula in the χ^2 equation:

$$\chi^2 = \sum \frac{(|O - E| - 0.5)^2}{E}$$

The values contained within the bars | | means 'take the absolute value', which means if there is a minus sign ignore it. If we calculate the χ^2 with the continuity correction, we find that $\chi^2 = 17.1$, and that the associated p with 1 df is still less than 0.001.

The problem with Yates' correction is that it makes the test a little conservative (*oh you just can't win*) so the type I error rate is now smaller than 0.05. This in itself isn't a problem, but it means that the test is now less likely to give a significant result, when it *should* be giving a significant result. The correction is a little bit controversial, as some people say it should always be used because otherwise you get the wrong result. Other people say it should never be used because otherwise you don't get the right result. Take your pick.

In fact, the correction only really matters when the sample size is relatively small so if the sample size is large, the correction makes little difference, and if the sample size is small there is a better test that we can use called *Fisher's exact test*. Let's look at it now.

FISHER'S EXACT TEST

Optional Extra: Fisher's tea test

There is a famous story of the development of the Fisher's exact test, which many believe to be apocryphal, although Salsburg (2001) has heard the story from someone who was there. Fisher's wife, Ruth, claimed that she could tell whether a cup of tea had had the milk poured in before or after the tea.

Fisher didn't believe her and so wanted to put the idea to the test. The problem is that the sample size needs to be large enough for the expected values to be above 5. This would require making a lot of tea using a lot of cups, and Fisher didn't want to do this. Instead he decided to work out a test that would work with smaller samples, and he came up with Fisher's exact test.

In case you're interested, Ruth could tell, every time.

The idea of **Fisher's exact test** is that for some events we can work out the exact probability of them occurring without needing to use test statistics and tables. For example, we know that if I toss a coin twice the probability of getting heads is 0.25. If I roll a die, the probability of getting a 6 is $\frac{1}{6}$.

We can do the same thing for data which are in a 2×2 contingency table (although we don't need to worry about how):

$$p = \frac{(A+B)!(C+D)!(A+C)!(B+D)!}{(A+B+C+D)!A!B!C!D!}$$

where the ! symbol means *factorial*, which means take the number and multiply it by every whole number below it down to 1. So, $4! = 4 \times 3 \times 2 \times 1 = 24$ and $8! = 8 \times 7 \times 6 \times 5 \times 4 \times 3 \times 2 \times 1 = 40,320$.

If we put the numbers into that equation, we get

$$p = \frac{(A+B)!(C+D)!(A+C)!(B+D)!}{(A+B+C+D)!A!B!C!D!}$$

$$= \frac{(24+6)!(7+23)!(24+7)!(6+23)!}{(24+6+7+23)!24!6!7!23!}$$

$$= 0.000011$$

Please forgive us for not showing each step – this leads to some staggeringly large numbers. The top row of the formula comes to about 5,115,413,423,836,020, 000,000, 000,000,000,000,000,000,000,000,000,000,000,000,000,000,000,000, 000,000,000,000,000,000,000,000,000,000,000,000,000,000,000,000,000. (Unless you have quite an expensive calculator, it won't be able to think about numbers that large.[3])

Fisher's exact test gives the probability of getting the exact result that was found in the study. However, we are not just interested in the exact result, we are interested in any result that is more extreme than the result we have. If someone tosses a coin 20 times and gets heads 16 times, we could ask what the probability was for every possible combination of numbers that is as extreme as this, or more extreme, find the probability, and then add them all up.

If we did do that, we will find that the probability was 0.000023. With Fisher's exact test there is no test statistic, and no need to look anything up in a table.

TEST SUMMARY

We have done three tests to examine the statistical significance of these data:

---

[3] We could do a bit of algebra, and simplify that. But you probably aren't very interested in that, and nor are we.

- The (Pearson) χ^2 test: χ^2 = 19.29, df = 1, p = 0.000011.
- The continuity-corrected χ^2 test: χ^2 = 17.1, df = 1, p = 0.000036.
- Fisher's exact test: p = 0.000023.

(Note that we would never normally bother to present this many decimal places for a probability value – we are just making a point.) The p-value of the exact test is in between the (liberal) Pearson χ^2 test and the (conservative) continuity-corrected χ^2 test.

Fisher's exact test is the most appropriate, as long as the sample size is sufficiently small that it can be calculated. If the sample is larger, there is little difference between the two types of χ^2 test.

Reporting the result

Here's how we would report the result of the Gale and Ball study: '*In the single goal group 20% (6/30) of the participants gave the correct answer to the 2-4-6 problem whereas in the dual goal group 77% (23/30) gave the correct answer. The odds ratio = 13.1, 95% CI = 3.84, 45.02.*'

MORE CATEGORIES

The χ^2 test can be used in larger tables than 2 × 2. If there were three groups, and four possible outcomes, we would have a 3 × 4 contingency table. We would calculate the expected values as before. We would then compute the sum of $\frac{(O-E)^2}{E}$ for each of the 12 cells. The degrees of freedom, as before, are given by:

$$df = (R - 1) \times (C - 1) = (4 - 1) \times (3 - 1) = 3 \times 2 = 6$$

It is difficult to calculate the odds ratio in this case. If you wanted to, you have to choose one group as the reference group and calculate the odds ratio for each of the other groups relative to that group. Unfortunately SPSS won't do this for you.

SUMMARY

We have looked at three ways to analyse independent designs with categorical data. The default test to use is the ever popular chi-square test. Although there are some limitations on its use it offers a good method for analysing a wide variety of data. If you follow the simple rules above you will be able to calculate the test, explain how it works and report your results correctly.

Test yourself answers

Test yourself 1

For the UK voters, they have used column percentages. For the US voters, they have presented row percentages. The two sets of values are not directly comparable.

DOING THIS IN SPSS

Common Mistake

In SPSS do *not* select **Analyze** ⇒ **Nonparametric Tests** ⇒ **Chi-Square.** This is something different.

In SPSS, you will have two variables, one of which defines the group people were in, and one of which defines the outcome. Select **Analyze** ⇒ **Descriptive Statistics** ⇒ **Crosstabs**. Put the outcome (called Outcome, in our case) into the **Row(s)** box. Put the Group (called Task, in our case) into the **Column(s)** box:

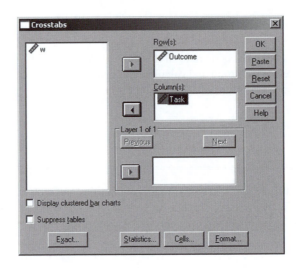

Click on **Statistics**:

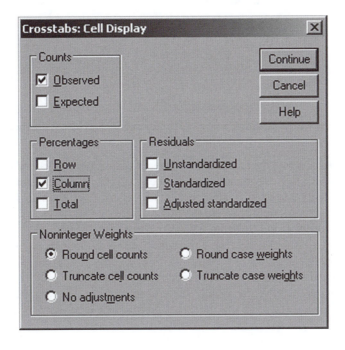

Tick **Chi-square**. Tick **Risk**. Click **Continue**. Now click **Cells**.

In percentages, tick **Column**. Click **Continue**. Then click **OK**.

The first output table is the contingency table. This shows the number, and percentage, of people giving each answer in each group. (Again, double-check that it's the percentage you want.)

Correct? * Task Crosstabulation

			Task		Total
			1 Single Goal	2 Dual Goal	
Correct?	0 No	Count	24	7	31
		% within Task	80.0%	23.3%	51.7%
	1 Yes	Count	6	23	29
		% within Task	20.0%	76.7%	48.3%
Total		Count	30	30	60
		% within Task	100.0%	100.0%	100.0%

The second table shows the Pearson chi-square, df and probability value (SPSS calls this Asymp. Sig., which is the asymptotic significance). If you have a 2×2 table, the second row is the continuity-corrected χ^2, along with df and probability (again, in the Asymp. Sig. Column).

The next row is the likelihood ratio – you can ignore this.

The next row is Fisher's exact test. This shows the probability only so you should look at the Exact Sig. (2 sided).

Linear-by-linear association can be ignored.

At the bottom of the table, SPSS tells you how many cells, and what percentage, have an expected value less than 5. If this number is greater than 25%, the χ^2 is not valid. *SPSS will give you no other warning.* It will continue to give all of the other statistics, even though they should not be interpreted.

Chi-Square Tests

	Value	df	Asymp. Sig. (2-sided)	Exact Sig. (2-sided)	Exact Sig. (1-sided)
Pearson Chi-Square	19.288[b]	1	.000		
Continuity Correction[a]	17.086	1	.000		
Likelihood Ratio	20.490	1	.000		
Fisher's Exact Test				.000	.000
Linear-by-Linear Association	18.967	1	.000		
N of Valid Cases	60				

a. Computed only for a 2 × 2 table
b. 0 cells (.0%) have expected count less than 5. The minimum expected count is 14.50.

The next table is titled Risk Estimate. The top row gives the odds ratio, and the 95% confidence intervals. The other rows give the odds ratio for each group but we are not interested in that (it's quite confusing).

Risk Estimate

	Value	95% Confidence Interval	
		Lower	Upper
Odds Ratio for Correct? (0 No / 1 Yes)	13.143	3.837	45.023
For cohort Task = 1 Single Goal	3.742	1.790	7.823
For cohort Task = 2 Dual Goal	.285	.145	.561
N of Valid Cases	60		

8

Relationships between variables: correlation and regression

What's in this chapter?

- Association
- Correlation
- Regression
- Interpreting correlation and regression
- Calculating correlation coefficients: Pearson and Spearman
- Causality
- Using SPSS

KEY TERMS

association
causal relationship
confidence interval
correlation coefficient
covariance
descriptive statistic
dicohotomania
equation for a straight line
eugenics
experiment

Fisher's z transformation
inferential statistic
Kendall's tau-a
line of best fit
non-parametric correlation
normal distribution
Pearson correlation coefficient
post hoc justification
power
proportion of variance

regression line   Spearman correlation
residual   standard deviation
sample statistics   standardised slope
scatterplot   statistical significance
Simpson's paradox   *y*-intercept

INTRODUCTION

So far in this book we have considered ways of comparing groups of individuals. In particular, we have looked at differences between groups. All our hypotheses so far have been along the lines of whether one set of scores is bigger, wider, more frequent etc. than another set of scores. Not all data are like that and sometimes we don't want to know about difference, we want to know about similarities or associations. For example, we might want to know if people who score higher on one measure also tend to score higher on another measure. This chapter looks at tests of association and how we can use them to predict scores.

ASSOCIATION

In experiments we can assign people to one group of participants or one condition of the independent variable. We have control over who does what and we can use this control to draw some conclusions about the independent variable. If we want to find out about the effects of alcohol on mood, we can divide our participants into two groups, give one group unlimited alcohol for a week and compare the moods of the two groups. This is an **experiment** and we can compare the differences between the scores and make some suggestions about the effect of alcohol on mood.

Much more common, however, would be to look at the effect of mood on drinkers by comparing the mood scores of people who admit they drink a lot of alcohol with people who do not drink much alcohol at all. In this case we have not been able to assign our participants to groups, and there might be a lot of differences between the two groups. Perhaps people drink more alcohol *because* of their mood state, and so our tests of difference will be harder to interpret. A more useful way of examining data of this kind might be to look at a range of personality and mood scores and see whether there is any **association** between them and the amount of alcohol that someone drinks.

Another type of question we might be interested in is whether there are similarities in the scores of family members on cognitive tests such as IQ. In fact, it was to investigate this particular question that correlations were first developed by Galton, and later by Pearson and Spearman. Do children in the same family achieve similar scores on IQ tests, and do children achieve scores similar to those of their parents? If this is the case then it might suggest a genetic component to individual differences in IQ scores. It was this genetic issue that interested Spearman and Pearson (both previously mentioned in this book) because they favoured eugenic solutions to social problems.

Optional Extra: Eugenics

Eugenics is the belief that by the careful choice of parents (selective breeding) we can create a generation of superior children. There is a remarkable amount of faith in this idea, even though there is very little evidence to support it. For example, bets are already being taken on the likelihood of David Beckham's children playing football for England.

Eugenics has a dark side in that the flip side of breeding superior children is the belief that some other people should be stopped from breeding or even killed to prevent their supposed inferior children being born.

We are interested, then, in finding a way to represent associations between scores. For example:

- Hulme, Hatcher, Nation, Brown, Adams and Stuart (2002) wanted to examine the relationship between measures of early sensitivity to phonological awareness and measures of early reading ability.
- Kozak, Strelau and Miles (2005) were interested in the correlation between measures of coping for twins. They wanted to see if the correlation between monozygotic (identical) twins was higher than the correlation between dizygotic (non-identical or fraternal) twins.
- McCann (2001, 2003) tested the 'precocity-longevity hypothesis'. He suggested that people who achieved very high success early in their life died earlier than people who achieved success later. He was, therefore, interested in examining the age of achievement, and the age of death, of people who had been elected president of the US, prime minister of the UK, or pope. In situations like these we can use correlation and regression.

Common Mistake: Inventing groups

This mistake is common amongst researchers as well as students. People want to compare groups so badly that they split their data, often at the mean or the median, into two groups and then compare high scorers with low scorers using one of the techniques described in the previous two chapters. Sometimes this makes statisticians angry and sometimes it makes them sad. Sometimes statisticians, such as Senn (2003), think of it as a disease which he called **dicohotomania**. Senn wrote of variables 'wastefully dichotomised to feed the numbers needed to treat (NNT) sausage machine' (we mentioned NNT in Chapter 7).

(Continued)

(Continued)

What did Senn mean by 'wastefully dichotomised'? He meant that when we take a rich continuous variable with lots of information and change it into a categorical variable (by dividing it into groups) we throw away a lot of that information (for more on this, see Cohen, 1983; Whitehead, 1993).

There is a further objection that is more theoretical. Suppose we have a group of participants, aged from 18 to 62. We decide to dichotomise at the half-way point, which is 40, to split people into young and old. What we are therefore saying is that, as far as our theory is concerned:

- An 18-year-old is the same as a 40-year-old.
- The difference between an 18-year-old and a 41-year-old is the same as the difference between a 40-year-old and a 41-year-old.
- Being 41 and being 62 are the same.

Whatever age you are, you probably find one of those statements insulting.

The problems of dichotomisation are not new, as Pearson (1900) wrote about them over 100 years ago. Some have suggested that Pearson was so obsessed with dichotomania, that he had an affliction of the opposite direction – **continuitis**. Pearson would never accept that a variable really was dichotomous and he would always seek the underlying continuous variable which had been dichotomised.

THE REGRESSION LINE

In order to show how we look at relationships between measures, we will use data from Hulme et al. (2002).[1] We have used a subsample of 35 children, randomly selected from the study. We will focus on two variables from the Hulme et al. study:

- Initial phoneme detection. Children were asked to listen to a word and repeat it. They were then asked which of three words started with the same sound.
- British Ability Scales (BAS) reading score, a standard measure of reading ability.

The data are shown in Table 8.1.

The first and most obvious way to summarise data where we are examining the relationship between two variables is to draw a **scatterplot**. We put one variable on the *x*-axis and another on the *y*-axis, and we draw a point for each person showing their scores on the two variables. Such a graph is shown in Figure 8.1.

---

[1] We would like to thank Charles Hulme for providing these data and allowing us to use them.

Table 8.1 *Raw data from Hulme et al. (2002)*

	BAS reading score	Initial phoneme score
1	33	26
2	5	15
3	51	29
4	14	15
5	11	15
6	9	15
7	5	21
8	2	13
9	3	19
10	16	27
11	15	26
12	36	23
13	9	14
14	2	8
15	43	25
16	14	15
17	3	13
18	11	9
19	48	26
20	16	27
21	3	13
22	2	6
23	8	16
24	9	13
25	8	17
26	20	22
27	3	6
28	12	13
29	5	11
30	2	13
31	3	14
32	19	29
33	16	8
34	3	22
35	6	11
Mean	13.29	17.00

If you look at Figure 8.1 you will see that the children who achieved the lower score on the phoneme test also scored the lower values on the BAS test, and likewise, the children who scored high on one also scored high on the other. There seems to be some relationship between the scores, so if we find another child who has scored very high on the phoneme test we might like to predict that they will also score high on the BAS test.

When we want to tell people about our results, we don't want to have to draw a lot of scatterplots because it takes a long time, and it uses a lot of paper.[2] We want to summarise and represent the relationship between these two variables with a number. We then want to calculate the confidence intervals for this number, and we want to be able to find out if the relationship is statistically significant. That is, we want to know what is the probability of

---

[2] Remember how sad we all got in Chapter 6 about all those needlessly long reports that waste so much paper.

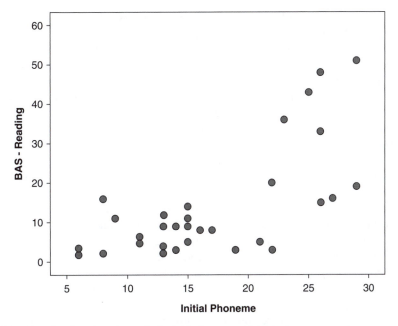

Figure 8.1   Scatterplot showing relationship between initial phoneme and BAS reading score

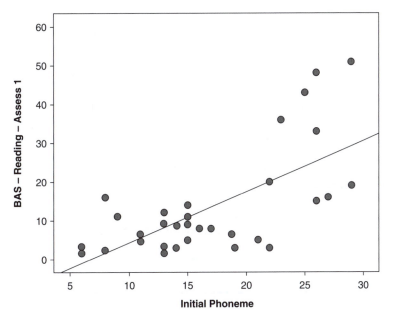

Figure 8.2   Figure 8.1 reproduced showing line of best fit

finding a relationship at least this strong if the null hypothesis that there is no relationship in the population is true.

So that we can think about how we might do this, we will draw a **line of best fit** on the graph – see Figure 8.2 (don't worry about how we know where to draw the line – we will come to that). We can describe this line by looking at its position on the page. We can describe how steep the slope of the line is and we can use this to tell us the predicted, or expected, score on the BAS, given a certain initial phoneme score. This is called the *regression line*. We can describe this line by giving its slope, in other words how steep it is. In this example, the slope is equal to 1.32 which means that for every 1 unit we move along the *x*-axis (horizontally), the line rises 1.32 units up the *y*-axis (vertically).

However, knowing the slope of the line does not tell us everything about it. We also need to know where to draw the line. To give the position of the line we also need to give its height. By convention we give the height at the point where the line hits the *y*-axis. The height is called the **y-intercept** or often just the *intercept*. It's also sometimes given another name, the *constant* (and you're going to have to trust us when we tell you that you don't need to know why). The intercept represents the expected score of a person who scored zero on the *x*-axis variable (initial phoneme). The intercept of our line is equal to −9.151.

Hold on (we hear you say), how can we expect that a person who scores zero on the initial phoneme test will score a negative number on the BAS reading? You can't score less than nothing. That's true, but we don't necessarily want to interpret this value, all it does is give the position of the line. It is often the case that the intercept doesn't make any sense. After all, no one scored 0, or even close to 0, on the initial phoneme score.

We can use the two values of slope and intercept to calculate the expected value of any person's score on the BAS reading scale, given their initial phoneme score. We find this using:

Expected BAS score = intercept + slope × initial phoneme score

The slope is sometimes referred to using the Greek letter β (beta – pronounced 'beater' by people from the UK, 'baida' by people from the USA, and correctly by people from Greece). The intercept is referred to in a couple of ways: sometimes it's called β as well, in which case we need to distinguish it from the slope, so we call the intercept β_0 and the slope β_1. Sometimes it is called α (alpha), but we think that this is a bit confusing because α is used to refer to several other things in statistics.

Tip: What's in a name?

At school you probably came across the **equation for a straight line,** which is

$$y = mx + c.$$

(Continued)

> *(Continued)*
>
> This is the same equation as
>
> $$y = \beta_0 + \beta_1 x$$
>
> Don't let the Greek symbols confuse you.

So, we can say that the expected or predicted score (that's your score on the *y*-axis variable so we will call it *y*) is given by

$$y = \beta_0 + \beta_1 x,$$

where *x* is the *x*-axis variable. This equation is called the *regression equation*.

Optional Extra: It's all Greek to me

Statisticians distinguish between **sample statistics**, which are calculated by taking a sample; and **population parameters**, which are the true values in the population.

 One rule that is stuck to *quite* closely (statisticians never stick to any rules very, very closely – that would make it too easy for students like you) is that a Greek letter represents a population parameter, and a normal letter represents a sample statistic. Of course, we can never truly calculate a population parameter, we can only *estimate* it. If we are estimating a population parameter we show this by putting a hat on it. So:

- $\bar{x}$ is the mean in our sample;
- μ is the Greek letter mu (pronounced 'myoo'), which is the equivalent of the Latin letter *m*, and is the mean in the population;
- $\hat{\mu}$ is μ with a hat on (pronounced 'myoo-hat') which is the estimate of our population mean. Because the estimate of our population mean is the sample mean, we say $\hat{\mu} = \bar{x}$.

 We came across this rule in Chapter 2 when we looked at the standard deviation. The standard deviation symbol is σ, the Greek letter sigma, because it is a population estimate. The sample standard deviation is given by *s*. Straight away, however, we can see that this rule is being broken because there is no hat on the σ.

Making sense of regression lines

Thinking about the relationship between two variables in this way can be very useful. We can make a prediction about one score from another score. We might be interested in, for example:

- The regression slope of job performance on prior qualifications (if you are an employer). We can work out the expected job performance of a person, based on their qualifications. The employer can therefore decide how much it is worth paying that person.
- The regression slope of grades on spending additional time doing college work (if you are a student). You can then try to decide how much work you should do (although we will come back to this issue).
- The regression slope of level of psychological disorders on time in therapy. Therapists may then be able to plan how long they should plan to give a person therapy.
- The regression slope of purchasing behaviour on some measure of personality. Advertisers can decide how they should advertise (and design) different products to appeal to different kinds of people.

Regression lines and equations have a big problem, and that is if we don't understand the scale(s) they are meaningless. If each point on a personality test is associated with a 10-point change in the score on a measure of job performance, is that a good thing? We don't know because we don't know what 1 point on the personality measure means and we don't know what 10 points mean on the job performance measure.

Notice that in the previous paragraph, we wrote things like 'regression slope of job performance on prior qualifications'. Why didn't we say 'the effect of prior qualifications on job performance'? The answer is that when there is a relationship between two variables, we can *predict* one from the other. We cannot say that one *explains* the other. We'll come back to this later on, but bear it in mind all the way through the chapter.

CORRELATION COEFFICIENT

We need some way of making the scales have some sort of meaning, and the way to do this is to convert the data into **standard deviation** units. If we have something approaching a **normal distribution** (as we often do), then the standard deviation means something to us and we show a normal distribution with standard deviations marked on it in Figure 8.3 (see page 208). If you are one standard deviation better than me you are quite a lot better than me. If you are 0.1 standard deviations better than me, you are only a little bit better than me. If this seems unclear at all, then go back and take a look at Chapter 3.

Instead of asking:

'if someone has an initial phoneme variable one point higher how much higher do we expect their BAS reading score to be?'

we could ask:

'if the initial phoneme score is *one standard deviation higher*, how many *standard deviations* higher would we expect the BAS reading score to be?'.

Talking in terms of standard deviations means that we are talking about standardised scores – we are not saying '1 point higher on this test', instead we are saying '1 standard deviation on this test'. Because we are talking about standardised regression slopes, we could call this the **standardised slope**. However, a much more common and more important name for the standardised slope is the **correlation coefficient**.

Now, it doesn't matter what units the scores are in because we understand what a standard deviation means. In order to convert the units, we need to know the standard deviation of each of the measures. In our reading example they are 13.334 for the BAS and 6.808 for the initial phoneme score.

If we know the slope, we can calculate the correlation using the formula

$$r = \frac{\beta \times \sigma_x}{\sigma_y},$$

where σ_x is the standard deviation of the variable on the x-axis (the horizontal one, which in this case is the initial phoneme score) of the scatterplot, and σ_y is the standard deviation of the variable on the y-axis (the vertical one, which in this case is the BAS reading score), and r is the correlation. (The letter r actually stands for regression, but most people ignore that because it is confusing.)

Tip

As you progress through your studies in psychology, you will find that the value r is used a lot. When people are talking about correlations, they will often refer to r, and they will expect you to know what it means. (Which is OK, because you will know what it means.)

If we pop our numbers into that equation:

$$r = \frac{\beta \times \sigma_x}{\sigma_y} = \frac{1.32 \times 6.808}{13.334} = 0.674$$

So our correlation coefficient is equal to 0.674.

Residuals

There is information in the graph that we don't seem to have summarised successfully. We want to know how well the regression line fits the data. That is, how far away the points are from the line. The closer the points are to the line, the stronger the relationship between the two variables. How do we measure this?

When we had one variable and we wanted to know the spread of the points around the mean, we calculated the standard deviation (σ). We used:

$$\sigma = \sqrt{\frac{\sum (x - \bar{x})^2}{N - 1}} = \sqrt{\frac{\sum d^2}{N - 1}}.$$

The square of the standard deviation is the variance. It's easier to calculate the variance because we just miss off the $\sqrt{}$ symbol:

$$\text{var} = \frac{\sum (x - \bar{x})^2}{N - 1} = \frac{\sum d^2}{N - 1}.$$

We can do the same thing with our regression data, but instead of making d the difference between the mean and the score, we can make it the difference between the value that we would expect the person to have, given their score on the x-variable, and the score they actually got. We can calculate their predicted scores, using

$$\hat{y} = b_0 + b_1 x$$

where b_0 is the intercept (-9.15), and b_1 is the slope (1.32).

For each person, we can therefore calculate their predicted BAS reading score, and the difference between their predicted score and their actual score. This difference is called the **residual**.

The first person has an initial phoneme score of 26. We calculate their predicted BAS score using

$$\hat{y} = b_0 + b_1 x$$

$$= -9.15 + 1.32 \times 26 = 25.16$$

Their residual score (the difference between the score they got and the score we thought they would get based on their initial phoneme score) is

$$\text{residual} = d = 33 - 25.16 = 7.84$$

However, if we want to calculate the equivalent of the variance, using the equation for σ^2 above, we need to square each person's score. For the first person we therefore calculate:

$$\text{residual}^2 = d^2 = 7.84^2 = 61.40$$

We can do this for every person's score and the results are shown in Table 8.2.

Table 8.2 *Raw scores, predicted BAS reading score, residual and residual squared*

	BAS reading score	Initial phoneme score	Predicted BAS reading score	d	d^2
1	33	26	25.16	7.84	61.40
2	5	15	10.65	−5.65	31.88
3	51	29	29.12	21.88	478.59
4	14	15	10.65	3.35	11.25
5	11	15	10.65	0.35	0.13
6	9	15	10.65	−1.65	2.71
7	5	21	18.56	−13.56	184.01
8	2	13	8.01	−6.01	36.08
9	3	19	15.93	−12.93	167.06
10	16	27	26.48	−10.48	109.91
11	15	26	25.16	−10.16	103.30
12	36	23	21.20	14.80	218.91
13	9	14	9.33	−0.33	0.11
14	2	8	1.41	0.59	0.35
15	43	25	23.84	19.16	366.95
16	14	15	10.65	3.35	11.25
17	3	13	8.01	−5.01	25.07
18	11	9	2.73	8.27	68.44
19	48	26	25.16	22.84	521.49
20	16	27	26.48	−10.48	109.91
21	3	13	8.01	−5.01	25.07
22	2	6	−1.23	3.23	10.45
23	8	16	11.97	−3.97	15.73
24	9	13	8.01	0.99	0.99
25	8	17	13.29	−5.29	27.94
26	20	22	19.88	0.12	0.01
27	3	6	−1.23	4.23	17.91
28	12	13	8.01	3.99	15.95
29	5	11	5.37	−0.37	0.13
30	2	13	8.01	−6.01	36.08
31	3	14	9.33	−6.33	40.02
32	19	29	29.12	−10.12	102.48
33	16	8	1.41	14.59	212.94
34	3	22	19.88	−16.88	285.09
35	6	11	5.37	0.63	0.40

If we sum the scores in the final column, we will get the value Σd^2, which is 3299.96. We can then put this into our equation:

$$\sigma^2 = \frac{\sum (x - \bar{x})^2}{N - 1} = \frac{\sum d^2}{N - 1} = \frac{3299.96}{35 - 1} = 97.06.$$

So the variance of the residuals is 97.06. But we don't know what that means do we?

Table 8.3 *Calculating the variance of the BAS score*

	BAS reading score	$x-\bar{x}$	$(x-\bar{x})^2$
1	33	19.71	388.65
2	5	−8.29	68.65
3	51	37.71	1422.37
4	14	0.71	0.51
5	11	−2.29	5.22
6	9	−4.29	18.37
7	5	−8.29	68.65
8	2	−11.29	127.37
9	3	−10.29	105.80
10	16	2.71	7.37
11	15	1.71	2.94
12	36	22.71	515.94
13	9	−4.29	18.37
14	2	−11.29	127.37
15	43	29.71	882.94
16	14	0.71	0.51
17	3	−10.29	105.80
18	11	−2.29	5.22
19	48	34.71	1205.08
20	16	2.71	7.37
21	3	−10.29	105.80
22	2	−11.29	127.37
23	8	−5.29	27.94
24	9	−4.29	18.37
25	8	−5.29	27.94
26	20	6.71	45.08
27	3	−10.29	105.80
28	12	−1.29	1.65
29	5	−8.29	68.65
30	2	−11.29	127.37
31	3	−10.29	105.80
32	19	5.71	32.65
33	16	2.71	7.37
34	3	−10.29	105.80
35	6	−7.29	53.08

No. We have exactly the same problem as we had with the regression line in that we didn't know the scale so we didn't know what it meant. We've got the same problem here and we've got a similar solution.

We want to know what that variance means in terms of the scale of the original BAS variable. How large is the variance of the residuals, compared to the variance of the BAS score. So, we calculate the variance of the BAS score. The formula as always is

$$\text{var} = \frac{\sum (x - \bar{x})^2}{N - 1} = \frac{\sum d^2}{N - 1}$$

Table 8.3 shows the calculation of the variance. The mean BAS score, is 13.29 (from Table 8.1). We then find $x - \bar{x}$ for each individual, and then square that value, and add them up:

$$\text{var} = \frac{\sum (x - \bar{x})^2}{N - 1} = \frac{6045.14}{35 - 1} = 177.80$$

The variance of BAS reading scores is 177.80. Therefore the proportion of variance that is residual variance is

$$\frac{97.06}{177.80} = 0.546.$$

The residual variance is 0.546, or 54.6% of the variance in BAS reading. We can think of this as the variance in the BAS score which is *not* explained by the initial phoneme score. But we want to know how closely the variables are related to each other, and we need this the other way around. The higher this value, the worse the relationship between the scores which is a little confusing. We can make this the other way around by subtracting it from 1:

$$1 - 0.545 = 0.454 = 45.4\%.$$

This is the proportion of variance in BAS reading that is explained by initial phoneme score.

However, this was in variance units. We want standard deviation units, because we understand them better. The standard deviation is the square root of the variance, so we can take the square root of this value:

$$\sqrt{0.454} = 0.674$$

Now hang on a minute. Isn't this the same value that we got for the standardised slope? Yes it is. This is the correlation coefficient:

$$r = 0.674$$

The value of the standardised slope and the value of the square root of the proportion of variance explained will *always* be the same value.

We therefore have two equivalent ways of thinking about a correlation.

- The first way is the *standardised slope*. It is the expected increase in one variable, when the other variable increases by 1 SD.
- The second way is the **proportion of variance**. If you square a correlation, you get the proportion of variance in one variable that is explained by the other variable.

INTERPRETING CORRELATIONS

A correlation is both a **descriptive statistic** and an **inferential statistic**. You can look it up in a table and find the probability value associated with the null hypothesis (that $r = 0$), just

(a)

$r = 0$

(b)

$r = 0.2$

(c)

$r = 0.4$

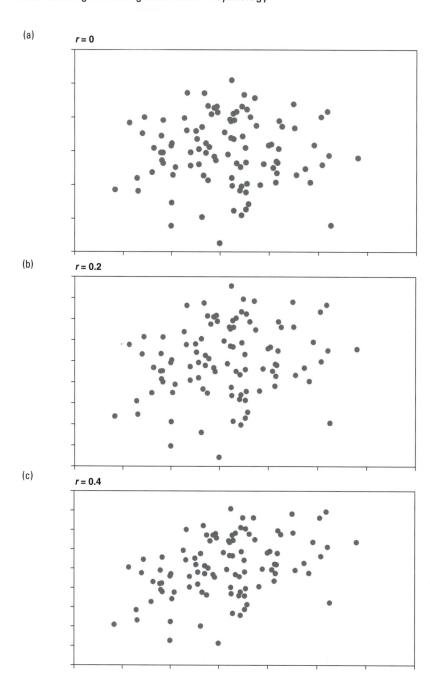

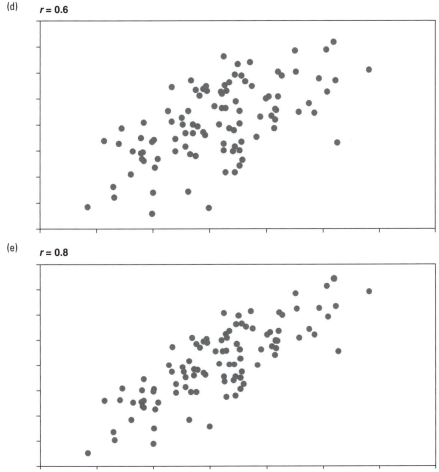

Figure 8.3   Two variables with correlation *r* equal to (a) 0, (b) 0.2, (c) 0.4, (d) 0.6, (e) 0.8

like *t* or *U*. However, you can also use it to describe the strength of the relationship between two variables. We have already seen the chart of the relationship between BAS reading and initial phoneme from Hulme et al. (2002).

We have generated data in which the correlation between two variables is equal to 0.0, 0.2, 0.4, 0.6 and 0.8 (and where the distribution of both is normal), shown in Figure 8.3. These will help you to understand the relationship between the scatterplot and the correlation.

Another way of thinking about correlation is to consider the size in terms of some sort of adjective. Various different schemes have been proposed, but the most commonly used comes from Cohen (1988). Cohen suggested:

- $r = 0.1$ – small correlation
- $r = 0.3$ – medium correlation
- $r = 0.5$ – large correlation

(note that these only really apply in what Cohen called social and behavioural sciences).

Common Mistake

A correlation around 0.5 is a large correlation. A correlation doesn't have to exceed 0.5 to be large. If you have a correlation of $r = 0.45$, you have a correlation which is approximately equal to a large correlation. It's not a medium correlation just because it hasn't quite reached 0.5.

Remember, these are very loose guidelines. Sometimes a correlation of 0.5 would be considered low. (For example, if the correlation between raters were only 0.5, we would probably be disappointed.)

CALCULATING THE CORRELATION COEFFICIENT

Although we have given you two ways to think about correlations, we haven't actually told you how to calculate them yet. Don't worry, we are going to do that now.

What we have been talking about so far is the **Pearson correlation coefficient**. Pearson was the same chap we encountered in the chapter on χ^2. This is a parametric correlation and makes the same assumptions made by other parametric tests: that the data are continuous and normally distributed. (Actually, as we'll see the normal distribution assumption is a bit tricky but more on that in a moment.)

Optional Extra: Product moments

The Pearson correlation coefficient is sometimes called the Pearson Product Moment Correlation Coefficient, which is quite a mouthful. However, it does tell us a tiny bit about where the formula comes from. If you did physics at school, you might remember that moments are used in levers. The moment is the length from the fulcrum (the pointy bit) multiplied by the weight on the lever. If you don't remember doing physics at school, you

(Continued)

(Continued)

might have played on a seesaw with someone who is a different weight from you. The same principle applies. The total moment is equal to the length from the centre, multiplied by the weight. The seesaw in Figure 8.4 will (approximately) balance – the 100-kg weight is twice as far from the centre as the 200-kg weight.

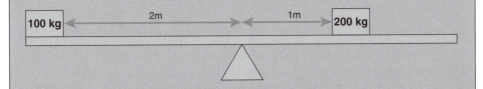

Figure 8.4   The seesaw will approximately balance because the 100kg weight is twice as far from the centre as the 200 kg weight

The same principle applies with the correlation. We find the length from the centre for each of the variables. In this case the centre is the mean, so we calculate the difference between the score and the mean for each variable (these are the moments) and then we multiply them together (this is the product). Because this value is dependent on the number of people, we need to divide it by N (and because it's related to the standard deviation, we actually divide by $N - 1$). This is called the **covariance**, and if we call the two variables x and y, the formula is

$$\text{cov}(x, y) = \frac{(x - \bar{x})(y - \bar{y})}{N - 1}.$$

We could also show you how the covariance relates to a scatterplot, but it all gets a bit too complex. If you are interested, you can see Miles and Shevlin (2001).

Just as before, we need to standardise this value by dividing by the standard deviations. However, this time, we need to divide by both standard deviations, so we multiply them together:

(Continued)

(Continued)

$$r_{xy} = \frac{\text{cov}(x, y)}{\sigma_x \times \sigma_y}$$

We can write this out in full, spelling out each part, as it were:

$$r_{xy} = \frac{\left(\dfrac{\sum[(x - \bar{x})(y - \bar{y})]}{N - 1} \right)}{\sqrt{\dfrac{\sum(x - \bar{x})^2}{N - 1}} \times \sqrt{\dfrac{\sum(y - \bar{y})^2}{N - 1}}}$$

You'll notice that there is a lot of dividing by $N-1$ going on. But they all cancel out (you've got N-1 on the top, and $\sqrt{N - 1} \times \sqrt{N - 1} = N - 1$ on the bottom), so you can remove them:

$$r_{xy} = \frac{\sum[(x - \bar{x})(y - \bar{y})]}{\sqrt{\sum(x - \bar{x})^2} \times \sqrt{\sum(y - \bar{y})^2}}$$

Finally, finding square roots is a bit of a pain, and we don't want to do it more than we have to. So instead of finding the square roots and then multiplying them together, it is easier to multiply the two values together, and then find the square root:

$$r_{xy} = \frac{\sum[(x - \bar{x})(y - \bar{y})]}{\sqrt{\sum(x - \bar{x})^2 \times \sqrt{\sum(y - \bar{y})^2}}}$$

That's the formula we are going to use.

The formula for the Pearson correlation between two variables, x and y, which we call r_{xy}, is given by:

$$r_{xy} = \frac{\sum[(x - \bar{x})(y - \bar{y})]}{\sqrt{\sum(x - \bar{x})^2} \times \sqrt{\sum(y - \bar{y})^2}}$$

As an example, we will use a study carried out by Roney, Mahler and Maestripieri (2003).[3] Roney et al. were examining the way that a male participant behaved towards a confederate whom the participant believed was really another participant. They measured a number of different variables. Two of them are:

- the participant rated how desirable the confederate would be as a romantic partner;
- the confederate rated how much the participant engaged in 'display' behaviour, for example trying to impress, showing off, talking about himself.

The results are displayed in Table 8.4.

---

[3] We'd like to thank Jim Roney for providing us with data, and giving us permission to use it.

Table 8.4   *Results from Roney et al. (2003)*

	Desirability of confederate (x)	Rating of display behaviour (y)
1	2.67	3.2
2	4	2
3	4.33	4
4	4.67	3.4
5	5	3.2
6	5	3.6
7	5	5.2
8	5	5.2
9	5	4.6
10	5.33	2.8
11	5.33	3
12	5.67	5.4
13	5.67	4.8
14	5.67	3.8
15	5.67	3.6
16	5.67	3.8
17	6	4.6
18	6	4.4
19	7	4.6

Before calculating a correlation coefficient, you should draw a scattergraph. This will help you in a number of ways.

- It will show you approximately what the correlation should be so if it looks like a strong, positive correlation, and your analysis shows it is –0.60, you have made a mistake.
- It will help you to detect any errors in the data, for example data entry errors.
- It will help you to get a feel for your data.

The scatterplot in Figure 8.5 shows no anomalous or strange data points. If we compare it with the previous scatterplots of different correlations we will be expecting to find a correlation of around 0.4–0.6.

Optional Extra: Jittering

We cheated a tiny bit in the scatterplot shown in Figure 8.5 – there were some places where two points were on top of each other, such as person 14 and person 16. In this case, rather than draw one dot on top of another, we have 'jittered' them – that is we have drawn them both a little away from where the dot should really be. Some programs will do that automatically.

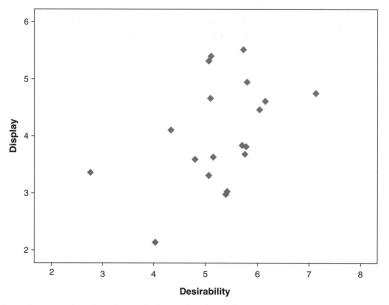

Figure 8.5   Scatterplot showing relationship of display behaviour and desirability

Calculating the Pearson Correlation

We will now show you how to calculate the correlation coefficient. As a reminder, here's the formula again:

$$r_{xy} = \frac{\sum[(x - \bar{x})(y - \bar{y})]}{\sqrt{\sum(x - \bar{x})^2 \times \sum(y - \bar{y})^2}}$$

Step 1: *Calculate the mean of each of the variables.*

To show how this works in the formula we have labelled our variables x (desirability) and y (display). We're sure you can work them out for yourself by now, but you can also take our word for it that $\bar{x} = 5.19$ and $\bar{y} = 3.96$.

Step 2: Calculate $x - \bar{x}$ and $y - \bar{y}$ for each case.

For the first case:

$$x - \bar{x} = 2.67 - 5.19 = -2.52$$
$$y - \bar{y} = 3.2 - 3.96 = -0.76$$

Table 8.5 *Calculation of Pearson correlation*

	Desirability of Confederate (x)	Rating of display behaviour (y)	$x - \bar{x}$	$(x-\bar{x})^2$	$y - \bar{y}$	$(y - \bar{y})^2$	$(x - \bar{x})(y - \bar{y})$
1	2.67	3.2	-2.52	6.35	-0.76	0.58	1.91
2	4	2	-1.19	1.42	-1.96	3.84	2.34
3	4.33	4	-0.86	0.74	0.04	0.00	-0.04
4	4.67	3.4	-0.52	0.27	-0.56	0.31	0.29
5	5	3.2	-0.19	0.04	-0.76	0.58	0.15
6	5	3.6	-0.19	0.04	-0.36	0.13	0.07
7	5	5.2	-0.19	0.04	1.24	1.54	-0.24
8	5	5.2	-0.19	0.04	1.24	1.54	-0.24
9	5	4.6	-0.19	0.04	0.64	0.41	-0.12
10	5.33	2.8	0.14	0.02	-1.16	1.35	-0.16
11	5.33	3	0.14	0.02	-0.96	0.92	-0.13
12	5.67	5.4	0.48	0.23	1.44	2.07	0.69
13	5.67	4.8	0.48	0.23	0.84	0.71	0.40
14	5.67	3.8	0.48	0.23	-0.16	0.03	-0.08
15	5.67	3.6	0.48	0.23	-0.36	0.13	-0.17
16	5.67	3.8	0.48	0.23	-0.16	0.03	-0.08
17	6	4.6	0.81	0.66	0.64	0.41	0.52
18	6	4.4	0.81	0.66	0.44	0.19	0.36
19	7	4.6	1.81	3.28	0.64	0.41	1.16
Σ				14.74		15.17	6.63

and then:

$$(x - \bar{x})(y - \bar{y}) = (-2.52) \times (-0.76) = 1.91$$

We'll do the same thing for each case and enter the results in Table 8.5.

Step 3: Find the sum of the column labelled $(x - \bar{x})(y - \bar{y})$. This gives us $\Sigma(x - \bar{x})(y - \bar{y})$. For our data this sum is 6.63.

Step 4: Find $\Sigma(x - \bar{x})$ *and* $\Sigma(y - \bar{y})^2$. These are shown in Table 8.5 above, 14.74 and 15.17, respectively.

Step 5: Put these values into the equation:

$$r_{xy} = \frac{\Sigma[(x - \bar{x})(y - \bar{y})]}{\sqrt{\Sigma(x - \bar{x})^2 \times \Sigma(y - \bar{y})^2}} = \frac{6.63}{\sqrt{14.74 \times 15.17}} = 0.44$$

Calculating confidence intervals

The **confidence intervals** for a statistic tell us the likely range of a value in the population, not just in our sample, and as we are interested in generalising beyond our sample, we would suggest that the confidence interval should be calculated whenever possible. (We looked at confidence intervals on page 94 with the mean.)

The problem with correlations is that their sampling distribution is a bit tricky. It's not even symmetrical, which means we can't add and subtract confidence intervals in the usual way. However, there is a transformation that we can use which makes the distribution symmetrical. We can use this to calculate the confidence intervals and then transform back to correlations. The transformation is called **Fisher's z transformation**. It's called a z transformation, because it makes the distribution of the correlation into a z distribution which is a normal distribution with mean 0 and standard deviation 1.

Step 1: Carry out Fisher's transformation.
The Fisher transformation is given by

$$z' = 0.5 \times \ln\left(\frac{1+r}{1-r}\right)$$

where r is the correlation. For our data $r = 0.44$, so

$$z' = 0.5 \times \ln\left(\frac{1+r}{1-r}\right) = 0.5 \times \ln\left(\frac{1+0.44}{1-0.44}\right) = 0.5 \times \ln(2.59) = 0.5 \times 0.95 = 0.48$$

Alternatively, if you want to save some effort, type = fisher(0.44) into Excel and get the same answer.

Step 2: Calculate the Standard Error.
This is given by:

$$se = \frac{1}{\sqrt{N-3}}$$

For our data $N = 19$, so

$$se = \frac{1}{\sqrt{N-3}} = \frac{1}{\sqrt{16}} = 0.25$$

Step 3: And now the confidence intervals. We use the formula

$$CI = z' \pm z_{\alpha/2} \times se$$

where $z_{\alpha/2}$ is the value for the normal distribution which includes the percentage of values that we want to cover. The value for the 95% confidence is (as always) 1.96. Plugging our values into this equation

$$\text{Lower CI} = 0.476 - 1.96 \times 0.25 = -0.01$$

$$\text{Upper CI} = 0.476 + 1.96 \times 0.25 = 0.97$$

Step 4: *Convert back to correlation.*
    We now know the confidence intervals of the correlation, but these are not in the right scale. We need to turn them back into correlations, using the reverse of the Fisher transformation. The formula is:

$$r = \frac{\exp(2z') - 1}{\exp(2z') + 1}$$

We need to do the calculation twice, once for the upper CI and once for the lower CI:

$$r = \frac{\exp(2z') - 1}{\exp(2z') + 1} = \frac{\exp(2 \times (-0.014)) - 1}{\exp(2 \times (-0.014)) + 1} = -0.01$$

$$r = \frac{\exp(2z') - 1}{\exp(2z') + 1} = \frac{\exp(2 \times 0.966) - 1}{\exp(2 \times 0.966) + 1} = 0.75$$

Alternatively, we can use the = fisherinv() function in Excel, and get the same answer.

Tip	
We came across ln (natural log) and exp (exponential) in the optional extra in Chapter 7.	

The confidence intervals of the correlation are therefore from −0.01 to 0.75.

Test yourself 1

(a)   Will the correlation be statistically significant at the 0.05 level?
(b)   Is the correlation equal to zero?

Answers are given at the end of the chapter.

Calculating the *p*-value

If you have calculated your correlation using a computer program, such as SPSS, then the probability value will be given to you by the program. If you haven't used a computer program, there are two ways to find the *p*-value associated with a correlation.

The first is to use a table such as Appendix 3. If we use this table, we look down the column of sample sizes until we find our sample size. We then read across and see if our value is higher than the critical value for each level of **statistical significance**. We can see that our value of 0.44 exceeds the critical value for significance at the 0.10 level but does not achieve significance at the 0.05 level.

If you really want to know the *p*-value, then you can convert the value for *r* into a value for *t*. You can then use this *t* value to obtain the exact *p*-value, using a program such as Excel. (That's actually how we calculate the tables that you find in the Appendix.) Rather than fill up the book with this sort of arcane detail, we've put it on the web instead – you can find it, and a range of related things, at www.jeremymiles.co.uk/usingstatistics).

Reporting the result

It is not common to report the confidence intervals of a correlation. We think that this isn't necessarily a good thing. We have seen that the confidence intervals convey information that the value of the correlation and the *p*-value alone do not provide. Here's how we would have reported the results of this correlation: *'The Pearson correlation between display and desirability was equal to 0.44 (95% CI –0.01, 0.75; p = 0.057).'*

CALCULATING THE REGRESSION LINE

When you know the correlation you can also calculate the position of the regression line. We know how to calculate the correlation (r) if we know the slope (β_1); we multiply by the standard deviation of *x*, and divide by the standard deviation of *y*:

$$r = \frac{\beta_1 \times \sigma_x}{\sigma_y}$$

A tiny little bit of algebra gives us

$$\beta_1 = \frac{r \times \sigma_y}{\sigma_x}$$

We know that the correlation between the display rating and the desirability rating is $r = 0.44$. The standard deviation of the display scores (σ_y) is 0.92, and the standard deviation of the desirability scores (σ_x) is 0.90. The slope of the regression line (β_1) is therefore given by

$$\beta_1 = \frac{r \times \sigma_y}{\sigma_x} = \frac{0.44 \times 0.92}{0.90} = 0.45$$

We know the slope of the line (β_1) but we don't know the height of the line (the intercept; β_0). We find the intercept (β_0) using the following equation:

$$\beta_0 = \bar{y} - \beta_1 \times \bar{x}$$

where $\bar{y}$ is the mean of the y-axis variable (display) and $\bar{x}$ is the mean of the x-axis variable (desirability):

$$\beta_0 = \bar{y} - \beta_1 \times \bar{x} = 3.96 - 0.45 \times 5.19 = 1.62$$

We can now use these two values (β_0 and β_1) to create a regression equation which will allow us to predict y (display behaviour) from x (desirability). We can use the predictions to draw a graph with the line of best fit on it (Figure 8.6). Note that we have extended the line to zero – you wouldn't normally do this.

Calculation of the probability value associated with the regression line follows a different procedure, but the result will be the same as the probability value for the Pearson correlation. It is also possible to calculate the confidence intervals for the regression line, but the calculation of these goes beyond the scope of this book.

DICHOTOMOUS VARIABLES

Two dichotomous variables

If your variables are both dichotomous (for example, yes/no, top/bottom, United/City) you can use the Pearson correlation formula. However, a much easier way is to calculate the value of χ^2 (see Chapter 7), and then use the phi (ϕ) correlation formula, which will give the same answer as using the r correlation:

$$\phi = r = \sqrt{\frac{\chi^2}{N}}$$

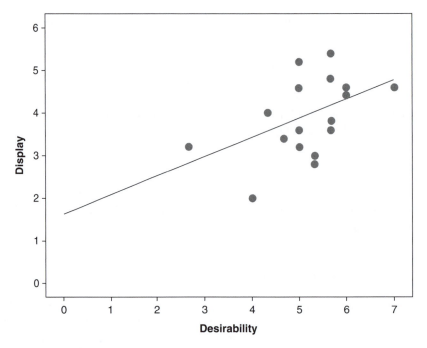

Figure 8.6   Scatterplot showing relationship between desirability and display, with line of best fit

The *p*-value of the correlation will be the same as the *p*-value for the x^2 (chi-square not *x* square) test because the two tests are just different ways of thinking about the same thing. (Understanding what a correlation means when both variables are dichotomous is a bit tricky, but you can do the calculation.)

One dichotomous variable

If one of your variables is continuous and the other is dichotomous you can use the point-biserial formula:

$$r = \frac{(\bar{x}_1 - \bar{x}_2) \times \sqrt{p \times (1 - p)}}{\sigma_x}$$

where x_1 and x_2 are the scores for *x* for group 1 and group 2, *p* is the proportion of people in group 1, and σ_x is the standard deviation of *x* (both groups together).

Tip
These formulae give exactly the same answer as the Pearson formula, but they are just easier to use. There is confusion though about which test to use. It's not uncommon on internet sites for people to ask 'How do I calculate the [point-biserial/phi] correlation in [name of computer program].' (You can see the sort of exciting internet sites that we hang out in.)

NON-PARAMETRIC CORRELATIONS

When we have data that do not satisfy the assumptions of the Pearson correlation because they are not normally distributed or are only ordinal in nature, we can use a **non-parametric correlation**. There are two different non-parametric correlations available to use; the Spearman correlation and the Kendall correlation.

Spearman rank correlation coefficient

There are two ways to find the **Spearman correlation**. We will demonstrate them using another pair of variables from Roney et al. (2003). Sometimes it is argued that response data that are measured on rating scales do not satisfy the criteria for continuous measurement, and that therefore non-parametric statistics should be used.

We'll have a go and see what we think afterwards. Along with display ratings, Roney et al. (2003) also recorded the testosterone levels of the participants before and after the interaction with the female confederate. The data are displayed in Table 8.6.[4]

Step 1: The first step should be to draw a **scatterplot** and examine the data for anything we don't expect, and to see what sort of relationship we will be looking for. This is shown in Figure 8.7. It shows a positive relationship (the upward slope of the pattern) and there do not seem to be any outliers (see page 27). We might guess that the correlation coefficient will be about 0.5.

Step 2: The next step is to rank the data in each group separately (see page 122). We assign the rank 1 to the lowest score, 2 to the next lowest, etc. Where two scores tie, we give them the average rank.

The first way to calculate the Spearman correlation is just to calculate a (Pearson) correlation, using the ranked data. The problem is that the Pearson formula is a bit fiddly, especially if you are not using a computer. A simplification of the Pearson formula is available, developed by Spearman, which works in the case where we have ranks. This is what

---

[4] Again, we'd like to thank Jim Roney for allowing us to use these data.

Table 8.6   *Display rating and change in testosterone levels, from Roney et al. (2003)*

	Display rating	Change in testosterone
1	5.4	1.16
2	4.8	1.01
3	3.6	1.07
4	3.8	.81
5	3.0	1.06
6	5.2	1.23
7	3.6	.96
8	3.4	.90
9	4.6	.97
10	3.2	1.35
11	2.0	.74
12	3.2	1.14
13	3.8	1.28
14	4.4	1.15
15	4.6	1.34
16	5.2	1.45
17	4.0	1.06
18	2.8	1.05
19	4.6	1.19

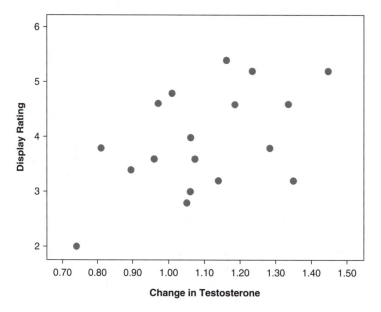

Figure 8.7   Scatterplot showing relationship between change in testosterone and display behaviour

we will use (although it does have a little problem, as we'll see). Make sure that you have kept the variables in order when you have done this.

Step 3: The next step is to find the difference between the ranks for each person, which we call *d*. The ranks and the difference between the ranks for each person are shown in Table 8.7.

Think about the differences in the ranks for a moment. If the person with the highest display score had the highest testosterone change score their difference would be zero. If the person with the second highest display score also had the second highest testosterone score their difference would also be zero. If we continued all the way down, with all the scores in the same order, the total of the *d*-scores would be zero. This would occur when the correlation was 1.

Similarly, if the person with the highest display score had the *lowest* testosterone change score the difference would be very large. If the person with the lowest display score had the highest testosterone change score, the difference would also be very large. If we carried on with each person being in the opposite place the total of the *d*-scores would be very high. The *d*-score total is on a scale, though sadly it is not a scale that we understand. We need to convert the scale into one that we do understand such as the correlation scale, which goes from −1.00 to +1.00.

Step 4: This is to use the formula that Spearman devised:

$$r = 1 - \frac{6 \times \sum d^2}{N^3 - N}$$

First we square each of the values of *d* (this is shown in Table 8.7), and add them up to get $\sum d^2$. If we do this, we get a total of 646.50. We put this into the equation, and work through it.

$$r = 1 - \frac{6 \times \sum d^2}{N^3 - N} = 1 - \frac{6 \times 646.5}{19^3 - 19} = 1 - \frac{3879}{6840} = 1 - 0.567 = 0.433.$$

However, there is a slight complication because the formula as we have given it is only valid when there are no ties in the data. We have got some ties in the data so the formula is not quite right. We have a calculated value of 0.433, though the true correlation between the two values is 0.431. We are not going to get upset about a correlation being wrong by 0.002 (we wouldn't normally even bother to report a correlation to 3 decimal places).

There are three ways to deal with this problem:

1. Ignore it. It doesn't make a lot of difference.
2. Use the Pearson formula on the ranks (although the calculation is harder than the Spearman formula).
3. Use a correction (again, because the probability that you are actually interested in this is pretty minimal, it's on the website: see http://www.jeremymiles.co.uk/usingstatistics).

Table 8.7 *Raw data, ranked data, and differences*

	Display rating	Change in testosterone	Rank display	Rank change in testosterone	d	d²
1	5.4	1.16	19.0	13.0	6.0	36.00
2	4.8	1.01	16.0	6.0	10.0	100.00
3	3.6	1.07	7.5	10.0	−2.5	6.25
4	3.8	.81	9.5	2.0	7.5	56.25
5	3.0	1.06	3.0	8.5	−5.5	30.25
6	5.2	1.23	17.5	15.0	2.5	6.25
7	3.6	0.96	7.5	4.0	3.5	12.25
8	3.4	0.90	6.0	3.0	3.0	9.00
9	4.6	0.97	14.0	5.0	9.0	81.00
10	3.2	1.35	4.5	18.0	−13.5	182.25
11	2.0	0.74	1.0	1.0	0.0	0.00
12	3.2	1.14	4.5	11.0	−6.5	42.25
13	3.8	1.28	9.5	16.0	−6.5	42.25
14	4.4	1.15	12.0	12.0	0.0	0.00
15	4.6	1.34	14.0	17.0	−3.0	9.00
16	5.2	1.45	17.5	19.0	−1.5	2.25
17	4.0	1.06	11.0	8.5	2.5	6.25
18	2.8	1.05	2.0	7.0	−5.0	25.00
19	4.6	1.19	14.0	14.0	0.0	0.00

If you do use the correction you will find that the correlation changes from 0.433 to 0.431 which is such a small change that it will make no difference to anything, ever. Finally,

Step 5: Significance.

We calculate significance of the Spearman correlation in the same way as the significance of the Pearson correlation. We can either use a computer, tables, or convert to a *t* statistic.

The *p*-value of a correlation of 0.431 is found to be 0.066, and is therefore not statistically significant.

It is not at all straightforward or easy to calculate confidence intervals for Spearman correlation and we need to use techniques which are way beyond the scope of an introductory statistics book, so we'll leave that for another day.

COMPARING SPEARMAN AND PEARSON

If we did a Pearson correlation on the same data we used with the above example we find that $r = 0.500$, $p = 0.029$, and the correlation achieves statistical significance.

What does this difference in the result tell us? One thing it tells us is that if we use a non-parametric test, such as a Spearman correlation, we tend to lose **power** (for more on power see Chapter 11). This happened because by converting our data to ranks we have thrown away some information about the actual scores. Although we could be strict and say that rating data are strictly measured at an ordinal level, in reality when there isn't a problem with the distributions we would always prefer to use a Pearson correlation because it gives a better chance of a significant result.

A curious thing about the Spearman correlation is how to interpret it. We can't really use either of the interpretations of the Pearson correlation. We can't say that it is the standardised slope that is the relative difference in the standard deviations, because the standard deviations don't really exist as there is not necessarily any relationship between the score and the standard deviation. We also can't say that it's the proportion of variance explained, because the variance is a parametric term, and we are using ranks, so the variance doesn't exist any more.

All we can really say about the Spearman correlation is that it is the Pearson correlation between the ranks. It shows how closely the ranked data are related.

An alternative non-parametric correlation, which does have a more sensible interpretation, is **Kendall's tau-a** (tau is the Greek letter τ, which is pronounced to rhyme with 'cow'). Kendall's tau-a is very rarely used, for two reasons. First, it's difficult to calculate if you haven't got a computer. Second, it's *always* lower than the Spearman correlation, for the same data (but the *p*-values are always exactly the same). Because people like their correlations to be high (it usually looks better) they tend to use the Kendall tau correlation less. The great advantage of Kendall's tau-a is that it has a meaningful interpretation. Suppose that you and a friend decided to give marks out of 10 for each statistical test, to rate how much you liked it (this is the sort of thing we do on those long winter evenings), and that Kendall's tau-a correlation was 0.7. This would mean that, if you took two tests, and asked your friend which they liked best, then you are 70% more likely to agree that you like the same one best, than you are to disagree. However, because Kendall's tau-a is pretty obscure, we've decided to write about it on the web page, which you can find at http://www.jeremymiles.co.uk/usingstatistics, rather than here.

CORRELATION AND CAUSALITY

The fact that two variables correlate does not mean there is a **causal relationship** between them, although it is often very tempting to believe that there is. You probably won't have noticed, but we have been very careful throughout this chapter to avoid using language that implied causation. We *didn't* write:

'*If a person's initial phoneme score went up 1 point, their BAS reading score would go up 1.32 points.*'

We *did* write:

'*If a person had an initial phoneme score 1 point higher, we would expect that their BAS reading score would be 1.32 points higher.*' (*Expect* is actually a technical statistical term, but we aren't going to worry about that for now.)

Causality is a very technical and tricky issue which we can't even begin to do justice to here.[5] We're going to put the tricky bits to one side for a while though, and think about causes and correlations.

---

[5] If you want a serious analysis of the tricky issues then have a look at the book by Pearl (2000). But be prepared for your brain to hurt. For a long time.

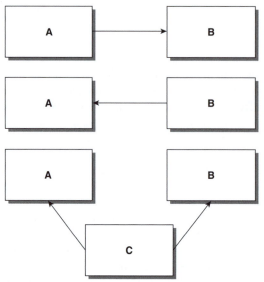

Figure 8.8   Three possible causal explanations for a correlation between *A* and *B*: *A* causes *B*, *B* causes *A*, and *C* causes both *A* and *B*

Let's say that we have a correlation between two variables, we'll call them *A* and *B*. There are three possibilities that you should consider (see Figure 8.8):

1.   that *A* causes *B*;
2.   that *B* causes *A*;
3.   that something else entirely (*C*) causes both *A* and *B*, and creates the correlation.

Let's think about some of our examples. We have seen that there is a correlation between initial phoneme detection and BAS reading score.

1.   Is it possible that initial phoneme detection is a cause of reading ability? Yes, this is feasible because detecting initial phonemes is part of reading, so if you are better at detecting initial phonemes you might be better at reading.
2.   Is there a mechanism by which being better at reading might improve initial phoneme detecting skill? It is possible that children who are better at reading will read more, and that they therefore practise initial phoneme detection.
3.   Is it possible that something else can cause both? What about general intelligence? Verbal ability? Speed of neural conduction? Any of these (or something else) could cause the effect.

The correlation between desirability and display narrowly failed to achieve statistical significance. What are the possible mechanisms for this relationship (assuming it turns out to be a real effect)? One would be that the more desirable the participant felt the female confederate to be, the more they engaged in display behaviour. Could it be that males who engaged in display behaviour then did a sort of **post hoc justification**? They need to explain why they acted this way, and do so with an explanation about the desirability of the confederate. (This sounds a little curious, but would be in line with the self-perception theory of Bem, 1972.) Could something else have caused both? Could it be that some people just display more, and that this kind of person finds more people attractive and desirable?

There are many examples of things which correlate where you would be tempted to draw a causal conclusion but such a conclusion would be erroneous. For example, if we measured the number of Christian ministers and the amount of whisky sold in each state of the USA in the year 1850, we would find a high correlation. Why?

Stop!

Think about the answer before you read on.

There is a very good reason. Those states with more people sold more whisky. They also have more ministers for the same reason that they sold more whisky – there are more people.

There are many variables that correlate without there being any causal link. The problem for us is that we commonly like to make inferential jumps to make statements about cause even when we don't have the evidence to back these up.

Optional Extra: The other Simpsons

Homer: Not a bear in sight. The 'Bear Patrol' must be working like a charm!
Lisa: That's specious reasoning, Dad.
Homer [*condescendingly*]:   Sure it is, honey.
Lisa: By your logic, I could claim that this rock keeps tigers away.
Homer: Oh, how does it work?
Lisa: It doesn't work; it's just a stupid rock!
Homer: Uh-huh.
Lisa: – but I don't see any tigers around, do you?
Homer: (Pause.) Lisa, I would like to buy your rock.
(*The Simpsons*, Season 7, Episode 23)

We can't emphasise enough that correlation does not mean causality. But actually, we can. We think that textbooks emphasise that correlation doesn't mean causality too much. Of course correlation doesn't mean causality, but, *causality does mean correlation*.

Test yourself 2

Why do these relationships exist?

(a)   On days when more ice cream is sold there are more deaths from drowning.
(b)   Boys who masturbate more have more acne.
(c)   The more children and grandchildren you have, the more likely you are to suffer a heart attack.
(d)   People who have written a book on statistics live longer, on average, than people who haven't written a book on statistics.
(e)   People who drink bottled water have larger babies than those who drink tap water.

Answer is given at the end of the chapter.

Correlation can certainly lead us in the direction of causality. If it could not then our knowledge about the world would be severely curtailed. Some people argue that the only way to determine causation is to carry out an experiment where we can manipulate the independent variable and measure its effect.

If we could only determine causation by experiment then astronomers would be pretty stuck. Astronomy is the ultimate observational science, yet this does not stop them making statements about causality. We don't read astronomy journals (*I check my stars in The Sun – Ed*) because, frankly, they are way too hard, but here are some quotes from the *New Scientist* magazine:

> Astronomers have spotted the first star known to be hurtling out of the Milky Way. And an encounter with the supermassive black hole at the galaxy's heart may be the *cause* of the star's exodus. (9 February 2005; emphasis added)

> In the early 1990s, astronomers spotted weaker X-rays coming from the same hydrogen cloud and suspected that radiation from the black hole was the *cause*. (5 January 2005; emphasis added)

> This overcrowding can *cause* the pulsars to lose or swap their partners in complex interactions that can produce 'truly exotic objects', says Ransom. (13 January 2005; emphasis added)

And on another well-travelled topic, without correlational evidence we would never suspect that smoking causes cancer in humans. The evidence for this can only ever be correlational because we can't assign people to smoking and non-smoking conditions and send them away for 20 years to see how much heart disease they develop. Of course, there are those who say that smoking does not cause cancer but they mainly work for cigarette companies. And they point at textbooks that say 'Correlation does not mean causation'.[6]

We've put a bit more discussion of why causation is tricky on the web at www.jeremymiles.co.uk/usingstatistics.

Optional Extra: Simpson's paradox

Simpson's paradox is a paradox that shows the danger of making causal statements from correlational data.[7] We are going to illustrate it with categorical variables, because that makes it much easier to think about, but it can still occur with continuous variables.

Let's say that Jeremy and Phil decide to see who can catch a Smartie in their mouth the most times. In the first week, Jeremy makes 100 attempts, and succeeds 60 times

(Continued)

---

[6] For more discussion of the links between causation and correlation, in relation to non-experimental research, have a look at the discussion in Abelson (1995).

[7] It's named after Edward H. Simpson. The H. *doesn't* stand for Homer (It's Hugh).

(Continued)

(that's a 60% success rate). Phil only tries 10 times, but succeeds 9 times, which is a 90% success rate. So Phil did better than Jeremy.

In the second week, Jeremy is determined to beat Phil. Jeremy tries to catch a Smartie 10 times, but only succeeds on one occasion. Phil tries 100 times, and succeeds 30 times. So Phil's success rate of 30% is higher than Jeremy's success rate of 10%. Phil declares himself to be the winner, having won in both weeks.

But Jeremy looks at the total scores: Jeremy made a total of 110 attempts, and succeeded 61 times. Phil also made 110 attempts, and succeeded only 39 times. Jeremy's success rate of 55% is much higher than Phil's success rate of 35%, so Jeremy declares himself to be the winner.

	Week 1	Week 2	Total
Phil	9/10	30/100	39/110
	90%	30%	35%
Jeremy	60/100	1/10	61/110
	60%	10%	55%

What was happening here? If we had simply correlated the two measures (person versus success) we would have got a different answer if we had done an overall measure, than if we had compared the individual weeks. What's happened here is that there is a third variable, that we have not taken into account. There is obviously some difference between the two weeks, which mean that Phil made 10 attempts in the first week, and 100 in the second week, but Jeremy's attempts were the other way around. We need to know what the difference is, and take it into account or we need to make sure that both Phil and Jeremy make the same number of attempts in each week.

A more serious example is in the 'low birthweight paradox' which is a real-life example of Simpson's paradox. A low birthweight baby is considered to be a baby with a birthweight of less than 2.5 kg. Babies of low birthweight have higher mortality than other babies. The babies of mothers who smoke also have higher mortality than other babies. Mothers who smoke are more likely to have low birthweight babies. However, those low birthweight babies born to mothers who smoke have *lower* mortality than low birthweight babies of mothers who do not smoke. This would imply that, if your baby is going to be small, you should take up smoking when pregnant to protect it. Obviously this isn't true. Can you see why this might happen? (Actually, it's quite complex. We suggest you look at the web pages ttp://en.wikipedia. org/wiki/Simpson%27s_paradox and http://en.wikipedia.org/wiki/Low_birth_weight_paradox.)

SUMMARY

This chapter has looked at the issue of correlations and regression. Much of the data we collect does not come from controlled experiments but from naturally occurring variables. The techniques of regression allow us to examine such data, look for patterns and draw conclusions about the relatedness of the different variables. Interpreting the data is controversial because it is common to make statements about causation even when they are not appropriate. Tests in this chapter looked at only two variables. The same principles can be applied to more than two variables, but the equations get even bigger, and this is outside the scope of this text.

Test yourself answers

Test yourself 1

(a) No. The confidence interval includes zero, so we know that it will not be statistically significant.
(b) No. We simply cannot reject the null hypothesis that the answer is equal to zero.

Test yourself 2

(a) On hotter days, more ice cream is sold. On hotter days, more people go swimming, so more people drown.
(b) At what age do boys get acne? (We'll leave the rest of that one for you to think about.)
(c) Heart attacks are primarily suffered by older people. Older people tend to have more children, and grandchildren.
(d) Writing a book on statistics takes quite a while. Some people die before they finish them (sometimes we thought we might). If you are one of the unfortunates who dies younger, then you will not write a book on statistics. People who have written a book on statistics must be older, when they die, than those who have not.
(e) There is a relationship between wealth and weight of newborn babies. People who are better off have heavier babies (another exercise would be to think about why this might be). People who are better off are also likely to drink more bottled water.

USING SPSS

To find the correlation between two variables, select **Analyze** $\Rightarrow$ **Correlate** $\Rightarrow$ **Bivariate**. Choose the variables you are interested in, and put them into the Variables box:

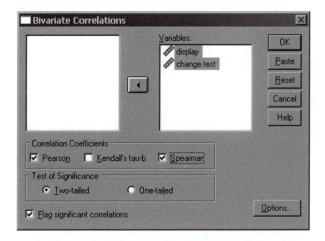

You can select the type of correlation – Pearson, Spearman and Kendall's tau-b (note that this is not the same as Kendall's tau-a) are available. Click **OK**.

In the following we run the correlation procedure twice, because parametric (Pearson) and non-parametric (Spearman) correlations are done by different procedures, so don't worry if you can't find both straight away. The parametric (Pearson) correlation output is shown first. Note that SPSS labels significant correlations with an asterisk (*).

Correlations

		Display Rating	Change in Testosterone
Display Rating	Pearson Correlation	1	.500*
	Sig. (2-tailed)		.029
	N	19	19
Change in Testosterone	Pearson Correlation	.500*	1
	Sig. (2-tailed)	.029	
	N	19	19

* Correlation is significant at the 0.05 level (2-tailed).

Next comes the Spearman correlation output:

Correlations

			Display Rating	Change in Testosterone
Spearman's rho	Display Rating	Correlation Coefficient	1.000	.431
		Sig. (2-tailed)	.	.066
		N	19	19
	Change in Testosterone	Correlation Coefficient	.431	1.000
		Sig. (2-tailed)	.066	.
		N	19	19

For each pair of variables, you are given the correlation, the *p*-value (called Sig. by SPSS) and the number of people who had a score for both variables.

Common Mistakes

1. Don't get the *r* and the *p* confused. They are very similar, both being numbers between 0 and 1. In the example above, for the Pearson correlation, $r = 0.500$, $p = 0.029$. It's horribly easy to write $r = 0.029$, $p = 0.500$, but the meaning is very, very different.
2. SPSS does give rather a lot of output for correlations, when we are really interested in two things: *r* and *p*. Don't copy the table (as we have done) and paste it in your report. Just write down what you need to.

Regression is a complex and flexible technique. SPSS gives a lot of output from regression, which means that it can be tricky to know what we are looking for. But let's do it anyway. Select **Analyze** ⇒ **Regression** ⇒ **Linear**. Put the predictor variable into the **Independent (s)** box, and the outcome into the **Dependent** box:

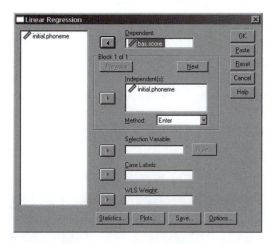

(Notice that SPSS's terminology is a bit different from ours. Where they say *independent* we say *predictor*, and where they say *dependent* we say *outcome*. We would rather not say dependent and independent unless we were really sure that the dependent variable really did depend on the independent variable – and that's not really a question that we can answer with statistics).

When you've done that, click **OK**.

SPSS gives you three tables as output, but the only one that we really need to care about is the last one, labelled coefficients.

Coefficients[a]

Model		Unstandardized Coefficients		Standardized Coefficients	t	Sig.
		B	Std. Error	Beta		
1	(Constant)	-9.151	4.604		-1.988	.055
	Initial Phoneme	1.320	.252	.674	5.239	**.000**

[a]Dependent Variables: BAS – Reading – Assess 1

We have highlighted in **bold** the parts that we need to look at. In the column labelled B we have two values, the constant (or intercept) and the slope. In the column labelled Standardized Coefficients (Beta) we have the Standardized Slope, which is the same as the correlation. In the final column we have the significance (*p*) values. A significance value is given for the constant and the slope, but the value for the constant is usually meaningless, and we can ignore it.

We now turn to scatterplots. A warning: most parts of SPSS don't change much with each new version. The instructions that we have given you so far in this chapter would have worked from 1993 to the present day (2006) in SPSS – most of the statistics don't look very different. In graphics, it's a different story. In the past few years, the graphics have changed several times. We are showing these procedures using SPSS 14.0 (which was released in 2005). Your version may look different.

Select **Graphs** ⇒ **Scatter/Dot**. Four types of graph are offered. The first, **Simple Scatter**, is the default, and this is what we want, so click **Define**.

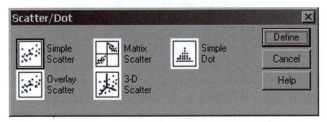

Put the variables you are interested in into the **Y Axis** and **X Axis** boxes, and click **OK**. Our scatterplot appears:

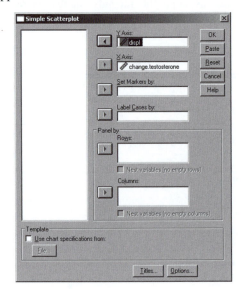

To add a line of best fit to that scatterplot, double-click on the scatterplot to open it. Then right click on a point – a context menu appears, select **Add Fit Line at Total**.

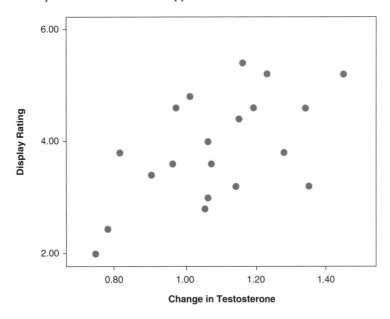

Your chart will then appear, with a line of best fit (and a value for R^2) on it.

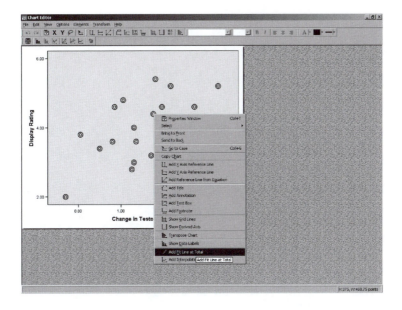

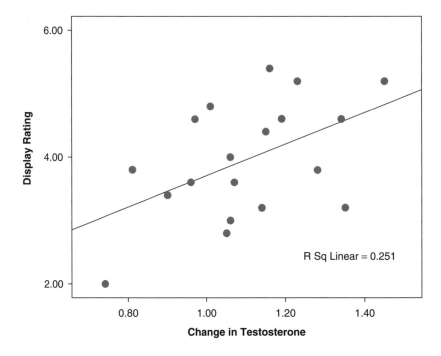

9

Introducing analysis of variance

What's in this chapter?

- What is ANOVA?
- Calculating ANOVA
- Post hoc testing
- Using SPSS

KEY TERMS

alpha inflation
analysis of variance
Bonferroni correction
box and whisker plot
confidence interval
degrees of freedom
effect size
error
factors
F-ratio
histograms
homogeneity of variance

mean squares
normal distribution
outcome variable
partition
post hoc tests
predictor variables
regression
statistical significance
sums of squares
t-test
type I error

INTRODUCTION

In this chapter we are going to introduce the ideas behind analysis of variance (ANOVA). ANOVA is a very flexible and general technique, and the principles can be applied to a wide range of statistical tests (including many that we have already encountered in this book). ANOVA has a wide range of applications, but many of those applications make some tricky assumptions about the data. Unlike the assumptions that we have encountered so far, which didn't make much difference as long as they weren't badly violated, the assumptions in some of the advanced applications of ANOVA can make a huge difference. For that reason, we recommend that you do some serious reading on ANOVA before using it in anger. In this chapter we look at the principles and practice of ANOVA so you can click the buttons to get the results, but also know what you are doing and what the results mean.

GETTING STARTED

Analysis of variance (ANOVA) requires us to think about our analysis in a slightly different way from other tests, but this is what makes it so flexible. In ANOVA we measure an **outcome variable** (also called a *dependent variable*). This outcome variable must be measured on a continuous scale, and it is called dependent because it depends on one or more **predictor variables**. These might be variables that we manipulate (like a treatment) or they might be variables that we simply measure (like sex). The way most people think about ANOVA is that these predictor variables are categorical, although continuous variables can also be used in the same framework. When the predictor variables are categorical, they are also called **factors** or *independent variables*.

Whenever we measure anything, we find differences. Measuring people on our outcome measure is no exception. These differences happen for two reasons: (a) because of the effect of the predictor variables (b) because of other reasons.

If we consider the Wright et al. (2005) study again on the effectiveness of two different treatments for chronic fatigue syndrome in children (we looked at this in Chapter 6, page 140), we had a predictor, which was treatment group, and we had an outcome, which was depression. People score differently on a depression measure for a very wide range of reasons, but we want to know whether one of those reasons was the treatment that was given. The differences between the scores on depression are represented by the variance of the depression score. (Remember that the variance is calculated using the difference between each person's score and the mean score. The further the scores are from the mean, the more different people are, and the higher the variance.)

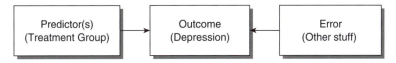

Figure 9.1   The outcome (depression) is affected by two different things – the predictor(s) that we know about (in this case, the intervention) and the other we don't know about (called error)

Some of the variance (difference between people) is due to the treatment, and some of the variance (difference between people) is due to other factors, of which there may be many including (a) how depressed the children were to start with (b) uncertainty in the measurement instrument (no measure is perfect), and (c) day-to-day changes in mood amongst the children. All of these other factors we lump together and call **error**, not because there is anything wrong, just because it is things we haven't measured (see Figure 9.1).

> ### Optional Extra: Why is it called error?
>
> The word error comes from the Latin word *errare*, meaning to wander or to stray. If people wander away from the mean, they are (statistically) errors.

We want to know two things. 1. How much of the variance (difference) between the two groups is due to the predictor variable (in this case, the treatment)? 2. Whether this proportion of variance is statistically significant, that is, is it larger than we would expect by chance if the null hypothesis were true?

CALCULATING THE PROPORTION OF VARIANCE

We can divide (statisticians sometimes say **partition**, because it sounds clever) variance into three different types:

1. The total variance.
2. Variance due to treatment, this is the differences *between* each group.
3. Variance due to error, this is the differences *within* each group.

In ANOVA the variance is conceptualised as *sums of squared deviations from the mean*, which is usually shortened to **sums of squares** and denoted by *SS*. So we have three sums of squares to calculate:

1. Total sum of squares, called SS_{total}.
2. Between-groups sum of squares. This is the variance that represents the difference between the groups, and this is called $SS_{between}$. Sometimes it refers to the between-groups sum of squares for one predictor, in which case it's called $SS_{predictor}$. In our case, the predictor is the treatment, so we would call it $SS_{treatment}$. The between-groups variance is the variance that we are actually interested in. We are asking whether the difference between the groups (or the effect of the predictor) is big enough that we could say it is not due to chance.
3. Error sum of squares, also called within-groups sum of squares. It's within the groups, because different people, who have had the same treatment, have different scores. And they have different scores because of error. So this is called either SS_{within}, or SS_{error}.

Let's have a look at some charts, to help us to think about this conceptually. Figure 9.2 shows two different possible results from an experiment. You can estimate the variance between the groups by looking at the difference between the two means of the groups, which in this example are also the two high points of the curve. You can estimate the variance within the groups by looking at the spread of the curve. Is it a fat one or a thin one? In the first study, shown in Figure 9.2(a), there is a small difference between the two groups, especially relative to the size of the variance within the groups. In the second study, shown in Figure 9.2(b), the variance within the groups is the same, but there is a greater difference (hence a greater amount of variance) between the groups. SS_{within} has stayed about the same, but $SS_{between}$ has grown.

(a)   (b)

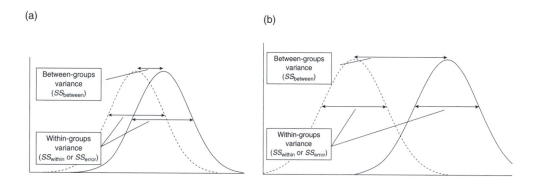

Figure 9.2   (a) Small and (b) Larger amount of between-groups variance, relative to within-groups variance

Calculating the sums of squares

We need to calculate the three kinds of sums of squares, total (SS_{total}), within groups (SS_{within}), and between groups ($SS_{between}$).

Calculating SS_{total}

We'll start off with SS_{total} which is the sum of the squared differences between the mean and each score. The formula is

$$SS_{total} = \sum (x - \bar{x})^2$$

where x is each score, and $\bar{x}$ is the mean of all scores.

Table 9.1 shows the calculation of the sums of squares for the CFS data we proceed as follows:

Step 1: Find $\bar{x}$, the mean of the scores for depression. This is equal to 12.2, and is shown in Table 9.1.
Step 2: Calculate x-$\bar{x}$, the difference between each score and the mean score.
Step 3: Calculate (x-$\bar{x}$)^2, by squaring the result of step 2.
Step 4: Find the sum of the squared values in step 3, to give

$$SS_{total} = \sum (x - \bar{x})^2 = 193.60$$

Calculating SS_{within}

The next stage is to calculate SS_{within}. The procedure is very similar, but this time we are looking for the sum of squares within each group. Rather than using the total mean, we use the mean for each group. We could write the formula as:

$$SS_{within} = \sum (x - \bar{x}_g)^2$$

This is almost the same as the formula for SS_{total}, except that we have put a little g on the $\bar{x}$ symbol. (We're sorry about that, it does make stuff look unnecessarily complicated when we do things like that, but we can't think of another way.)

Table 9.1 *Calculation of total sums of squares*

Group	Score	$\bar{x}$	$x - \bar{x}$	$(x - \bar{x})^2$
Pacing	11		1.80	3.24
Pacing	11		3.80	14.44
Pacing	9		−3.20	10.24
Pacing	18		5.80	33.64
Pacing	3		0.80	0.64
		12.2		
Active rehabilitation	14		−1.20	1.44
Active rehabilitation	16		−1.20	1.44
Active rehabilitation	9		−3.20	10.24
Active rehabilitation	18		5.80	33.64
Active rehabilitation	13		−9.20	84.64

We carry out the same procedure as before:

Step 1: Find $\bar{x}_g$, *the mean of the scores for depression for each group.* These are 14 for the pacing group, and 10.4 for the active rehabilitation group, and are shown in Table 9.2.

Step 2: Calculate $x - \bar{x}_g$, *the difference between each score and the mean score for the group.*

Step 3: Calculate $(x - \bar{x}_g)^2$, *by squaring the result of step 2, shown in column 5.*

Step 4: Find the $S (x - \bar{x}_g)^2$, *by adding up each of the values. This comes to 161.2.*

Now we know $SS_{within} = 161.2$.

Calculating $SS_{between}$

There's an easy way to calculate $SS_{between}$, and there's a hard way. If you are a tiny bit like us, we suspect that you don't even want to know about the hard way. So we aren't going to tell you. We're just going to do the easy way. And the easy way is very easy.

We know that there are three kinds of sums of squares, total (SS_{total}), between ($SS_{between}$) and within (SS_{within}). You might have realised from the name total sums of squares, that this is the, erm, total. And you'd be right. And given that there are only two other kinds, they must add up to the total. So:

Table 9.2 *Calculation of SS_{within}*

Group	Score	$\bar{x}_g$	$x - \bar{x}_g$	$(x - \bar{x}_g)^2$
Pacing	14		0.00	0.00
Pacing	16		2.00	4.00
Pacing	9	14	−5.00	25.00
Pacing	18		4.00	16.00
Pacing	13		−1.00	1.00
Active rehabilitation	11		0.60	0.36
Active rehabilitation	11		0.60	0.36
Active rehabilitation	9	10.4	−1.40	1.96
Active rehabilitation	18		7.60	57.76
Active rehabilitation	3		−7.40	54.76

$$SS_{total} = SS_{within} + SS_{between}$$

A really small bit of algebra tells us that

$$SS_{between} = SS_{total} - SS_{within}$$

So we put our numbers into the equation:

$$SS_{between} = 193.6 - 161.2 = 32.4$$

Calculating the effect size

We want to know how large the effect of the treatment has been. This is the same as asking what proportion of the total variance (or total sum of squares) the treatment effect has been responsible for. This is just $SS_{between}/SS_{total}$. This statistic is known as an **effect size**. It goes under two different names (which in our analysis are the same, but in more advanced applications can differ); these are R^2 or η^2 (that's the Greek letter eta, so it's pronounced eta-squared). So

$$R^2 = \eta^2 = \frac{SS_{\text{between}}}{SS_{\text{total}}}$$

$$= \frac{32.4}{193.6} = 0.167.$$

The proportion of variance due to the treatment is 0.167, or 16.7%, and therefore 83.3% is due to other things, which we call error.

Calculating statistical significance

To calculate the **statistical significance** of the effect of treatment, we use the sums of squares again. However, the statistical significance is dependent on the sample size, and we don't use that in the calculation of R^2.

To calculate the statistical significance, we first need to calculate the **mean squares**, often written as MS. It might not surprise you to find that we have MS_{within} for mean squares within groups, and MS_{between} for mean squares between groups. We don't have MS_{total} though.

When we find the mean of things, we divide by the sample size, N. Remember when we calculated the standard deviation we divided by $N - 1$? Well, it's similar in this situation, we don't divide by N, we divide by the degrees of freedom (explained in Chapter 4, page 91).

Step 1: Calculate the degrees of freedom.
There are three sets of degrees of freedom, called df_{total}, df_{between} and df_{within} (or df_{error}). As you might have come to expect:

$$df_{\text{total}} = df_{\text{between}} + df_{\text{within}}$$

To calculate df_{total} we use

$$df_{\text{total}} = N - 1$$

So in our example

$$df_{\text{total}} = 10 - 1 = 9$$

To calculate $df_{between}$, we use the number of groups (which we'll call g, but you don't need to remember that beyond the next line):

$$df_{between} = g - 1$$

So in our example

$$df_{between} = 2 - 1 = 1$$

(OK, you can forget what g means now.)

The easiest way of calculating df_{within} is to use:

$$df_{within} = df_{total} - df_{between}$$

So

$$df_{within} = 9 - 1 = 8$$

Step 2: Calculate the mean squares.
We do this by dividing the sums of squares by the degrees of freedom. For $MS_{between}$:

$$MS_{between} = \frac{SS_{between}}{df_{between}}$$

$$= \frac{32.4}{1} = 32.4$$

For MS_{within}:

$$MS_{within} = \frac{SS_{within}}{df_{within}}$$

$$= \frac{161.2}{8} = 20.15$$

Step 3: Calculate F.
Finally we calculate the relative size of the two values, by dividing $MS_{between}$ by MS_{within}. This gives us the test statistic for ANOVA, which is called F, or sometimes the **F-ratio**. Just like the other test statistics that we have encountered, F doesn't meananything, we just use it to calculate the probability. For our example,

$$F = \frac{MS_{\text{between}}}{MS_{\text{within}}}$$

$$= \frac{32.4}{20.15} = 1.68$$

Step 4: Calculate the p-value.

To find the probability associated with F we need to have two sets of degrees of freedom, the between and the within. These are usually reported as df = 1, 8. Using a computer program we can find the probability associated with a value of F as high as 1.68, with 1, 8 df. We type

$$= \text{fdist}(1.608, 1, 8)$$

into Excel, and the answer is 0.24. The value is greater than 0.05, and so we cannot reject the null hypothesis. This study has not provided evidence that there is any difference between the two methods.

ANOVA and *t*-tests

If you turn back to Chapter 6, you will find that when we analysed the same data with a *t*-**test**, the *p*-value was also 0.24. We shouldn't be surprised by this – ANOVA and the *t*-test are exactly the same test, just a different way of thinking about the result (when we have two groups). In fact, if we take the value of *t* (which was 1.27, in case you don't remember) and square it, we get 1.64, which is the value of *F*. This is a general rule when there are two groups:

$$F = t^2.$$

Optional Extra: *F*

Where do all these letters come? Why is it the *t*-test for example, and not the *j*-test? Usually there is no good reason. The *F* Name is a little different. Unlike most of the others, it does stand for something – Snedecor named it *F* after Fisher and not a naughty word as many people think. (We came across Fisher in the Fisher's exact test, and will come across him again in Chapter 11, where he plays an important role.)

> ## Common Mistake: Don't forget the degrees of freedom
>
> Students often fail to report the degrees of freedom to go with a value for F. Without the degrees of freedom, the F is meaningless.

So, you might well be asking, if we covered t-tests in Chapter 6, why are we doing it again in Chapter 9? The reason is that the t-test is restricted to comparing two groups, whereas ANOVA extends in a number of useful directions. It can be used to compare three groups (or more), it can be used to calculate the p-value associated with a regression line, and it can be used in a wide range of other situations.

Understanding ANOVA

Before we move on to the other applications, let's have a look at what ANOVA is doing. Figure 9.3(a) shows two (normally distributed) **histograms**, plotted on the same chart. The difference between the means is small (it's actually one standard deviation, in case you are interested), relative to the size of the standard deviation. Remember that the F-ratio is given by $MS_{between}$ / MS_{within} – because $MS_{between}$ is small, F will be small, and hence less likely to be statistically significant.

Now compare Figure 9.3(b). Here, the within-groups variance is about the same, but the between-groups variance is larger (the means are now 2 standard deviations apart), because $F = MS_{between}/MS_{within}$, F will be larger, and all other things being equal, the p-value will be lower.

ASSUMPTIONS IN ANOVA

When there are two groups, ANOVA is equivalent to a t-test, and it therefore makes the same assumptions as a t-test, and it makes these assumptions regardless of the number of groups that are being compared.

Normal distribution within each group

This is another one of those tricky ones about the **normal distribution**. We do not assume that the outcome variable is normally distributed – despite what you may read or think. What we do assume is that the data *within each group* are normally distributed.

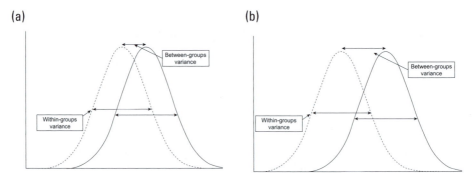

Figure 9.3   (a) Small and (b) larger between-groups variance

Homogeneity of variance

As with the *t*-test, we assume that the standard deviation within each group is approximately equal, which is often referred to as **homogeneity of variance** (the variance being the square of the standard deviation). However, as with the *t*-test, we don't need to worry about this assumption, if we have approximately equal numbers of people in each group. It is possible to test for this, using Levene's test, but the comments that we made when we discussed the *t*-test are still relevant. (If you've forgotten, here's the gist of it. When it matters if we have violated the assumption, Levene's test isn't very good. When it doesn't matter the Levene's test is good, but we don't care.)

ANOVA COMPARING THREE GROUPS

The nice thing about ANOVA is that it naturally extends to three groups. The formulae are all the same (although we have an extra issue to worry about, which we'll come to later). However, even though the formulae are the same, we are still going to work through them, and show you how to do it.

We will use some data from a study by Dorahy, Middleton and Irwin (2005).[1] These researchers wanted to examine responses, on a measure of dissociative experiences, of people who had been diagnosed as suffering from dissociative identity disorder (DID), and compare them with controls. There is a problem with finding a suitable control group for a condition such as this. If we use a control group of people who are suffering from no psychiatric disorder, and we find a difference, we don't know if this is because the difference is caused

---

[1]We would like to thank Martin Dorahy for providing these data.

by DID, or if it is caused by having been diagnosed with a psychiatric disorder. An alternative is that we use a control group of individuals who have been diagnosed with a psychiatric disorder unrelated to the condition, but of similar severity – for example, a major depressive disorder. However, if we find a difference between these two groups, we don't know which condition has made people different. The solution employed by Dorahy et al. is to use two control groups: one group of 11 people who had been diagnosed with no psychiatric condition, and one group of 11 people who had been diagnosed with major depressive disorder.

The outcome measure (dependent variable) used was the Dissociative Experiences Scale (DES) developed by Carlson and Putnam (1993), that can be used to assist in the diagnosis of DID. It contains items such as: '*Some people have the experience of finding new things among their belongings that they do not remember buying. Mark the line to show what percentage of the time this happens to you.*' The data from the study are shown in Table 9.3.

Common Mistake: Entering data incorrectly

We've put the data into three columns, because it saves space. When you enter the data into a computer program, you should not enter them in this way – it tells the computer that each person was measured three times, once in each group. This is obviously wrong, but the computer won't know that.

Table 9.3   *Data from Dorahy et al. (2005) study*

DID group	Depressed control	Non-psychiatric control
71	57	14
38	29	3
69	25	17
28	1	20
42	23	31
60	10	12
61	8	24
33	10	10
63	9	5
53	7	5
89	45	23

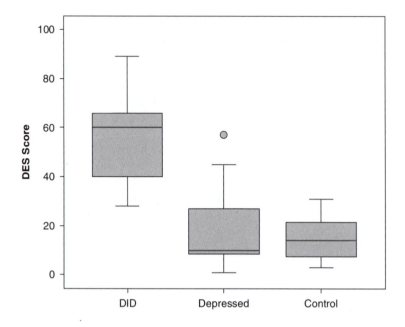

Figure 9.4 Box and whisker plot of Dorahy et al. data

As always, we should begin by exploring our data, to ensure that the assumptions of normal distribution and homogeneity of variance were not violated. This should also give us some idea of the results that we expect, and avoid any nasty surprises along the way.

A **box and whisker plot** of the data is shown in Figure 9.4 (box and whisker plots are described in Chapter 2, page 42). The three groups all appear to have a distribution that at least approximates a normal distribution, and the width of the distribution is approximately equal as well, therefore we can happily use ANOVA (although, as with the *t*-test, the distribution assumption is less important when there are equal numbers in each group). In addition, the graph shows that the group who are scoring the highest are the DID group, and that the psychiatric controls, and the non-psychiatric controls seems to be scoring similarly.

Again, we need to calculate η^2, to see how large the effect is, and the *F*-ratio, to see if the effect is significantly different from zero. The formula for R^2 or η^2 (remember they are a different name for the same thing) is:

$$R^2 = \eta^2 = \frac{SS_{\text{between}}}{SS_{\text{total}}}.$$

The formula for F is:

$$F = \frac{MS_{between}}{MS_{within}}.$$

So to calculate both of these, we are going to need to know the sums of squares.

Calculating sums of squares

There are three sums of squares to be calculated: the total sum of squares (SS_{total}), the within-groups sums of squares (SS_{within}) and the between-groups sums of squares ($SS_{between}$).

Total sum of squares

Just as in the two-group example, the total sum of squares is given by:

$$SS_{total} = \sum (x - \bar{x})^2$$

The data and the calculation are shown in Table 9.4. The steps are as follows:

Step 1:   Find $\bar{x}$, the mean of the scores for the DES. This is equal to 30.15, and is shown in column 3 of Table 9.4.
Step 2:   Calculate $x - \bar{x}$, the difference between each score and the mean score, shown in column 4.
Step 3:   Calculate $(x - \bar{x})^2$, by squaring the result of step 2, shown in column 5.
Step 4:   Find $\Sigma(x - \bar{x})^2$, by adding up each of the values. This comes to 17,820.24. This is our value for the total sum of squares.

Calculating within groups sums of squares (SS_{within})

Calculating SS_{within} with multiple groups is a repeat of the procedure that we used for two groups. The formula is:

$$SS_{within} = \sum (x - \bar{x}_g)^2$$

(You need to remember again that $\bar{x}_g$ is the mean score for group g.)

Table 9.4 *Calculation of Total sums of squares*

Group	DES score	$\bar{x}$	$x - \bar{x}$	$(x - \bar{x})^2$
DID	71	30.15	40.85	1668.60
DID	38		7.85	61.60
DID	69		38.85	1509.20
DID	28		−2.15	4.63
DID	42		11.85	140.39
DID	60		29.85	890.93
DID	61		30.85	951.63
DID	33		2.85	8.11
DID	63		32.85	1079.02
DID	53		22.85	522.05
DID	89		58.85	3463.14
Depressed	57		26.85	720.84
Depressed	29		−1.15	1.33
Depressed	25		−5.15	26.54
Depressed	1		−29.15	849.81
Depressed	23		−7.15	51.14
Depressed	10		−20.15	406.08
Depressed	8		−22.15	490.69
Depressed	10		−20.15	406.08
Depressed	9		−21.15	447.39
Depressed	7		−23.15	535.99
Depressed	45		14.85	220.48
Control	14		−16.15	260.87
Control	3		−27.15	737.20
Control	17		−13.15	172.96
Control	20		−10.15	103.05
Control	31		0.85	0.72
Control	12		−18.15	329.48
Control	24		−6.15	37.84
Control	10		−20.15	406.08
Control	5		−25.15	632.60
Control	5		−25.15	632.60
Control	23		−7.15	51.14

1. Find $\bar{x}_g$, the mean of the scores for DES for each group. These are shown in column 3 of Table 9.5.
2. Calculate $x - \bar{x}_g$, the difference between each score and the mean score for the group, shown in column 4.
3. Calculate $(x - \bar{x}_g)^2$, by squaring the result of step 2, shown in column 5.
4. Find $\Sigma(x - \bar{x}_g)^2$, by adding up each of the values. This comes to 7319.09.

Table 9.5   *Calculating SS_within*

Group	DES score	$\bar{x}_g$	$x - \bar{x}_g$	$(x - \bar{x}_g)^2$
DID	71	55.18	15.82	250.21
DID	38		−17.18	295.21
DID	69		13.82	190.94
DID	28		−27.18	738.85
DID	42		−13.18	173.76
DID	60		4.82	23.21
DID	61		5.82	33.85
DID	33		−22.18	492.03
DID	63		7.82	61.12
DID	53		−2.18	4.76
DID	89		33.82	1143.67
depressed	57	20.36	36.64	1342.22
depressed	29		8.64	74.59
depressed	25		4.64	21.50
depressed	1		−19.36	374.95
depressed	23		2.64	6.95
depressed	10		−10.36	107.40
depressed	8		−12.36	152.86
depressed	10		−10.36	107.40
depressed	9		−11.36	129.13
depressed	7		−13.36	178.59
depressed	45		24.64	606.95
control	14	14.91	−0.91	0.83
control	3		−11.91	141.83
control	17		2.09	4.37
control	20		5.09	25.92
control	31		16.09	258.92
control	12		−2.91	8.46
control	24		9.09	82.64
control	10		−4.91	24.10
control	5		−9.91	98.19
control	5		−9.91	98.19
control	23		8.09	65.46

Calculating between groups sums of squares ($SS_{between}$)

When we calculated the between-groups sum of squares, $SS_{between}$, with two groups, there was an easy way, and a hard way. We still think the easy way is the best way: we know that

$$SS_{between} = SS_{total} - SS_{within}$$

Putting our numbers in gives us:

$$SS_{between} = 17,820.24 - 7319.09 = 10,501.15$$

Calculating the effect size

We now have our three sums of squares, and so calculating the effect size is the same as it was with two groups (and will be with as many groups as we care to find).

$$R^2 = \eta^2 = \frac{SS_{between}}{SS_{total}}$$

$$= \frac{10,501.15}{17,820.24} = 0.589.$$

A very substantial 58.9% of the variance (differences) in the DES score are associated with the predictor variable.

Calculating statistical significance

The next stage is to calculate the statistical significance of that effect. The formula is the same for the two-group analysis:

$$F = \frac{MS_{between}}{MS_{within}}$$

where MS denotes the mean squares. The mean squares are equal to the sum of squares, divided by the appropriate degrees of freedom, so:

$$MS_{between} = \frac{SS_{between}}{df_{between}}$$

$$MS_{within} = \frac{SS_{within}}{df_{within}}$$

Step 1: Calculate the degrees of freedom.
As with the two-group situation, we make our life a little easier by calculating df_{total} first.

$$df_{total} = N - 1$$

where N is the total sample size. So in our example,

$$df_{total} = 33 - 1 = 32$$

Calculating $df_{between}$ is done using

$$df_{between} = g - 1$$

So in our example,

$$df_{between} = 3 - 1 = 2$$

With the sums of squares, adding the between and within gives the total. It's the same with the degrees of freedom:

$$df_{total} = df_{within} + df_{between}$$

Again, a teeny bit of arithmetic gives:

$$df_{within} = df_{total} - df_{between}$$

So

$$df_{within} = 32 - 2 = 30$$

Step 2: Calculate the mean squares.
Now we are ready to calculate the mean squares:

$$MS_{between} = \frac{SS_{between}}{df_{between}} = \frac{10,501.15}{2} = 5250.58$$

$$MS_{within} = \frac{SS_{within}}{df_{within}} = \frac{7319.09}{30} = 243.97$$

Step 3: Calculate F.
Finally we can calculate F:

$$F = \frac{MS_{between}}{MS_{within}} = \frac{5250.58}{243.97} = 21.52$$

Step 4: Calculate the p-value.
As we can now find the probability value associated with F, using the two values for degrees of freedom, 2 and 30. Using MS Excel, we type

$$= fdist\ (21.52, 2, 30)$$

The resulting probability value is less than 0.001, indicating that the probability of finding an effect that large in the sample, if the population effect were zero, is extremely low.

Hence, I can reject the null hypothesis, and conclude that there is a difference amongst the three groups.

Summary of formulae for calculating F

Just so you don't have to go through all that again, we'll repeat the formulae.

Here are two different ways to calculate F:

$$F = \frac{MS_{\text{between}}}{MS_{\text{within}}}$$

$$F = \frac{SS_{\text{between}}/df_{\text{between}}}{SS_{\text{within}}/df_{\text{within}}}$$

To calculate degrees of freedom:

$$df_{\text{total}} = N - 1$$

$$df_{\text{betweeen}} = g - 1$$

$$df_{\text{within}} = df_{\text{total}} - df_{\text{between}}$$

where g is equal to the number of groups.

For the sums of squares:

$$SS_{\text{total}} = \sum (x - \bar{x})^2$$

$$SS_{\text{within}} = \sum (x - \bar{x}_g)^2$$

$$SS_{\text{total}} = SS_{\text{within}} + SS_{\text{between}}$$

POST HOC TESTING

You thought we'd finished, didn't you? We almost have, but there's an extra complication that we need to sort out first. We said that we have found that there are *differences* between the groups, but we didn't say what those differences were.

More formally (we don't usually like to be formal, but stick with us here), ANOVA tests the null hypothesis that:

$$\bar{x}_1 = \bar{x}_2 = \ldots = \bar{x}_k$$

where $\bar{x}_1$ is the mean of group 1, $\bar{x}_2$ is the mean of group 2, and so on, all the way up to $\bar{x}_k$, which means as many groups as we have. In the case of two groups, this is not a problem, because if the mean of group 1 is different from the mean of group 2, that can only happen in one way (the way that it happens is that the mean of group 1 is different from the mean of group 2, but bear with us).

However, when we reject a null hypothesis when there are three or more groups, we aren't really saying enough. We are just saying that group 1, group 2, group 3 (and so on, up to group k) are not the same. But unlike the two-group solution, this can happen in lots of ways. We would just say that:

$$\bar{x}_1 = \bar{x}_2 = \bar{x}_3 = \ldots \bar{x}_k$$

is not true. But is that because groups 1 and 2 are different from 3? Or is it because group 1 is different from groups 2 and 3? Or maybe group 1 is different from group 3, but group 3 is not different from group 2. Or maybe group 1 is different from groups 2 and 3, and group 2 is also different from group 3. And so on, and when there are 4 or more groups, it becomes more complex.

To answer the question of where the differences come from, we need to do **post hoc tests**. 'Post hoc' is Latin, and it just means 'after this'. Post hoc tests are tests that we do after we do analysis of variance.

Post hoc tests are based on t-tests, which we saw in Chapter 6. To do post hoc tests with three groups, we do three tests: group 1 vs. group 2, group 1 vs. group 3, and group 2 vs. group 3.

Optional Extra: How many post hoc tests?

To find out how many post hoc tests will be required, we use the formula

$$\frac{k(k-1)}{2}$$

where k is the number of groups. For three groups we therefore need to have 3 tests. For four groups there will be 6 tests. For five groups there will be 10 tests. As you can see, the number of tests required grows faster than the number of groups, which can cause problems.

We could just do three t-tests to compare the three groups, but this would cause a problem, called **alpha inflation**. To understand this problem, we need to understand that alpha is the type I error rate. A type I error is where we reject a null hypothesis that is true. You might like to go and have another look (or even a first look) at Chapter 4, if this is unfamiliar.

The probability value that we choose as a cut-off (usually 0.05) is referred to as our **type I error** rate. That is, it is the probability of getting a significant result in our test, if the population effect is actually zero. When we do three tests, we use a cut-off of 0.05, and therefore we think that the probability of a type I error is still 0.05. We call 0.05 our *nominal* type I error rate, because that is the type I error rate we have named. The problem is that the type I error rate has risen above 0.05, and it is no longer our true type I error rate. To understand why, consider this example.

Tossers

If someone keeps tossing a coin what is the probability that they can toss heads 10 times in a row? The answer is $1/(2 \times 2 \times 2 \times 2 \times 2 \times 2 \times 2 \times 2 \times 2 \times 2) = 1/2^{10} = 1/1024$, which is pretty close to 1 in 1000. This is a pretty small number. If you came to me, and threw heads 10 times in a row, I would be rightly impressed at your good luck (or more likely, I would wonder how you cheated). However, if you told me that there is a student in the university who tossed heads 10 times in a row, you would be right. There are about 10,000 students in the university, so if we tested each student, in their coin tossing ability (and none of them cheated) we would find about 10 who would toss 10 heads in a row. (There aren't actually *exactly* 10,000 students in either of our universities, but it makes the sums easier.)

What we have done is *capitalise on chance*. We have taken the fact that these things happen by chance occasionally, and made out that this is something special.

When we do multiple *t*-tests, following an ANOVA, we are also at risk of capitalising on chance. The probability that one of those tests will be statistically significant is not 0.05 (remember that's our nominal type I error rate), but is actually closer to three times 0.05, or 0.15, about 1 in 7, so our actual type I error rate is much higher than our nominal rate. Hence, we need to perform some sort of modified test and we can't use our plain ordinary *t*-test, as we had planned. There are many, many different post hoc tests that we could choose to carry out, (SPSS, for example, will do 18 different kinds of post hoc tests). We are only going to look at one, known as **Bonferroni correction**.

Optional Extra

Interestingly (well, we think it's interesting), Bonferroni didn't have a great deal to do with Bonferroni correction. The proof required for Bonferroni correction relies on Boole's inequality (which Bonferroni extended, but this extension wasn't needed for Bonferroni correction). It was actually first applied by Dunn (1961) and hence is sometimes known as Dunn's correction. This is a further example of Stigler's law of eponymy, which we described in Chapter 2, page 20.

BONFERRONI CORRECTION

Doing three *t*-tests, and then multiplying the *p*-values by 3 seems too easy, doesn't it? Suspiciously easy? So easy, you might think that it was more complicated than that? You'd be right.

We've been assuming that we have homogeneity of variance (it's an assumption of ANOVA and the *t*-tests), and we're still making this assumption. What we should really do is to calculate the pooled standard error, and then calculate three *t*-tests using this pooled standard error. However, there are two reasons why we are not going to do this. First, it's rather tricky. Secondly, it is so unintuitive that we don't think there's a great deal to be learned by exploring this approach. If you are interested, a brief guide to the formulae is given in Roberts and Russo (1999), and a more detailed discussion can be found in Maxwell and Delaney (2004).

Optional Extra: Bonferroni correction formulae

If you just want to know the formulae, you can use the SPSS Statistical Algorithms documentation, which comes with SPSS, or is available on their website at http://support.spss.com. (To find post hoc tests, you need to look in Appendix 10.) Andy Field's book '*Discovering Statistics Using SPSS*' covers most of the tests that SPSS does that you might be interested in.

Test yourself 1

What is homogeneity of variance, and why is it important?

Answer is given at the end of the chapter.

Test yourself 2

Calculate whether each of the following results is statistically significant. (Use either method, or ideally both.)

(a) $p = 0.003$, 4 groups compared
(b) $p = 0.010$, 5 groups compared

(c) $p = 0.060$, 3 groups compared

(d) $p = 0.002$, 10 groups compared

Answers are given at the end of the chapter.

Bonferroni corrected confidence intervals

When we had two groups, in Chapter 6, we calculated the standard error, and then calculated the confidence interval, based on multiplying the standard error by the critical value for t, at the 0.05 level. We carry out the same procedure, except we are no longer using the 95% level. We have to adjust alpha by dividing by 3, to give 0.0166. We then calculate the critical value for t, using this new value for alpha.

The means and standard deviations of the Dorahy et al. (2005) data are given in Table 9.6. The first stage is to calculate the difference between each of the means, and the standard error of the difference between each of the means. (We won't go through this again, it's in Chapter 6, page 143). The results are shown in Table 9.7.

To calculate the **confidence intervals**, we need to know the critical value of t. When we used 0.05, we could have used either a table or a computer to find the critical value. However, we are now using the value of alpha corrected for the number of tests that we are doing. We are going to be doing three tests, so we need to use $0.05/3 = 0.0166$. Most books don't have that sort of table, so we are forced to use a computer.

Before we can determine the critical value, we need to know the degrees of freedom (df). The df are calculated in the same way as we saw for the t-test, in Chapter 6, that is, $df = N - 2$, where N is the total sample size for the two groups we are comparing. In our case, each of the groups is the same size, with 11 people in it. $N - 2$ is $22 - 2 = 20$ for each comparison.

To find the critical value, we can use Microsoft Excel, entering:

$$= \text{tinv} (0.05/3, 20)$$

Table 9.6 *Means and standard deviations of three groups*

Group	Mean	SD
DID	55.18	18.460
Depressed	20.36	17.614
Control	14.91	8.994

Table 9.7   *Difference between means, and standard errors of three groups*

Comparison	Difference	Standard error
DID – Depressed	34.82	7.69
DID – Control	40.27	6.19
Depressed – Control	5.46	5.96

Table 9.8   *Difference between means, and standard errors of three groups*

Comparison	Difference	Standard error	Critical value	Lower 95% confidence limit (Difference – se × critical value)	Upper 95% confidence limit (Difference + se × critical value)
DID – Depressed	34.82	7.69	2.61	14.73	54.91
DID – Control	40.27	6.19	2.61	24.11	56.43
Depressed – Control	5.46	5.96	2.61	−10.10	21.02

We use 0.05/3, because 0.05 is the value of alpha we want to use, and 3 is the number of comparisons we want to make. We use 20, because we have 20 degrees of freedom. This gives us the critical value of 2.61.

The confidence intervals reveal (Table 9.8) that both of the control groups differ from the DID group, with the confidence intervals not crossing zero. The two control groups do not differ from one another – the confidence interval does include zero.

Bonferroni corrected statistical significance

Calculation of statistical significance is also straightforward once we have the standard errors of the differences. The calculations are shown in Table 9.9. The value for t is equal to the difference divided by the standard error of the difference. We then look up the probability value associated with a value of t this large, using the degrees of freedom (which are still equal to $N - 2$). We have to use a computer to find the probability value. We are going to be multiplying it by 3, so we need it to be accurate. (Note that in the table, we have presented 7 decimal places.) You would not normally do this in any report that you wrote. We also have a significance reported column, which shows what you would write in your report.

Table 9.9 *Calculation of significance values*

Comparison	Difference	Standard error	t (difference/se)	df (N–2)	Significance (uncorrected)	Significance (corrected = uncorrected × 3)	Significance reported
DID – Depressed	34.82	7.69	4.53	20	0.0002040	0.0006120	< 0.001
DID – Control	40.27	6.19	6.50	20	0.0000025	0.0000074	< 0.001
Depressed – Control	5.46	5.96	0.92	20	0.3685368	1.1056103	1.00

Optional Extra: The hard way (for the sake of completeness)

We said that we did that the easy way, and that there is a hard way, which is more accurate. If we did do it the correct (and hard) way, our confidence intervals would be:

	Lower Bound	Upper Bound
DID – depressed	17.93	51.71
DID – control	23.38	57.16
Depressed – control	−11.43	22.34

In addition, the true *p*-values would be 0.0000367, 0.0000037, 1.0000000. The values are slightly different, but the interpretation is the same.

Optional Extra: Problems with Bonferroni correction

Bonferroni correction has two advantages for us. First, it controls our type I error rates, which means that we don't go making spurious statements. Second, it is easy to understand. Whenever we do multiple tests, we can Bonferroni correct by multiplying the probability value by the number of tests, and treating this as the probability value. (Or equivalently, dividing our cut-off by the number of tests, and rejecting only null hypotheses that have significance values lower than that cut-off.)

(Continued)

(Continued)

However, Bonferroni correction has a problem in that it is a very unwieldy and very blunt tool. If you want to chop down trees, you use a chainsaw. A chainsaw is (relatively) easy to use, and chops down trees quickly. Bonferroni correction is a bit like a statistical chainsaw: it's straightforward to use, and gets the job done. If you want to perform brain surgery, a chainsaw is still relatively easy to use, and it still gets the job done. However, there are times when you want something a bit more precise than a chainsaw, especially when the aim is not just to chop, but instead to chop carefully, and in the right place.

The problem with Bonferroni correction is that the p-values required for statistical significance rapidly become very small. Let's look at an example of why this is a problem. Imagine in our study we decide to compare two groups, and we find that the significance of the difference between them is 0.03. We would have achieved a statistically significant result, and we would reject the null hypothesis.

However, what would have happened had we added a third group to our study? Even if the data from the first two groups *had not changed*, we would have to multiply the p-value by 3, hence the significance of the difference would become $0.03 \times 3 = 0.09$. Despite the data being exactly the same, we would no longer reject the null hypothesis.

Optional Extra: Analysis of variance and regression: two of a kind?

All analysis of variance can be thought of as a case of **regression**, which can, in turn, be thought of as a special case of the general linear model. When these techniques were first being used, people knew this. The trouble is that regression can be very hard work if you haven't got a computer (and back in the days when this sort of thing was being done for the first time, no one had a computer). An analysis could take literally days. However, in the special case where you have categorical predictors (and equal numbers in each group), it was possible to do the analysis in a different way, which made life much easier. This approach was called analysis of variance (ANOVA).

However, the formulae for regression and ANOVA look nothing like each other, which makes people believe that they are doing different and unrelated things.

SUMMARY

We have looked at the workhorse of psychology statistics that is ANOVA. It is commonly used, and sometimes even understood by the people who use it. We have explained the hows and whys of ANOVA and shown that, even though the equations are messy, the principles are straightforward. Understanding the rationale of a statistical allows you to recognise what it can tell you and also what it cannot tell you.

Test yourself answers

Test yourself 1

Homogeneity of variance means that the variances (standard deviations) of each of the groups that we are investigating are approximately equal. This is an assumption made by ANOVA and t-tests, and it is important for two reasons.

First, we use the variance to estimate the standard error (and hence the confidence intervals and p-values). If we can assume homogeneity of variance, we can pool the variances from each group. If we estimate the variance with a larger number of people, the standard error will be smaller (because $se = \sigma/\sqrt{N}$). And a smaller standard error means reduced confidence intervals, and lower p-values.

Second, and perhaps more importantly, if we can assume homogeneity of variance, the calculations are much, much easier.

Test yourself 2

(a) Four groups means that 6 comparisons are made (remember $k(k-1)/2$), we can therefore multiply the p-value by 6, to give $0.003 \times 10 = 0.018$, which is statistically significant. Alternatively, we can adjust the value of alpha, by dividing by 6 – this gives $0.05/6 = 0.0083$ as our new cut-off. The p-value of 0.003 is still below the new cut-off, and hence the result is statistically significant, whichever way we work it out.

(b) When 5 groups are compared, 10 comparisons are made. We can therefore multiply our obtained p-value of 0.010 by 10, to get a value of 0.100, which is no longer statistically significant. Alternatively, we can divide our value of alpha by 10, to obtain 0.005. The p-value that we have is larger than our new, Bonferroni-corrected, alpha, and so the result is not statistically significant.

(c) When comparing three groups, we make three comparisons, so the Bonferroni corrected p-value is $0.06 \times 3 = 0.18$, which fails to achieve significance at the 0.05 level. Alternatively, we can divide the alpha cut-off by 3, to give $0.05/3 = 0.017$, and again, our value of 0.06 fails to achieve statistical significance at this level. (You might have noticed that this wasn't statistically significant before we did any corrections, so you could have saved the effort of doing them).

(d) When comparing 10 groups, we will carry out 45 tests (given by $10(10-1)/2$). This means that we can Bonferroni correct our p-value, to give $0.002 \times 45 = 0.09$, which fails to achieve significance at the 0.05 level. Alternatively, we can correct our p-value cut-off by dividing the cut-off by the number of tests, giving $0.05/45 = 0.0011$. Again, we can see that the p-value fails to achieve statistical significance.

USING SPSS

Select **Analyze** $\Rightarrow$ **Compare Means** $\Rightarrow$ **One-Way ANOVA**. You get the following window:
The **Dependent List** box is used for your outcome variable(s). These must be continuous.

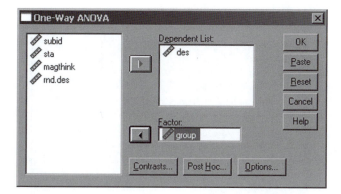

It's a list, because SPSS allows you to put more than one variable in there. In our example this is the DES because this is the dependent variable we are interested in. The factor contains the variable that defines the groups and this *must* be a categorical variable.

Clicking first on the **Post Hoc** button gives you a selection of post hoc tests, in the following window:

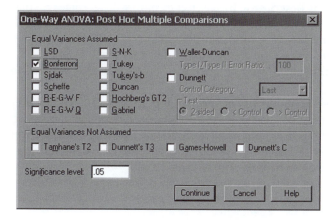

We don't really know why, but one day, someone who works at SPSS woke up and said 'Let's put 18 different post hoc tests into the one-way ANOVA command', and other people agreed. We find this many post hoc tests too much for our brains to deal with. We've discussed the Bonferroni post hoc test in this chapter, and we don't even know a book that will tell you about all of those tests; so we suggest you don't worry about them.

We'll tick **Bonferroni**, click **Continue** and move on.

Clicking on **Options** gives the following window:

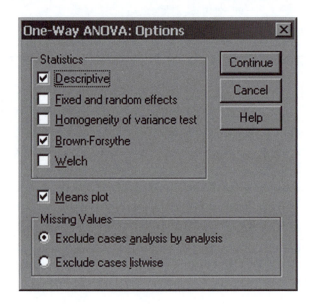

The first option is **Descriptive**. If we select this, we will get some descriptive information about each group. We probably should know all this anyway because we should have explored (and made friends with) our data sufficiently well before we did this test, but it's worth asking for, in case we get any surprises that we didn't expect.

Fixed and random effects you can ignore, unless you study statistics for a good many more years.

If we ask for a **Homogeneity of variance test**, SPSS will carry out Levene's test, which won't tell us much that's useful. If we are worried about the homogeneity of variance, there are two corrections that are possible in SPSS: the **Browne–Forsythe** correction and the **Welch** correction. We aren't going to go into how these are done, but you can use them if you are worried about homogeneity of variance.

The first output table comes under the heading Descriptives. For each of our three groups, and for all three groups combined, we are given some descriptive statistics. It's worth looking at these, to make sure that the data look approximately like you expect them to.

Descriptives

Dissociative experiences scale

	N	Mean	Std. Deviation	Std. Error	95% Confidence Interval for Mean		Minimum	Maximum
					Lower Bound	Upper Bound		
DID	11	55.0938	18.33125	5.52708	42.7787	67.4089	27.96	88.89
Depressed	11	20.2922	17.71916	5.34253	8.3883	32.1961	.89	57.14
Control	11	14.8939	8.94078	2.69575	8.8874	20.9004	3.39	31.15
Total	33	30.0933	23.56680	4.10245	21.7369	38.4497	.89	88.89

Next, we get the overall ANOVA:

ANOVA

Dissociative experiences scale

	Sum of Squares	df	Mean Square	F	Sig.
Between Groups	10473.202	2	5236.601	21.522	.000
Within Groups	7299.407	30	243.314		
Total	17772.609	32			

Notice that this table contains the parts we discussed: sums of squares, df, mean squares and F. Finally, there is a table in which every group is compared with every other group. (Notice that the standard error is a little smaller than ours, because SPSS uses a pooled standard error – we didn't, because it's really hard to work out if you're not a computer.)

Multiple comparisons

Dependent Variable: dissociative experiences scale

Bonferroni

(I) group	(J) group	Mean Difference (I-J)	Std. Error	Sig.	95% Confidence Interval	
					Lower Bound	Upper Bound
1 DID	2 depressed	34.80159*	6.65123	.000	17.9358	51.6674
	3 control	40.19994*	6.65123	.000	23.3341	57.0657
2 depressed	1 DID	-34.80159*	6.65123	.000	-51.6674	-17.9358
	3 control	5.39835	6.65123	1.000	-11.4674	22.2641
3 control	1 DID	-40.19994*	6.65123	.000	-57.0657	-23.3341
	2 depressed	-5.39835	6.65123	1.000	-22.2641	11.4674

The mean difference is significant at the .05 level.

10

Analysing questionnaires and measurement instruments

KEY TERMS

Bland–Altman limits of agreement
citations
classical test theory
coefficient alpha
Cohen's kappa
correlation
Cronbach's alpha
internal consistency
line of best fit

line of equality
psychometric
reliability
split-half method
standardised alpha
temporal stability
test–retest reliability
true measure
variance

INTRODUCTION

We live in a world that constantly surveys its population. Questionnaires are big business, and statisticians have developed ever increasingly sophisticated ways to analyse this wealth of data. Questionnaires are also the most common way of collecting data in applied areas of psychology. This chapter introduces some simple psychometric principles and techniques of analysis such as coefficient (Cronbach's) alpha, and other measures of reliability.

MEASUREMENT

In psychology, we spend a great deal of our time measuring things, and a great deal of our time thinking about how to measure things. The problem that we have is that the things we try to measure aren't like the things people in other sciences try to measure.

We try to measure things like extraversion, intelligence, attitude and attractiveness, which are all hidden qualities or qualities that are perceived by observers. How do we measure those things? Sometimes by seeing where someone has put a tick on a questionnaire and sometimes by asking someone (a knowledgeable expert) what they think about something (for example, in Chapter 8 we saw that each participant had a display rating).

Let's unpack that a bit. We want to measure something, but it's not a real thing. It's a thing that exists inside people's heads or in their behaviour, like intelligence or extraversion. Because it's not a real thing, we'll call it a psychological construct. But the act of measuring that thing doesn't involve *directly* measuring that thing, instead it involves measuring an *effect* of that thing.

People who are of higher intelligence will put more ticks in the correct boxes than people who are of lower intelligence. The thing we are interested in (intelligence) and the process that we are using to measure that thing (counting ticks) are very, very different. This is not the case in most sciences, where the thing that we are measuring, and the process that we are using to measure it, are very similar. Let's look at two examples from other sciences:

- To measure how effectively something kills bacteria, you put some of it on some bacteria, and see how many die.
- To measure the temperature at which something melts, you heat it up until it melts, and then measure the temperature.

The construct that you are interested in (the killing of bacteria, the melting point) is almost indistinguishable from the process that you use to measure it (bacteria killed, temperature when it melts). This is not the case with our psychological examples.

Because of this difficulty we must, where possible, ensure that two things are true about our measures: that they are reliable and that they are valid. Reliability refers to whether a test measures *something* well. In this chapter we are going to look at the issue of reliability and how we can calculate how reliable our data are. Validity is whether that measure actually measures what it is supposed to measure.

RELIABILITY

A test is reliable if it satisfies the following conditions:

- It is an accurate measure.
- The results are dependable.
- Using the measure again, will I get the same answer?

Unfortunately, **reliability** means two different things, and they are not both always appropriate as ways to assess the reliability of a measure. The two meanings are:

- *Temporal stability.* That is a posh way of saying unchanging over time – that is, the measure does not change over time. If I measure your height today, and I measure your height tomorrow, if my tape measure is reliable, I should get the same answer.
- *Internal consistency.* This is a more complex idea. It is based on the fact that a test comprises multiple items – for example, an intelligence test contains a large number of items that ask about intelligence, and these items should all measure the same thing.

Optional Extra: Classical test theory

The framework we are working with in all these discussions is called **classical test theory**. Classical test theory has, as the name suggests, been around for quite a while. Its alternative, which we are not going to look at, is called item response theory (IRT). IRT is a different way of thinking about measurement, and has some advantages that mean that it is used in testing intelligence and abilities much more. The people who devise things like the Scholastic Aptitude Test (SAT), which is commonly used in the USA for determining university and college entry, use IRT to develop their scales. For an introduction to IRT, and for a look at its implications, see Embretson and Hershberger (1999).

TEMPORAL STABILITY

Temporal stability is often known as **test–retest reliability**. It means that, if we measure something once, and then measure it again at some later time, we get a similar score. However, there are a few issues that we need to consider.

Most importantly, what is the time period between test and retest? Although this is a commonly asked question, there is no answer apart from 'it depends'. If a measure is found to change over time, it may be because the measure is poor. Alternatively, it may be because the thing you are measuring has changed.

Some traits might be reasonably stable. We might expect intelligence, for example, to be particularly stable, and there is evidence to support this. Deary, Whiteman, Starr, Whalley and Fox (2004) followed up a group of people who had taken a test of intelligence at age 11, and then repeated the *same test* 67 years later. They found a correlation of 0.66 between the measures, suggesting that intelligence is stable over 67 years. Harding and Golombok (2002) examined the ability of gay men to measure the length and girth of their partner's penis using paper strips. They found that for length $r = 0.60$ and for girth $r = 0.53$ which are both relatively low values and suggests that this technique is not a reliable way of measuring penis dimensions. However, because of the time period involved there may be an alternative explanation for the low correlations in that it may be that the dimensions of erect penises vary over time (we'll leave it to the reader to think of things that might cause this variability).

The obvious answer to this problem is to use a shorter time period. The problem with a shorter time period, however, is that people can remember their previous answers and may keep them the same for fear of looking inconsistent. If I ask you today 'how much do you like that book on statistics you are reading?', and then ask you the same question tomorrow, you will be likely to remember your answer, and give the same answer so that you don't look like a mad person who changes their mind.

Temporal stability is assessed in two ways. One, the most common, is through the use of correlation. The two measures are correlated, and the correlation indicates the degree of stability of the measure. Higher correlations indicate higher stability, though, as ever, it is not quite that simple. The problem with using correlation is that correlations measure whether there is a *linear* relationship between scores. In other words, whether the people who had the highest scores in the group at time 1 also have the highest scores in the group at time 2. A high correlation value tells you that the rank order of the scores is relatively constant but does not confirm that the actual scores are the same. They might all have improved or the responses might have stretched out with people at the bottom scoring even lower while people at the top scored even higher. Correlation is not the same as agreement.

A second way of measuring stability over time is to use the **Bland–Altman limits of agreement**. This was devised and first appeared in 1981, and then again two years later (Altman & Bland, 1983), but the paper that is almost always cited is Bland and Altman (1986). (You can find these papers and more on Martin Bland's website at http://www-users.york.ac.uk/~mb55.) Although this is a very common method in health and medical research, it isn't often used in psychology, probably because psychologists don't know about it (and they don't know about it, because it isn't often used in psychology; see how we're kind of stuck here?) Anyway, we are going to change that by writing about it. But first, an optional extra.

Optional Extra: Journalology

When we say that something is very common or popular amongst scientists, how do we know? Or how do we know that a scientific method or discovery is important? We might say that a lot of our friends use it, but that might be because we hang out with weird friends. The reason why we know is *citations*. When a journal article includes a reference to a paper or a book, this means (usually) that the authors of that paper have read it and thought it was worth repeating. So every time your paper appears in the references of another article you notch up another citation. Citations are how we know that research that we publish is appreciated by other researchers.

(Continued)

(Continued)

It sounds like rather hard work to track down all the occasions that your paper might have been cited, but luckily this is done for us, by some people called the Institute for Scientific Information (or ISI, for short, they've got a website at wwwisiknowledge.com). For example, by searching on that website, we can find that Banyard and Shevlin's (2001) seminal paper, called 'Responses of football fans to relegation of their team from the English Premier League: PTS?' and published in the *Irish Journal of Psychological Medicine*, has been cited 4 times. With the best will in the world you can only see this as a pitifully low level of citation, and the article remains a hidden classic in the annals of psychology.

If we now go back to the Bland–Altman limits of agreement method and look at its citation rating we find a very different story. We mentioned that the method was published in three different journals. The first (Altman and Bland, 1983) was published in *The Statistician*, that paper has been cited 181 times, and is the most cited paper ever published in that journal. The second (Bland and Altman, 1986), which was a simplified version of the first one, was published in *The Lancet*, that paper has been cited 10,587 times, and is the most cited paper ever published in that journal. A third paper (Bland and Altman, 1999) was published in *Statistical Methods in Medical Research*, and has been cited 339 times, and is the most cited paper ever published in that journal. So you can see that it's not just us saying that this is an important method – the truth is out there.

We will illustrate the problem with the **correlation** using some data from Wetherell, Crown, Lightman, Miles, Kaye and Vedhara (2006). The researchers were looking at causes of stress. If we want to examine stress in a laboratory, it's sometimes useful to stress people without hurting them, and they used a technique to do just this. They asked people to breathe in a mixture of 35% carbon dioxide and 65% oxygen. The body finds this stressful as the only reason you would normally have that much carbon dioxide in your lungs would be if you were being suffocated or strangled. They then collected saliva and measured the level of cortisol, which is a hormone that the body produces under stress. The cortisol was measured 10 minutes after breathing the gas mixture, and 30 minutes after breathing the gas mixture.

The data are shown in Table 10.1. If you were to calculate the correlation between these two measures, you would find that it were 0.92, and highly significant. There is therefore a strong linear relationship between the two measures.

We can demonstrate the linear relationship with a scatterplot showing the **line of best fit** (see Figure 10.1). This shows that all the points are pretty close to the line, as we would expect if the correlation is high. This means that, if we know someone's score at time 1, we can make a pretty good guess what their score will be at time 2. However, it doesn't mean that they have the same score.

A better representation than the line of best fit might be the **line of equality** (see Figure 10.2). That is, the line that all the points would lie on if the person had scored the same for both measures.

Table 10.1 *Results of Wetherell et al. study*

Number	10 mins post CO_2	30 mins post CO_2
1	1.32	1.15
2	1.36	1.36
3	1.09	0.94
4	1.36	1.23
5	0.78	0.88
6	0.95	0.87
7	1.05	0.98
8	0.90	0.91
9	1.44	1.49
10	1.29	1.24
11	1.10	0.97
12	0.83	0.58
13	0.56	0.79
14	0.80	0.70
15	0.55	0.43
16	1.19	1.04
17	0.74	0.71
18	1.32	1.17
19	0.71	0.69
20	1.13	1.11
21	1.31	1.29
22	1.02	0.87
23	0.96	1.00

The Bland–Altman limits of agreement approach

If a person scores *higher* at time 1 than time 2, their point lies above the line and if they score *lower* at time 1 than time 2, their point lies below the line. You can see that most people's points lie below the line, meaning we would expect their score at time 2 to be lower than their score at time 1, so despite the high correlation, they are not scoring the same.

The next question, then, is how different the scores are likely to be. The mean difference is easy, and we can calculate that the average score drops by 0.06 between time 1 and time 2. Not everyone's drops that much, however, and some people's score even goes up. What we want to know is, what is the range of values within which a person's score is likely to be, or in other words, what are the limits of agreement. To do this, we use the *Bland–Altman limits of agreement approach.*

The bad news here is that we don't know of a computer program that can work this out for us. The good news, though, is that it's very easy.

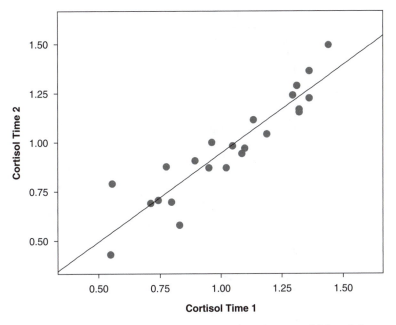

Figure 10.1   Relationship between cortisol at time 1 (10 mins post CO_2) and time 2 (30 mins post CO_2) with line of best fit

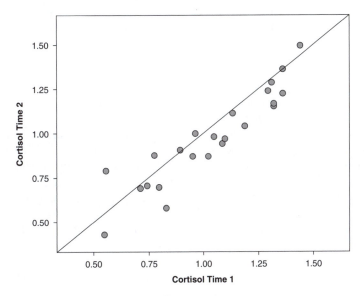

Figure 10.2   Scatterplot with line of equality

Table 10.2 *Calculation of the limits of agreement*

	10 mins post CO_2	30 mins post CO_2	Difference	Mean
1	1.32	1.15	0.17	1.235
2	1.36	1.36	0	1.36
3	1.09	0.94	0.15	1.015
4	1.36	1.23	0.13	1.295
5	0.78	0.88	−0.1	0.83
6	0.95	0.87	0.08	0.91
7	1.05	0.98	0.07	1.015
8	0.9	0.91	−0.01	0.905
9	1.44	1.49	−0.05	1.465
10	1.29	1.24	0.05	1.265
11	1.1	0.97	0.13	1.035
12	0.83	0.58	0.25	0.705
13	0.56	0.79	−0.23	0.675
14	0.8	0.7	0.1	0.75
15	0.55	0.43	0.12	0.49
16	1.19	1.04	0.15	1.115
17	0.74	0.71	0.03	0.725
18	1.32	1.17	0.15	1.245
19	0.71	0.69	0.02	0.7
20	1.13	1.11	0.02	1.12
21	1.31	1.29	0.02	1.3
22	1.02	0.87	0.15	0.945
23	0.96	1	−0.04	0.98

Step 1. For each person, calculate the difference between their time 1 score and their time 2 score (this is shown in Table 10.2).

Step 2. Draw a scatterplot, with the mean score for each person (from Table 10.2) on the x-axis (see Table 10.2), and the difference on the y-axis. (see Figure 10.3).

Step 3. Find the mean of the difference scores. In our example, this is 0.06. This means that, on average, people were 0.06 higher at time 1 than time 2.

Step 4. Find the standard deviation of the difference score. In our data this is found to be 0.10.

Step 5. Find the 95% limits of agreement. If our data are normally distributed, we expect 95% of our sample to lie with 1.96 (or approximately 2) standard deviations of the mean difference, so the limits of agreement are given by

$$\text{Lower limit} = \text{mean} - 2 \times \text{SD} = 0.0591 - 2 \times 0.1049 = -0.1507$$

$$\text{Upper limit} = \text{mean} + 2 \times \text{SD} = 0.0591 + 2 \times 0.1049 = 0.2689$$

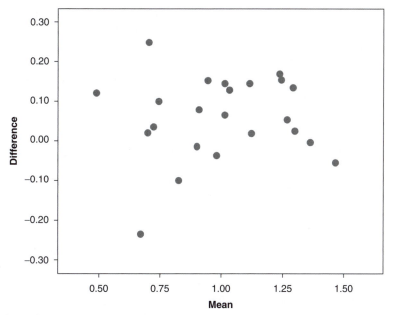

Figure 10.3   Mean plotted against difference

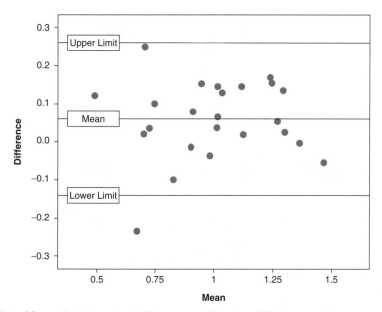

Figure 10.4   Mean plotted against difference, with mean difference and upper and lower limits marked

This means that for any particular score at time 2, we would expect the time 1 score to be 0.6 higher. However, it is likely that it will vary around this, and it will be between 0.15 lower, and 0.27 higher.

Step 6. Add horizontal lines to the scatterplot, showing the limits of agreement, and the mean difference (Figure 10.4). One way of checking the plot is to see if approximately 95% of cases do lie between the upper and lower limits. We would therefore expect 1 in 20 cases to fall outside the limits of agreement. In our data, we have 23 cases and one of them does fall outside the limit.

The difficult thing to do is to decide whether your limits are sufficiently small to say that the measures do agree with each other. This is not an answer that the statistics can give, so you have to decide, from your knowledge of the measure, whether the results are sufficiently similar that they could be said to have not changed.

Test yourself

A researcher develops two versions of a test of non-verbal reasoning for children. The two versions of the test are designed to be interchangeable and equivalent. They give the test to a group of children, and calculate the correlation, which they found to be 0.92. Which of the following statements can be said to be true?

(a) The two tests give very similar scores.
(b) Knowing someone's score on one test will give a prediction about the average score we would expect someone to get on the other test.
(c) Knowing someone's score on one test will give us the likely range of values for the other test.

Answers are given at the end of the chapter.

INTERNAL CONSISTENCY: COEFFICIENT ALPHA

'Measure twice, cut once' is a common saying (*if you say so – Ed*). It refers to work with materials. If you're making some curtains, for example, and don't measure it quite right then when you cut the material you find you have to cut it again to make it fit. The better approach is to take extra care with the measure so you are not messing about later on. Of course you might choose to buy standard length curtains, which also solves the problem.

When people say 'measure twice, cut once' they might not realise it, but they are talking about the internal consistency of a measure. Let's explain:

If you want to know how extravert someone is, you don't ask them one question:

- 'Do you often tell jokes at parties?'

Similarly, if you want to know how intelligent someone is, you don't just ask them one question:

- 'Which number comes next: 1, 4, 9, 16, 25, …'.

The reason why we don't do this, is that each time we measure something, using an item or using a tape measure, we are likely to make errors. In the case of measuring the material using a ruler, we will get the measure wrong, maybe because the ruler slipped a little. In the case of the question about extraversion, it may be that the respondent is extravert but can't remember jokes. In the case of the measure of intelligence, it may be that the person was asked the same question yesterday. (The question we used comes up in lots of intelligence tests, and once you know the answer it's easy. Oh, the answer is 36, by the way.) So what do we do? We measure twice, or even more than twice. We measure the thing we are trying to measure lots of times. Each time we measure something, the accuracy of the overall measurement should increase.

Optional Extra: Lots of essays to write?

Why do you have to do so many essays and exams? Although it may seem as if your tutors set assignments simply to be cruel, this is not the case and they do it for good reasons. Although your tutors probably do enjoy being cruel, they almost certainly don't enjoy marking assignments. The good reason is that each assignment is attempting to measure something like 'your knowledge and skill at psychology'. This is a somewhat tricky thing to measure, and so to ensure that it is measured as accurately as possible, so that you leave with the correct grade, the more times it is measured (and hence the more assignments you write) the better. Sorry.

If you're interested, this sort of issue is discussed in Newstead and Dennis (1994) and Newstead (2004).

So, we know that the more times we ask a question, the more accurate the measure becomes; that's easy. But how close are we likely to be? Well, that depends on how accurate the questions are, in the first place. Imagine that we were using a very, very accurate laser to measure a 10 cm square of paper. If we measure once, we know we are going to be very close to the right length. If we measure 10 times, we know we will be incredibly close to the right length. However, if we estimated the size of our square by asking the next 10 people we met to draw a square that estimates the size of our paper, then the average of all their answers probably wouldn't be very close. However, the more people we asked, the more accurate the answer would be. But let's imagine that we didn't know anything about measuring and let's pretend we don't know if asking people is any better than using a special clever laser device that's extremely accurate. How would we know which was the better way of measuring – or, in other words, which was the more *reliable* way of measuring?

It's easy because we just have to see how close together the different measures are. If the measures are all close to each other, we know that the average measure is likely to be close to the **true measure**. If the measures are all far apart, it's likely that the average measure is further from the true measure.

Optional Extra: What's a true measure?

In **psychometric** theory, we have to assume that for whatever we are measuring there is a 'true score' for any individual. That's easy when it comes to the size of a square because there is a true score for any square. However, it's not necessarily so easy to say that a measure of intelligence, for example, has a 'true score'. We have to distinguish between true score intelligence and true score motivation, because people who try hard will probably do better. If there isn't a 'true score' this doesn't really work.

The second issue about true score is harder to think about. With the size of a square, there is an objective size of a square. We said that if you averaged everyone's guesses about the size of the square, you will eventually get to the size of the square. That wasn't strictly true. People might be biased so we might find that the average value given for the size of the square was 11 cm, not 10 cm. If we were really interested in the size of the square this would be a problem. Luckily for us, psychological measures aren't like physical measures in that there are no external units like metres to base the measures on. In our psychological measures if we say that someone scored 11 on a test, we cannot take a ruler and say 'Ah! but the real score is 10!'. In psychology we use all our measures *relatively*, so we just say that Phil scores 10 points higher than Jeremy on a measure of procrastination. It doesn't matter what the true score is, it just matters that he is 10 points higher.

We measure how far apart measures are with the standard deviation or **variance** (remember that the variance is just the square of the standard deviation i.e. var = sd^2). So, we can calculate the variance of the measures and then we have some idea of how far apart the measures are. We would expect that the measures using the laser would have a smaller variance than the measures using people's guesses, hence we know that we will get a good estimate from the laser with fewer measures than it took to get a good estimate just by asking people.

We've got one more problem. In our example so far, we've got two measures: one is good, and therefore has a small variance (the laser), and one is bad, and therefore has a large variance (asking people). The final problem that we have is that when we collect psychological data we don't have two measures, one of which we know to be better, we've only got one measure and we don't know if it is good or bad. And if we don't know if it's good or bad, we don't know how large the variance needs to be to show that our measure is good or bad.

Coefficient alpha

We can estimate how good or bad our measure is by comparing the variance of scores for individuals taking the test with the variance of scores on the test items. We can calculate the variance within a measure, so we ask lots of people to assess the size of our square, or we give a large number of questions to a person, add up each person's score, and get the variance of that. So, we have two measures of variance: the variance between the items (within a person) and the variance between the people. Now, as you can imagine, this takes rather a lot of working out – we need to calculate a variance for every person that we measure and, as we saw in Chapter 2, if calculating variance once is a bit fiddly, calculating it for every person is a pain.

When we know these two variances we can calculate something called **Coefficient Alpha** (or often **Cronbach's alpha**) which was first described in a paper by Cronbach (1951) though he wasn't the first person to talk about this sort of thing (see Stigler's law, page 20). Alpha can be thought of in lots of ways, but the most useful is that it is an estimate of the correlation between the true score and the measured score. That is, it tells us how close our measured score, that we get from the test, is to our true score. We know that this sounds a bit weird – how can it estimate a correlation with something that we can't measure, and can't even be sure exists? Well, it can, but it's a bit technical and lots of books on psychometrics cover this. We recommend you to either of our favourites, which are Nunnally and Bernstein, (1992) and Streiner and Norman (2003).

We don't want to have to calculate a lot of variances, because it's hard work. If we can assume (or make) the variance of each item equal, we can use a much simpler formula instead, which is based on the correlations, called **standardised alpha**. (We've still got a lot of correlations to calculate though.) We calculate the average correlation, which we call $\bar{r}$, and use this in the following formula.

$$\alpha = \frac{k \times \bar{r}}{1 + (k - 1) \times \bar{r}}$$

where k is the number of items in the scale.

Let's look at an example. Hughes, Galbraith and Torrance (2005) were interested in how well children thought they could do in different subjects at school.[1] They asked children to respond to the following statements about each subject:

1.   I can understand what is taught in [subject].
2.   I can do an excellent job on the problems and tasks assigned for [subject].
3.   I can learn what I need to do for [subject].
4.   I can organise my work in [subject].
5.   I can get a good grade in my [subject] GCSE.

---

[1] Thanks to Mark Torrance of Staffordshire University for allowing us to use these data.

Table 10.3 *Correlations between items*

English Q1	1.000				
English Q2	0.779	1.000			
English Q3	0.794	0.787	1.000		
English Q4	0.722	0.724	0.764	1.000	
English Q5	0.702	0.722	0.734	0.722	1.000
Maths Q1	0.332	0.262	0.297	0.246	0.262	1.000
	English Q1	English Q2	English Q3	English Q4	English Q5	Maths Q1

The response was on a 7-point scale, from 'not well at all' to 'very well'.

Table 10.3 shows the correlations between the five items for English, and the first item for maths. We find the mean correlation (excluding the 1.000s) and then enter that into the formula. The mean correlation is 0.589, and there are six items, so $k = 6$. We pop the numbers into the formula and calculate away.

$$\alpha = \frac{k \times \bar{r}}{1 + (k - 1) \times \bar{r}}$$

$$= \frac{6 \times 0.589}{1 + (6 - 1) \times 0.589}$$

$$= \frac{3.534}{1 + 5 \times 0.589}$$

$$= \frac{3.534}{3.945}$$

$$= 0.896$$

(By the way, if we didn't want to make the assumption that the variances are equal, and calculated alpha the long way around, it comes to 0.892, so it doesn't matter too much in this case, and we can take the simpler route with confidence.)

A useful thing to do sometimes is to calculate the value of alpha without one of the items in the scale. We can then see if that item fits in well with the rest of the items. In our example, we have five questions about English, and one question about maths. It seems likely that the maths question may not be improving the scale, so we would calculate alpha with that item removed. If we were to remove the item, and recalculate alpha, we find that the reliability increases to 0.94. If we remove any other item from the scale, we find that the reliability would decrease (remember that longer scales are more reliable, so adding an item to the scale should make alpha increase.) We can use this technique to select and reject items and therefore increase the reliability of our scale.

Common Mistake: Reversing items

Many questionnaires measuring personality and attitudes have 'reverse-scored' items. That is, some items ask the question one way:

Do you like to tell jokes to groups of people?

Others ask a similar question, but in the opposite direction:

Would other people describe you as quiet?

Obviously the two items are asking similar questions, but in different directions. If you say 'Yes' to the first, you are likely to say 'No' to the second. Hence, you need to reverse-score the items before you attempt to calculate alpha.

Optional Extra: Alpha and split-half reliability

A second method to assess the reliability of a test is to use the **split-half method**. We divide the test into two smaller tests, and correlate the two. A higher correlation between the measures is indicative of higher reliability. However, the split-half correlation suffers from one obvious problem, and one not so obvious.

The obvious problem is that there is more than one way to split a test. If you split the items into halves in different ways, you'll find that you get a different test–retest correlation.

The less obvious problem is that the two tests are shorter. We've already said that a shorter test is a less reliable test, so we are likely to underestimate the reliability of the test, unless we account for this.

Coefficient alpha solves both of these problems. First, alpha is the average of all the split-half correlations that you could do. Second, alpha takes into account the test length, and corrects for it.

Although you often read about split-half correlation in textbooks, it's almost never used in practice. It is, however, a useful way to think about alpha, which is why we've put it here.

How high should alpha be?

It's often asked how high alpha should be before you can say that your scale is reliable. Unfortunately, and not altogether surprisingly, there's not a very easy answer. One value that is mentioned a lot is 0.7. If your alpha is above 0.7, then the reliability is 'high enough'. High enough for what, you might ask, but let's not go there.

Optional Extra: Why 0.7?

In Chapter 8, we explained that the square of the correlation gave the proportion of variance shared by two variables. If we think of alpha as a correlation, then squaring 0.7 gives 0.49, which is just under 0.5. If your value of alpha is higher than 0.7, then more than half of the variance in the measure is 'true score variance'.

Values of alpha tend to vary according to the kind of measure that you are using. For example, the Eysenck Personality Questionnaire (EPQ) measures three personality traits: extraversion (E), neuroticism (N) and psychoticism (P). The underlying constructs of extraversion and neuroticism are clearer and better defined than psychoticism, and so the alphas for extraversion and neuroticism tend to be higher. Miles, Shevlin and McGhee (1999), for example, found alphas above 0.8 for N and E, but less than 0.7 for P (shown in Table 10.4).

Table 10.4 *Alphas for the difference subscales of the EPQ*

Scale	Group	Alpha
Extraversion	Male	0.849
	Female	0.862
Neuroticism	Male	0.833
	Female	0.824
Psychoticism	Male	0.543
	Female	0.622

Can alpha be too high?

Yes, is the short answer. If alpha is very high (let's say 0.95 or greater), there are two possible things going on. First, your items may be very highly correlated. This means that they are all measuring the same thing to such an extent that they are all almost the same question. For example, a measure of extraversion should reflect all the different aspects of extraversion (warmth, gregariousness, assertiveness, activity, excitement seeking, positive emotions). If your alpha of a measure of extraversion is 0.95, it is unlikely that it is measuring all those different things.

Table 10.5   *Alpha, given different values of mean correlation and numbers of items*

Number of items	$r = 0.4$	$r = 0.3$	$r = 0.1$
2	0.57	0.46	0.18
3	0.67	0.56	0.25
4	0.73	0.63	0.31
5	0.77	0.68	0.36
10	0.87	0.81	0.53
20	0.93	0.90	0.69
30	0.95	0.93	0.77
40	0.96	0.94	0.82
50	0.97	0.96	0.85
60	0.98	0.96	0.87
70	0.98	0.97	0.89
80	0.98	0.97	0.90
90	0.98	0.97	0.91
100	0.99	0.98	0.92

However, the second way of making the alpha very high is to have a longer test. The longer the test, the higher alpha will be. There isn't a statistical problem with the test having a high value for alpha if that value has arisen because of the length of the test, but there might be a practical one.

Let's explore this a little in Table 10.5. This shows three different values for the mean correlation between items and numbers of items from 2 to 100. Notice that as the number of items increases, the reliability increases. In fact, even with a mean correlation between the items of 0.1 you can, with enough items, obtain a respectable value of alpha.

We said that there's nothing statistically wrong with this, and there isn't. But asking people to complete a 100-item questionnaire could be a problem:

- People are going to get bored, and stop concentrating, or just stop, before they get to the end.
- People are never going to agree to take part in a study of yours again (so no test–retest data for you).
- You're going to need to use a lot of paper.[2]

Looking at the table, you could have got an alpha of 0.77 (which isn't bad at all) with a 30-item questionnaire, and avoided those problems. In short, if your alpha is very high, you may well have too many items in your questionnaire, and you can cut it down.

---

[2] Which is bound to make somebody sad.

RELIABILITY FOR CATEGORICAL DATA: COHEN'S KAPPA

With categorical data, we need a slightly different way of thinking about reliability – a correlation isn't really useful any more. The most common problem where this occurs is when two raters are attempting to make decisions about something, for example, whether an individual is depressed or not, or whether a face is happy or not. Although we could calculate the (phi) correlation coefficient (see page 219) this doesn't really tell us what we want to know. The problem with categorical data is that you can get a lot of agreement that appears just by chance so it looks like we agree when actually we don't.

Let's look at an example. Sid and Chardonnay go to the races. They watch the horses go by and try to decide which ones to put their money on. Sid is very good at this. Chardonnay, however, has no idea, but doesn't want to look stupid in front of Sid. Chardonnay knows that 90% of the time, Sid says he shouldn't put his money on a horse. Chardonnay has no idea what he's saying, but she knows that 90% of the time she should say no, so she does this randomly. They both look at 100 horses, and make a decision about whether it's worth placing a bet. The results are shown in Table 10.6. At first, it appears that the two have agreed to say no 81 times, and to say yes once, so overall they have agreed 82 times (which, handily, is 82% of the time). They have disagreed a total of 18 times, so Chardonnay feels that she has got away with her ignorance.

Table 10.6   *Results of study of gambling*

		Sid says		
		No	Yes	Total
Chardonnay	No	81	9	90
says	Yes	9	1	10
Total		90	10	100

However, let's think about this a bit more. We know that Sid was going to say no (about) 90% of the time, and so he would say no about 90 times. We know that Chardonnay was also planning to say no about 90% of the time. If we calculate what 90% of 90% is, we find it's 0.90×0.90, which makes 0.81, or 81%. It turns out that we would have expected agreement about saying no 81% of the time, which is exactly what we have got. Similarly, if Chardonnay says 'yes' 1 time in 10, and Sid says 'yes' 1 time in 10, we would expect both of them to say 'yes' 1 time in 100, giving another 1% agreement. We got a total of 82% agreement, which is exactly what we would have expected to get by chance.

Cohen's kappa is a measure of agreement. Specifically, it is the proportion of agreement, excluding the amount which is chance agreement. In the above example, we got 82%

agreement, which is exactly what we would have got by chance. There is no more agreement than by chance, and so our Cohen's kappa is zero.

We can think of Cohen's kappa as the proportion of agreement that is above the level we would expect by chance.

Let's look at a more serious example so we can see how kappa is calculated. Feldman, Cohen, Doyle, Skoner and Gwaltney (1999) were interested in looking at how different people responded to being exposed to a cold virus. They took two different measures of whether a person had a cold: a subjective measure, and an objective measure. For the subjective measure they asked the participant if they had any symptoms of a cold (congestion, runny nose, sneezing, etc.). For the objective measure they collected and weighed all the participant's used tissues, and performed nasal washes to test for viral infection. (We don't really know what a nasal wash is, and we're glad that we don't do that kind of research.)

Of their 276 people, they found that 77 (28%) had a cold by both measures; 32 (12%) said they didn't have a cold, but did have the presence of viruses, which suggested they actually did have a cold; 32 (12%) said they had a cold, but the objective measures said they didn't; and 135 (48%) didn't have a cold by either measure.

We can see that 28% + 48% = 76% showed agreement between both measures of whether they had a cold or not, but we would like to know how much agreement there was above the level which we would expect by chance.

Calculating kappa

Step 1: Enter the data into a contingency table, such as shown in Table 10.7. Notice that we have labelled the cells *A*, *B*, *C* and *D*. The cells where there is agreement are *A* and *D*, the cells where there is disagreement are *B* and *C*.

Table 10.7   *Contingency table showing results from Feldman et al.*

		Subjective Measure		
		Yes	No	Total
Objective	Yes	*A*: 77	*B*: 32	109
Measure	No	*C*: 32	*D*: 135	167
	Total	109	167	276

Step 2: We calculate the expected frequencies (which we encountered in Chapter 7, on page 184) – but only for cells A and D. In case you have forgotten (and let's face it, it's not the sort of thing that you need cluttering your head) expected values are calculated using:

$$E = \frac{R \times C}{T}$$

where E is the expected value, R is the row total for the cell, C is the column total for the cell and T is the grand total. For cell A, the expected value is:

$$E = 109 \times 109/276 = 43.0$$

For cell D, the expected value is:

$$E = 167 \times 167/276 = 101.0$$

Step 3: Calculate kappa (κ), for which the formula is

$$\kappa = \frac{(A + D) - (E(A) + E(D))}{N - (E(A) + E(D))}$$

Where A and D are the values in cells A and D, and E(A) and E(D) are the expected values for cells A and D (which earlier we just called E), and N is the total number of people. Substituting our numbers into the formula gives us:

$$\kappa = \frac{(A + D) - (E(A) + E(D))}{N - (E(A) + E(D))}$$

$$= \frac{(77 + 135) - (43 + 101)}{276 - (43 + 101)} = \frac{212 - 144}{276 - 144} = \frac{68}{132} = 0.51$$

Interpretation of kappa

Altman (1991) – yes, that's the same one as Bland and Altman – suggested the following guidelines:

- Less than 0.20: poor agreement
- 0.20 to 0.40: fair agreement
- 0.40 to 0.60: moderate agreement
- 0.60 to 0.80: good agreement
- 0.80 to 1.00: very good agreement

Of course, these are only guidelines. You should interpret kappa in terms of what you are doing. The fact that kappa was 0.5 (moderate agreement) in two ways of deciding if someone has a cold may well be interesting, and we could happily describe that as moderate agreement. However, if we were deciding whether a person should be thrown off their university course for failing, and we only had a kappa of 0.5, that would be rather poor agreement.

Extending kappa

Kappa can be extended in three ways: multiple raters, multiple categories, and ordinal data.

- *Multiple raters.* We have only shown how kappa is calculated with two raters, but the number of raters can be increased, and the principle is the same – how much agreement is there above that which we would expect by chance? With three raters we need to have a 2×2×2 contingency table, which is quite hard to think about, and the difficulty of thinking about it increases rapidly each time we add a rater.
- *Multiple categories.* We can extend kappa to multiple categories, for example, two psychiatrists may decide whether a patient is depressed, anxious, both, or neither. Again, the principle remains the same, kappa is still the amount of agreement we have above that which we would expect by chance.
- *Ordinal data.* We can use kappa when we have categories which are ordinal – that is, they go in an order. An example of this might be if we asked two raters to decide if two children were friends, were neutral, or disliked each other. These categories are not completely unrelated because they go in a clear order: friends, neutral, enemies. In this case, we use weighted kappa. We weight the level of disagreement by the distance between the measures. If friends scores 3, neutral 2, and enemies 1; then a rating disagreement of friends versus neutral scores 1 because it is a minor disagreement as the categories are adjacent. On the other hand, a rating of friends versus enemies scores 2, as the categories are not adjacent and this is therefore a bigger disagreement. Of course, the problem here is deciding what the distances are. From friends to neutral seems like a smaller jump than from neutral to enemies. Sometimes people square the distance between them, if the scores are 1 unit apart, they score 1, if they are 2 units apart, they score 4, etc.

SUMMARY

This chapter has looked at the measurement of psychological qualities. It has shown why you can't just take numbers at face value and why you need to calculate the level of reliability of your test, and shown you how to do it. It has also looked at some of the pitfalls of using the standard tests of reliability and what you should do about them.

Test yourself answer

(a) No. There is no reason why they give similar scores – a high correlation means that there is a strong linear relationship between the two sets of scores.
(b) As long as we have sufficient information to calculate the regression line, then we can know this (means and SDs of the two measures, along with the correlation).
(c) No, we cannot calculate the likely score on one test, based on the other if we only know the correlation.

USING SPSS

Test–retest reliability (correlation)

Doing test–retest reliability in SPSS is just a matter of using correlation, so, if you don't mind, have a look at Chapter 8, where this is shown. Thanks.

Bland–Altman limits of agreement

SPSS does not automatically calculate the limits of agreement, but it's not very hard.

The first stage is to draw a scatterplot of the data, with a line of equality (not a line of best fit). Select **Graphs ➢ Scatter/Dot**:

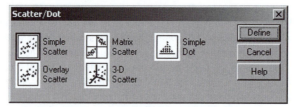

Make sure that **Simple Scatter** is selected (it will be if you haven't done anything else), and click **Define**.

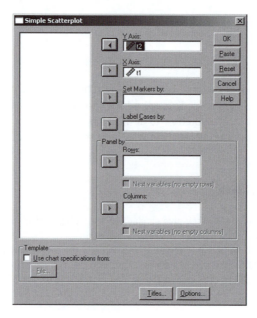

Put one of your measures in the X **Axis box**, and one in the **Y Axis box** (it doesn't really matter which way around) and click **OK**.

A scatterplot appears in the Output window. Double-click on that scatterplot to edit it. Then right-click on the graph, and a context menu appears. From this, select **Add Reference Line from Equation**.

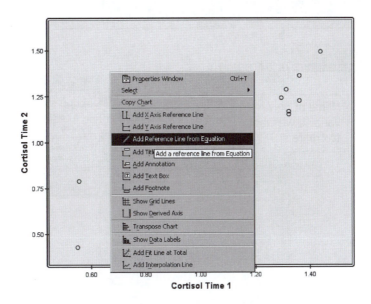

Set **Y-Intercept** to 0, and **slope** to 1.

Click **Apply**, and the line appears on your graph.

The next stage is to compute the mean of the two scores, and the difference between the two scores. To do this, we use the **Transform ➤ Compute command**. The **Compute Variable** dialog box is shown below:

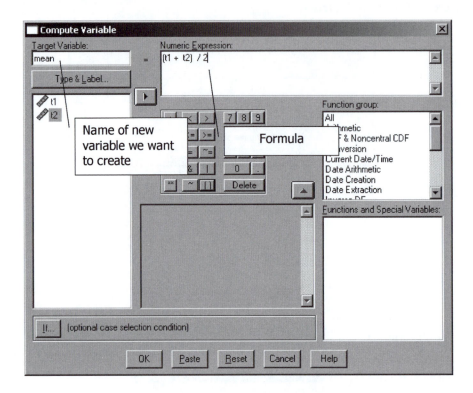

In the box on the left, we type the name of the new variable we want to create. In the box on the right, we type the formula that creates that variable. (Notice that there's an equals sign between them.) In the case of the mean, in the formula box, we write:

$$(t1 + t2) / 2$$

In the case of the difference, in the formula box we write:

$$t1 - t2$$

We then find the mean and standard deviation of the difference. There are many ways to do this; however, we can use **Analyse ➤ Descriptive Statistics ➤ Descriptives**:

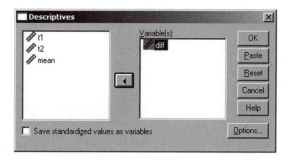

Select the variable called diff, and click **OK**.

Descriptive Statistics

	Mean	Std. Deviation
diff	.06	.105
Valid N (listwise)		

We then use the formula on page 180 to calculate the upper and lower limits of agreement. This gives a difference of 0.06, with limits from −0.15 to 0.27.

To draw the scatterplot, select **Graphs ≻ Scatter/Dot**.
Put mean in the X Axis box, and diff on the Y Axis box. Click **OK**.

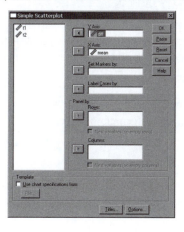

Double-click the chart to edit it, and then right-click on the chart. The context menu pops up:

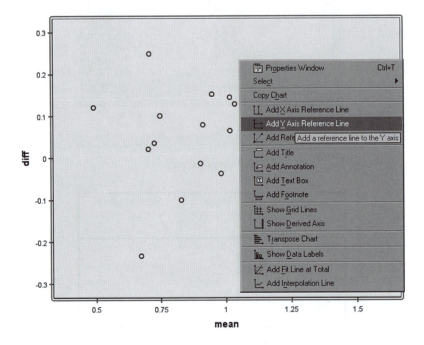

Click on **Add Y Axis Reference Line**, and change the value in the box to 0.06.

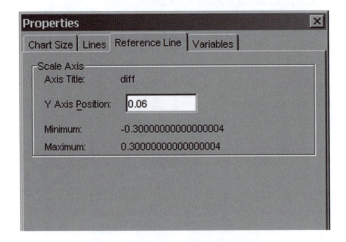

Right-click again, and add another line for the upper limit at 0.27, and again for the lower limit, at −0.15. Your graph will then look like Figure 10.4.

Coefficient alpha

SPSS calculates alpha using the Reliability Analysis command. Select **Analyze** ➔ **Scale** ➔ **Reliability Analysis**. Select the variables you are interested in, and put them into the **Items** box.

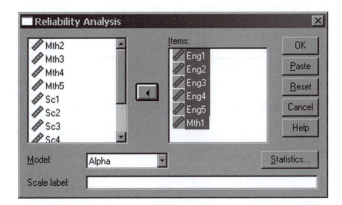

Notice that the model that is selected is Alpha by default. Click on **Statistics**.

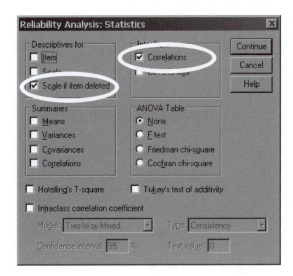

Select **Scale if item deleted** and **Inter-Item Correlations**. Press **Continue** and OK.

The first part of the output is the reliability statistics. Two values for alpha are given: the usual value and the standardised value.

Reliability Statistics

Cronbach's Alpha	Cronbach's Alpha Based on Standardized Items	N of Items
.892	.896	6

Next are the inter-item correlations:

Inter-Item Correlation Matrix

	Eng1	Eng2	Eng3	Eng4	Eng5	Mth1
Eng1	1.000	.779	.794	.722	.702	.332
Eng2	.779	1.000	.787	.724	.722	.262
Eng3	.794	.787	1.000	.764	.734	.297
Eng4	.722	.724	.764	1.000	.722	.246
Eng5	.702	.722	.734	.722	1.000	.262
Mth1	.332	.262	.297	.246	.262	1.000

Finally, there is a table showing the scale properties if each item is not included. Of most interest to us is the final column: Cronbach's alpha if item deleted.

Item-Total Statistics

	Scale Mean if Item Deleted	Scale Variance if Item Deleted	Corrected Item-Total Correlation	Squared Multiple Correlation	Cronbach's Alpha if Item Deleted
Eng1	24.4585	29.165	.828	.715	.855
Eng2	24.6941	29.296	.811	.711	.858
Eng3	24.4857	29.263	.842	.748	.854
Eng4	24.5185	29.135	.782	.664	.862
Eng5	24.6063	29.335	.773	.635	.864
Mth1	24.6655	35.180	.313	.115	.935

Kappa

SPSS calculates kappa using the Crosstabs command – the same one we used to calculate χ^2. First though, a couple of warnings: SPSS will only calculate kappa for two measurements or raters. Second, SPSS will assume that the measures are categorical, not ordinal, and will not do weighted kappa.

To calculate kappa in SPSS, select **Analyse → Descriptive Statistics → Crosstabs**. Put one of the variables into the row, and one of them into the columns (it doesn't matter which way around).

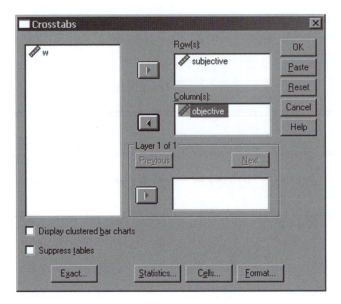

Click on **Statistics**, and choose **Kappa**.

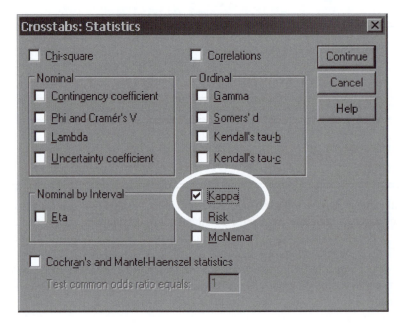

Press **Continue** and **OK**.

The output comes in two parts. First, the contingency table – this just reproduces what we already knew:

		Objective		Total
		No	Yes	
Subjective	No	135	32	167
	Yes	32	77	109
Total		167	109	276

Second, the kappa statistics:

		Value	Asymp. Std. Error[a]	Approx. T[b]	Approx. Sig.
Measure of Agreement	Kappa	.515	.053	8.553	.000
N of Valid Cases		276			

a. Not assuming the null hypothesis
b. Using the asymptotic standard error assuming the null hypothesis

11

Thinking some more about statistics

What's in this chapter?

- Problems with significance tests
- Power analysis
- Meta-analysis
- Bayesian analysis

KEY TERMS

Bayesian statistics
confidence intervals
effect size
frequentists
meta-analysis
null hypothesis
power analysis

prosecutor's fallacy
p-value
replicability
significance tests
type I error
type II error

INTRODUCTION

We've called this chapter 'Thinking some more about statistics'. You might be surprised by that. In fact you might be thinking that we've just spent almost a whole book doing quite a lot of thinking about statistics, and now you are saying that we have to think more? In the book, we've been thinking about how to *do* statistics and, in particular, we've been interested in calculating *p*-values. What we've been thinking about less is *why* we do statistical analysis (and calculate *p*-values), and what those analyses (and *p*-values) *mean*.

So, here's what we're going to do. In the first half of the chapter, we will look at some of the problems of significance testing. In the second half of the chapter, we will look at some of the solutions that have been suggested for these problems.

PROBLEMS WITH SIGNIFICANCE TESTS

There are two problems with **significance tests**.

- They don't tell us what we want to know. This is bad enough. But it's made worse by the second problem.
- People think they *do* tell us what we want to know.

Let's reiterate a little of Chapter 4, and remember what a *p*-value actually is, using a test yourself box.

Test yourself 1: What is a p-value?

Suppose that an experiment has been done, and a ***p*-value** of 0.01 has been found. Assume that everything about the study has been done correctly, including the assumptions of the test and the calculations. Which of the following statements can we say is true? You can agree with as many or as few of them as you like.

(a) You have absolutely disproved the null hypothesis (that is, there is no difference between the population means).
(b) You have found the probability of the null hypothesis being true.
(c) You have absolutely proved your experimental hypothesis (that there is a difference between the population means).
(d) You can deduce the probability of the experimental hypothesis being true.
(e) You know, if you decide to reject the null hypothesis, the probability that you are making the wrong decision.
(f) You have a reliable experimental finding in the sense that if, hypothetically, the experiment were repeated a great number of times, you would obtain a significant result on 99% of occasions.

Answers are given at the end of the chapter.

What does a *p*-value tell us?

A *p*-value doesn't tell us any of the things we saw in the box, so what does it tell us? It tells us the probability of an effect of that magnitude (or larger) occurring, if the null hypothesis is correct. Cohen (1994) wrote a famous and highly cited (614 times, when we checked) attack on the use of *p*-values. He thought about calling the use of *p*-values Statistical Hypothesis Inference Testing (think about that) but decided instead on null hypothesis significance testing (NHST). As Cohen put it, 'a *p*-value does not tell us what we want to know, and we so much want to know what we want to know that, out of desperation, we nevertheless believe it does' (p. 997).

What we want to know is 'the probability that the null hypothesis is correct, given that we have got this result'. This sounds very similar to what we said, but it's not, and we'll try to explain why. Because understanding this is a bit tricky, we are going to explain it in two different ways. Before we do that we need a bit of shorthand to make it a bit more readable. Instead of writing 'a result of at least this magnitude' we'll write *D*, and instead of 'null hypothesis is true' we'll write *H*. We hope using these abbreviations will make it a bit more readable.

First explanation

If we have a low *p*-value, this means that the probability of *D* is low if *H* holds. But this does not translate into the probability of *H* given that *D* is true.

Given that you are British, the probability that you are the prime minister is very low. Does this mean that, given that you are the prime minister, the probability that you are British is also low? It does not. Similarly, if the probability of *D*, given *H*, is low, this doesn't tell us much about the probability of *H*, given *D*.

Second explanation

The second way of explaining is called the **prosecutor's fallacy** – this is a fallacy whereby people (usually the prosecutor) believe that they have stronger evidence of guilt than they do, based on probabilities.

Let's consider that there has been a murder. The police have a DNA sample from the murderer, and test people in the country until they get a DNA match (*D*). This happens, and the DNA matches you. (Uh oh.)

The police say that only one person in a million matches that DNA, therefore the chances that you did not commit the homicide (*H*) are one in a million. The police are saying that the probability of you not being the murderer (*H*, the null hypothesis) given the DNA match (*D*, the data) is one in a million. Looks like you are in trouble. Unless, of course, you have read this book. Then you calmly explain to the police that they are getting their probabilities wrong and, in fact, they have used the prosecutor's fallacy. Their one in a million is not the probability of *H* given *D*. The one in a million is the probability of *D* (getting a DNA match) given *H*, that the person who matched the DNA is not the murderer. Given that there are (about) 60 million people in the country, there are probably about 60 people who match, who didn't do the murder and you are just unlucky enough to be one of them. The probability that you are not the murderer is therefore not 1 in 1,000,000, it's close to 59/60 or about 0.98.

What does a *p*-value not tell us?

Let's look again at the questions in the above test yourself box.

(a) You have absolutely disproved the null hypothesis – that is, there is no difference between the population means (34% of students agreed with this, 15% of professors/lecturers, 10% of professors/lecturers teaching statistics).

We know we haven't disproved the null hypothesis. We have found that there is some evidence against it though we don't really know how good that evidence is.

(b) You have found the probability of the null hypothesis being true (32% of students agreed with this, 26% of professors/lecturers, 17% of professors/lecturers teaching statistics).

Nope, we don't know that either.

(c) You have absolutely proved your experimental hypothesis – that there is a difference between the population means (20% of students agreed with this, 13% of professors/lecturers, 10% of professors/lecturers teaching statistics).

We haven't disproved the null, so we certainly haven't proved the alternative.

(d) You can deduce the probability of the experimental hypothesis being true (59% of students, 33% of professors/lecturers, 33% of professors lecturers, 33% of professors/lecturers teaching statistics).

Nope. We can't deduce the probability of it being false, either.

(e) You know, if you decide to reject the null hypothesis, the probability that you are making the wrong decision (68% of students, 67% of professors/lecturers, 73% of professors/lecturers teaching statistics).

This is an interesting one. It was the most popular amongst all groups, and a higher proportion of the professors/lecturers who taught statistics agreed with it than the students. It's still wrong. But the reasons are a bit more complex than the other statements, so we are going to come back to this, when we look at some of the alternatives that have been suggested.

(f) You have a reliable experimental finding in the sense that if, hypothetically, the experiment were repeated a great number of times, you would obtain a significant result on 99% of occasions (41% of students, 49% of professors/lecturers, 37% of professors professors/lecturers teaching statistics).

This is another subtle one. We can know the probability of replication, but it's hard to work out and it's not the sort of thing you can do in your head. We'll come back to this one as well.

Common Mistakes: Using significance tests when you don't have to

The use of significance tests is so pervasive in psychological research that people want to do them really, really badly. They want to do them so badly that they try to squish their data into a significance test, whether it's appropriate or not. People often ask us what sort of statistical test they should do on their data. They say things like:

- 'I think that no 5-year-old children will be able to complete this task. What test should I use?' There is no answer. The only way to reject the null hypothesis that no 5-year-old children can do the task is to give it to *every* 5-year-old child in the world, and show that none of them can do it. If none can, the *p*-value is zero. If any can, the p-value is one.
- 'I think that the standard deviation of this group will be small'. Uh-huh. So what's the null hypothesis? That the standard deviation is large? How large? We have to have a clear null hypothesis to test against, or there is no way of doing a test.
- 'I think that the mean number of questions people will get right is greater than zero'. (These people have often done a statistical test already and sometimes it's significant, sometimes it's not.) If one person gets one question right, the mean is greater than zero.

OK, so we have some problems with significance tests. But what if we pretend all those problems don't exist? Would significance tests be OK? No, they still wouldn't be OK. There are even more reasons why significance testing is flawed.

Nil versus null hypotheses

Our **null hypothesis** is almost always that a difference or a correlation is zero. (There's nothing inherent in significance testing procedures that forces this on us, it's just what everyone uses, almost all the time.) Using a difference of zero is a bit strange, isn't it? What's so special about zero (this is what Cohen has called the 'nil hypothesis') and why do we use a nil hypothesis for a null hypothesis every time?

If we believe that zero is an appropriate null hypothesis, we have to believe that zero is a possible answer. That is, that zero is a likely effect in the population. Is it? Let's look back at some of the examples we've seen in this book.

- In Chapter 5 we looked at the effect of cricket helmets. Is it likely that cricket helmets have absolutely no effect? That is, there would be no difference in the helmet wearers and the

- non-helmet wearers, even if we tested everyone in the world? (We are suggesting it is likely, if we do a significance test with a zero null hypothesis.)
- In Chapter 6 we looked at two treatments for chronic fatigue syndrome. Are we suggesting that there may be absolutely no difference in their effectiveness? Not even the teeniest little bit? (We are, if we do a significance test with a zero null hypothesis.)
- In Chapter 6, we also looked at birth order of people with two conditions. Are we saying that birth order might have absolutely zero effect on your probability of being diagnosed with schizophrenia? Not even a 0.00000000001% higher chance – which could be caused by the elder siblings of schizophrenics driving them to the doctor to get them diagnosed? (We are, if we use a significance test with a zero null hypothesis.)

As Cohen (1988) has put it, 'all null hypotheses ... are false'. Because everything (that we might study) has an effect on everything (that we might study). We are going through the procedures (on which we have spent a lot of pages and a lot of words in this book) to find out if we can reject the null hypothesis. We know that we can reject the null hypothesis before we start. The null hypothesis is wrong. A non-significant result just tells us that we don't know the direction of the effect, whether it is positive, or negative.

Statistical significance and replicability

Another area of confusion in statistical significance testing is **replicability**. We looked at this in (f) above: 'You have a reliable experimental finding in the sense that if, hypothetically, the experiment were repeated a great number of times, you would obtain a significant result on 99% of occasions.' This is wrong. We can calculate the probability of actually replicating a result, at a given significance level. The methods are a bit tricky though, and so rather than cover them here, we direct you to the web page (www.jeremy miles.co.uk/usingstatistics). Let's give the answers here:

First, we carry out a study, and get a p-value of 0.05. You then carry out a study which *exactly* replicates ours in every way (same random sample drawn from same population, same procedure, same measures, same researchers, same time, same day, same room, etc.). What is the probability that you will get a p-value of 0.05 *or less*?

The answer is 50%. Half the time you will successfully replicate my study, and half the time you will not.

What if my p-value was 0.01. What then is the probability that your *exact* replication will give a p-value of 0.05 or less? Think about that before you read on.

You would think that $p = 0.01$ was a reasonably significant result. If we were famous researchers in some area, and you had failed to get a significant result when our result was $p = 0.01$, we would be likely to get into a (perhaps heated) debate. We would try to find flaws in each other's research. We would discuss what was wrong with the other person's procedure or method or measures or laboratory or personality. (You thought scientists were beyond that sort of thing, didn't you? They're not.) We would *not* say, 'Ah well, that happens about a quarter of the time'. Which, in fact, is what does happen. Your probability of getting a p-value less than 0.05 is about 0.73, so slightly more than a quarter of the time, you will fail to replicate my study. But because we don't understand what that p-value means, instead of using our research to build up scientific knowledge in an area, the replication will just lead to obfuscation and confusion. Tversky and Kahneman (1971) suggest that if you replicate a study, you should actually have a larger sample than the original sample.

Schmidt (1996) suggested that this feature of statistical significance testing actually makes it deceptive and harmful. Significance testing creates boundaries and gaps where none exist. The use of significance testing means that we find it hard to build upon knowledge, and so in psychology we don't get an accumulation of knowledge. Findings don't build on other findings, to help us to advance the science. Instead, we have lots of disparate findings but we don't understand which ones are linked by showing the same effect, and which ones are showing different effects. We don't understand when it matters how we measure extraversion, and when it doesn't matter. We can't work out what aspects of a treatment for depression make a difference, and what don't make a difference.

What does a non-significant result mean?

We've seen in the section above that a statistically significant result isn't as useful and informative as we might think. Doing a statistical test is a bit like looking for something. If we find it, we know it's there. If we don't find it, it might still be there, but we just didn't find it.

Test yourself 2

If you do not achieve a statistically significant result in your study, which of the following should you do:

(a) Accept the null hypothesis.
(b) Fail to reject the null hypothesis.
(c) Reject the experimental hypothesis.
(d) Fail to accept the experimental hypothesis.

Answer is given at the end of the chapter.

It is sometimes tempting to try to develop studies that attempt to prove a null hypothesis – you can't do this. You can only say that you have failed to find evidence against the null hypothesis. That does not mean that you have found evidence for it. Absence of evidence is not evidence of absence.

Common Mistake: Stating the obvious

It is very common for students to get this wrong. The worst case of this is where they write something like '25 out of 51 (49%) of participants in group A answered the question correctly, 24 out of 41 (59%) of participants in group B answered the question correctly (OR = 0.68, 95% CI = 0.30, 1.56; $p = 0.363$), therefore the proportions in the two groups are *the same*'. You don't need a significance test to be told that 49% is not the same as 59% – they are plainly not the same.

A non-significant result is only a failure to find evidence that the two groups (or whatever) are different.

Some defences of significance testing

Significance tests are not all completely bad. There are a number of defences that have been put forward for significance testing, sometimes general, and sometimes specific.

Wainer (1999, p. 212) suggested that we could have 'one cheer for null hypothesis significance testing'. Wainer put forward a number of suggestions where a dichotomous result would be interesting, and a highly significant result of a test would be informative and useful. One example Wainer gives is the first known example of a significance test being used (Arbuthnot, 1710, cited in Wainer). Arbuthnot wanted to test the null hypothesis that 'number of supreme beings (gods) = 0' against the alternative hypothesis that 'number of supreme beings (gods) > 0'. Wainer suggests that a highly statistically significant result would be both interesting and informative. (Incidentally, Arbuthnot found what he said was convincing evidence against the null hypothesis.)

A stronger defence was put forward by Frick (1997). He suggests that theories in psychology often make predictions which are only ordinal, or in other words, X will be bigger than Y, and Y will be bigger than Z. (Compare this with theories in, say, physics, which often give exact values for parameters. For example, Einstein predicted in 1915 that the gravitational pull of the sun would deflect light by 1.75 seconds of arc. When readings were taken during an eclipse in 1919 the observed values were found to be 1.98 ± 0.16 and 1.61 ± 0.40 seconds of arc, respectively, which was taken as clear confirmation of Einstein's prediction.) If that's the sort of claim we want to make, then null hypothesis significance tests will serve us fine.

Why 0.05?

The final point that opponents of significance tests make is the arbitrary use of 0.05 as a cut-off for alpha. It seems to be fixed in stone, but no one has ever suggested this. Fisher, who developed much of the logic behind significance tests, suggested that it is one of many appropriate values. He thought that a person who always used 0.05 showed a lack of statistical sophistication (Gigerenzer, 2004), and that a respectable researcher would never use a fixed level. (Gigerenzer also wrote that your chance of finding this written in a psychology text was close to nil. We are glad to prove him wrong.)

Optional Extra: Gerd Gigerenzer

Gigerenzer is a cognitive psychologist, historian of statistics, philosopher and all-round egghead. He often writes about the use of statistics from the perspective of a cognitive psychologist, for example in the book *Cognition as Intuitive Statistics* (Gigerenzer and Murray, 1987). He also has written about the history of statistics, from a cognitive/ philosophical perspective. In his book *The Empire of Chance* (Gigerenzer et al., 1989) he discusses how and why people started using statistical tests when they did, noting that the mathematics had existed for a couple of hundred years, but no one had thought of developing statistical tests. He has written a great deal on the ways in which statistics are interpreted, for example in a book chapter called 'The Superego, the Ego, and the Id in statistical reasoning' (Gigerenzer, 1993). (We like this because he calls the current teaching of statistics 'bastardised'; Jeremy once wrote a job application letter with the word 'bastard' in it, to see if he could still get the job. He didn't.) He has discussed the impact of a failure to understand statistics in real-life arena, such as the book *Calculated Risks: How to Know When Numbers Deceive You* (Gigerenzer, 2002). This book explains how a failure of policy makers to understand statistics can lead (and has led) to some public health catastrophes such as a decision in Florida that people should be told of the results of their HIV tests. This was catastrophic because no one understood, or explained to the recipients, that a positive result still probably means that they are not HIV positive. Some people lost their jobs, some were divorced, some committed suicide, as a result of the (probably false) information.

WHAT SHOULD WE DO INSTEAD?

We've seen that use of significance testing is considered by many people to be bad. So, what should we do instead? Unfortunately, there is no straightforward answer. (If there was, we'd all be doing it.) There are several things that can either supplement or potentially replace conventional significance tests, and we'll have a look at them now.

Power analysis

Power analysis is a supplement to significance testing, and not a replacement for it. If we think about whether or not we get a statistically significant result, there are three things that have an effect on this.

1. Alpha: the *p*-value cut-off. The smaller the value of alpha that we use, the harder it is to get a significant result.
2. Sample size: the more people we have in the study, the more likely it is that we will get a significant result.
3. The population effect size. The population effect size is the size of the effect in the population from which we have taken our sample. There are many different measures of effect size – in fact there is a different one for each statistical test. The simplest to think about is the correlation. The population correlation is the size of the correlation, if we were to assess everyone in the population. The larger this is, the easier it will be to get a significant result.

If we know these three values, we can calculate the fourth value we are interested in:

4. Power or beta. Where alpha is the probability of making a **type I error** (a false positive), beta is the probability of making a **type II error** (failing to spot an effect). The power of the study is given by 1–beta, and the power of the study is the probability of getting a significant result, given that the effect in the population is equal to the **effect size.** (We met beta in Chapter 8.)

Power analysis involves calculations that are really, really hard. Luckily, there are computer programs that will do the calculations for us – and, even better, some of them are free. A couple that we like are *GPower* and *PS: Power and Sample Size* (and they are linked from the site: www.jeremymiles.co.uk/usingstatistics). If we tell such programs three of the values that are required in a power analysis, they will tell us the fourth. There are two ways to use power analysis: a priori, when you are planning a study, and post hoc, when you are evaluating a study.

A priori power analysis

Suppose we are planning a study to find a correlation. We should decide on a value for the smallest correlation that would still be interesting. We might do this based on prior research, or we might do it based on the ability to predict particular values. If we were a bit more desperate, we might choose to base it on Cohen's criterion which we met in Chapter 8: a small correlation is 0.1, a medium correlation is 0.3 and a large correlation is 0.5. In our example we think that we might be interested in finding a medium correlation, and we are going to use a value of alpha of 0.05.

We then need to decide on the power. If there is a medium (r = 0.3) correlation in the population, how likely do we want it to be that we will find that? This is a rather hard question, and it is often moderated by the sample size (but we'll come to that in a minute). Again, there are conventions and some people use 0.80, that is, they want an 80% chance of a significant result. Others prefer 0.90 or, in other words, a 90% chance of a significant result.

Table 11.1 shows the sample size required to detect correlations of different sizes. To use the table, we look at the correlation that we are interested in detecting, in the left-hand column. We then select the power to detect a statistically significant effect (using alpha = 0.05) and read the number off to reveal the required sample size.

Table 11.1 *A priori power table for correlations.*
Values show sample size required for given population
effect size and power

	Power	
r	**90%**	**80%**
0.05	4195	3134
0.10	1043	779
0.15	459	343
0.20	255	191
0.25	160	120
0.30	109	82
0.35	78	59
0.40	58	44
0.45	44	33
0.50	34	26
0.55	27	21
0.60	21	17
0.65	17	13
0.70	14	11
0.75	11	9
0.80	9	7
0.85	7	3

For our analysis, we want to be able to detect a correlation of $r = 0.3$. For our study to have 80% power, that is, an 80% chance of a significant result, we would require a sample size of 82 individuals (if the population correlation is 0.3). For our study to have 90% power, we would require 109 people. That is, for a power increase of just over 10%, we need about a third more people.

Power analysis before a study is carried out makes our study more useful because we ensure that we have some idea of what we are looking for, and we ensure that we have a decent chance of finding it. Many journals (particularly in medicine) insist that when you write your study, you present a rationale for the sample size that you use. Power analysis better enables us to interpret a non-significant result because it allows us to say 'if there is an effect, it's probably no bigger than [the effect size that the study was powered to find]'.

Post hoc power analysis

Very closely related to a priori power analysis is post hoc power analysis. In a post hoc power analysis we aim to interpret a non-significant result. If a researcher says 'the result was not statistically significant, therefore the null hypothesis is true' we know that they are wrong. If the researcher failed to reject the null hypothesis, we might ask how large the

Table 11.2   *Table for post hoc power analysis. Values show power for given sample size and population correlation*

Correlation	$N = 100$	$N = 200$
0.15	0.32	0.57
0.18	0.44	0.73
0.21	0.57	0.86
0.24	0.69	0.94
0.27	0.79	0.98
0.3	0.88	0.99
0.33	0.93	1.00
0.36	0.97	1.00
0.39	0.99	1.00
0.42	1.00	1.00
0.45	1.00	1.00

population correlation is likely to be. Table 11.2 shows a power table for post hoc analysis. If a research carried out a study, with $N = 100$, and found a non-significant result, what does this mean? Reading the $N = 100$ column in the table, shows that the study only had a 57% chance of detecting an effect of $r = 0.21$. If an effect of $r = 0.21$ might have been considered important, then the study did not have enough power.

It's not a great idea to use post hoc power analysis in your own study. If you carry out a study and then find that the result is not statistically significant, this may not be the result you were looking for. If you then say 'however, a post hoc power analysis shows that we didn't have a large enough sample', someone will ask 'so why did you do the study?'. Only use post hoc power to understand the results of other studies.

Confidence intervals

Many authors who are against significance testing suggest greater use of **confidence intervals**, as either an alternative or an adjunct. Throughout this book, we have attempted to emphasise confidence intervals because they solve some of the problems that we encountered with significance tests. We saw the problems that we might encounter when two people carried out studies, and compared them using only the p-values. A statistically significant value in one study, combined with a non-statistically significant value in the other study, is seen as disagreement.

Figure 11.1 shows the results of two studies. Study 1 has a significant result ($p < 0.07$; we can see this from the fact that the confidence interval of the difference does not cross zero. Study 2 has a result that is not statistically significant because the confidence interval does cross zero. If we only considered the p-value, it is possible that we would

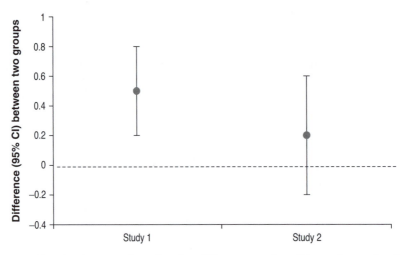

Figure 11.1   Result of two studies, showing difference and confidence intervals of difference: study 1 is statistically significant, study 2 is not

consider these studies to be in conflict with one another, and we would have to think of reasons why one gave a statistically significant result and the other did not. If instead we look at the confidence intervals, there is no disagreement. Both studies suggest a range of possible values for the population parameter, and there is considerable overlap. Confidence intervals can make us all be friends.

Meta-analysis

Meta-analysis is advocated by a number of opponents of significance testing – in particular, Schmidt (who we encountered earlier) and his co-worker Hunter, who worked together in developing meta-analysis. Schmidt and Hunter pull no punches in their attacks on significance testing. They wrote a book chapter called '*Eight common but false objections to the discontinuation of significance testing in the analysis of research data*' (Schmidt & Hunter, 1997). In this chapter, they say: 'Statistical significance testing retards the growth of scientific knowledge; it never makes a positive contribution' (p. 37). Later they say: 'Do not use significance testing in data analysis. Instead use confidence intervals and point estimates in individual studies, and meta-analysis in integrating findings across multiple studies' (p. 61).

So what does meta-analysis do that's so great? Meta-analysis combines the results of multiple studies, to treat them as if they were one large study. It then examines the studies, to see if they are actually different or not. If it appears that they are different, it is

Table 11.3 *Results of six studies on counselling for alcoholics*

Treatment Group			Control Group			*p*	OR	95% confidence limits	
Total number	Number relapsed	% relapsed	Total number	Number relapsed	% relapsed			Lower	Upper
20	6	30	31	14	45	0.381	0.520	0.158	1.710
28	10	36	63	34	54	0.119	0.474	0.189	1.187
53	25	47	53	28	53	0.437	0.685	0.318	1.472
103	48	47	112	63	56	0.173	0.679	0.396	1.162
25	12	48	54	33	61	0.341	0.615	0.237	1.595
54	29	54	66	40	61	0.349	0.676	0.323	1.415

possible to enter explanatory variables at the level of the study, which can explain the difference between the studies.

Let's look at a simple example. Six studies were carried out looking at the effect of counselling versus usual care for alcoholics. The results of the six studies are shown in Table 11.3. For each study, we show the number in each group (treatment and control) and the number and percentage in each group who relapsed. We also show the *p*-value, the odds ratio and the 95% confidence intervals. Notice first that in every study, a higher proportion of people in the control group than in the treatment group relapsed into drinking. Notice also that for each study, the results are not statistically significant. In fact, they are never even close to statistically significant. If we were to evaluate each of these studies separately, we would conclude that there is no evidence that the counselling is better than usual care.

However, rather than treat these as separate studies, we could treat them as one large study (as long as the results are consistent with that). We could combine the results of the studies, and treat it as one study with 242 participants. This is called a meta-analysis (*meta* meaning 'beyond' or 'higher'), and we show the results of such an analysis in Figure 11.2. For each of the studies, there is a square, which shows the odds ratio, and a horizontal line, which extends to the 95% confidence limits (except where the confidence limits are too far away, and then it shows an arrow).

At the bottom of the diagram is a diamond. The centre of the diamond shows the overall odds ratio, and the edges of the diamond extend to the overall 95% confidence intervals. Notice that the confidence intervals now do not cross zero, and hence the result is statistically significant.

At the bottom of the figure, there are two tests carried out. The first is the test of heterogeneity which tests the null hypothesis that each study can be thought of as one member of a population from a random sample of studies. In our example, this test is not statistically significant, and therefore we cannot reject the null hypothesis that all the studies are from the same sample. Second is the test for the overall effect which examines the

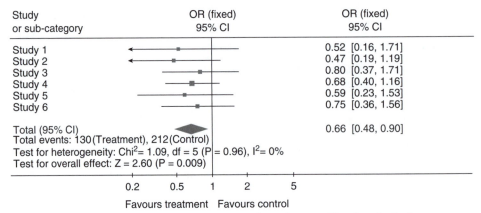

Figure 11.2 Results of meta-analysis of six studies of counselling for alcoholism

overall effect of all the studies combined, and gives us a *p*-value of 0.009. If we look at the individual studies we might conclude that there was no evidence for the effect of counselling, but by combining the evidence from each study we have a much better estimate of the effect, and have evidence that counselling is effective for alcoholics.

Now let's add one more study to the table:

| Treatment Group | | | Control Group | | | | | 95% confidence limits | |
Total number	Number relapsed	% relapsed	Total number	Number relapsed	% relapsed	*p*	OR	Lower	Upper
60	45	75	75	35	47	0.32	2.333	1.122	4.854

Notice that for this study, the relapse rate is much higher in the counselling group than it was in the control group, which is the opposite effect of the other studies. In fact it suggests that having no treatment is better than having counselling. Also notice that this time, the result is statistically significant.

Now that this study has been added, the overall result is no longer statistically significant (Figure 11.3). However, the test for heterogeneity is statistically significant; *p* = 0.008. This means that we can no longer assume that the studies are all sampled from the same population of studies. In fact, looking at Study 7, it appears that the result of this study is very different from the others. We might want to think about why this is the case, and compare this study with the others, in terms of its sample, quality, methodology or measurement, and see if this is able to explain the difference. It is likely that we will exclude this study from our analysis.

Rossi (1997) presents an example of where a reliance on significance testing has caused a piece of knowledge to be effectively lost, where meta-analysis could have saved

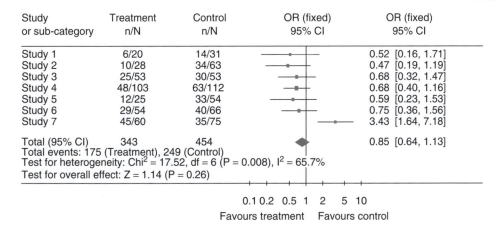

Figure 11.3   Results of meta-analysis of seven studies of counselling for alcoholism

it. Spontaneous recovery was proposed as a memory mechanism in the late 1940s by Underwood (1948; cited in Rossi, 1997). Around 40 studies were carried out investigating the effect of spontaneous recovery, and about half of them found a statistically significant result, and about half didn't. Ultimately research on spontaneous recovery faded away, and people no longer believed it existed as a phenomenon. Underwood didn't put it into the final editions of his textbook on memory.

However, as we have seen, not having a statistically significant result is not necessarily an indication that something does not exist. Rossi demonstrates that, had someone carried out a meta-analysis of the research, spontaneous recovery would have been demonstrated as a robust phenomenon and would have a place in memory texts today. However, because this analysis was not done, spontaneous recovery has been, effectively, forgotten about, and lost from knowledge. The work that was carried out was wasted, and the effect will need rediscovering in the future.

Bayesian analysis

Bayesian statistics was developed by Thomas Bayes, who lived from 1702 to 1761. His theorem was published after he died, in 1762, and has given rise to what is now known as Bayesian statistics. Sometimes, statisticians divide themselves into Bayesians and **frequentists**, and the two camps do not necessarily get along. When we have discussed probability we have done it from a frequentist perspective. We talk about probability as being the long-run frequency, if we were to repeat the experiment lots of times. Bayesians say that our probabilities are based on analysing lots of experiments that don't exist. Bayesian probabilities are based on likelihoods of two competing hypotheses.

The great thing about Bayesian analysis is that it can tell us what we really want to know: the probability that the null hypothesis is true. Let's have a look at why Bayesian statistics is great, and explain a bit about how Bayesian statistics works.

Optional Extra: Songs by Bayesians

There are a number of songs by Bayesians, about doing Bayesian statistics. A lot of these are collected in 'The Bayesian Songbook', and you can read these, and play them from http://www.biostat.umn.edu/~brud/cabaret.htm (linked from the book website). Most of the songs are about how the Bayesian approach to statistics is better than the frequentist approach. Here's just a snippet of one of them. It's called 'Bayesian Believer' and it's sung to the tune of 'I'm a believer' by The Monkees.

> I thought inference was just a fairy tale,
> Confused by stats and probability
> Frequentist approaches (doo-doot doo-doot)
> Made no sense to me (doo-doot doo-doot)
> Summarizing evidence by *p*?!
>
> Then I saw Tom Bayes – Now I'm a believer,
> Without a trace – of doubt in my mind,
> [I'm a] Bayesian (oooh) – Oh I'm a believer –
> I couldn't *p* now if I tried!

By the way, if you have ever sung this song then the probability that you have many friends is less than 0.0001.

Suppose that there is a disease which is prevalent in the population, and this disease has no symptoms in its early stage (this example relates directly to the example of HIV that we looked at on page 308, but we have changed the numbers to make it simpler.) We have a test for the disease, and we know that the test gives the correct answer 99% of the time. We test a person in the population (let's say it is you). The test says that you have the disease. What is the probability that you actually have the disease? If you are like almost everyone that we ever ask this question to, you will say that it is 99% certain that you have the disease.

If you think about that for a minute, you will realise that it isn't true. We have tested a null hypothesis, that you don't have the disease, and the result has told us that $p = 0.01$. But this *p*-value is *not* the probability that the null hypothesis is true, that is, it is not the probability that you don't have the disease. It is the probability of getting the result, if you don't have the disease. It's not $p(H_0)$, but $p(D|H_0)$, where p(hypothesis) is the probability of the hypothesis being true and | means *given*.

We need to know the probability that you actually *don't* have the disease. We need to know an additional piece of information, before we can work that out, and that piece of information is the *prior probability*. The prior probability is the probability that the null hypothesis was true, *before we tested you*. In other words, it is the proportion of people who have the disease in the population from which you are drawn. Let's say that we know that this is 1%, or 0.01.

There are two ways to work out the probability that you have the disease. There is the quick way, which is hard to understand, and there is the slow way, which is easy to understand. We'll do the quick and hard one first:

The quick way

$$p(H_0|D) = \frac{p(D|H_0)P(H_0)}{p(D|H_0)p(D) + p(D|H_1)p(H_1)}$$

where H_0 is the null hypothesis, H_1 is the alternative hypothesis (that you have the disease), and D is the result – in our case, it's a positive result. The bar | means 'given' so $p(H_0|D)$ is the probability that the null hypothesis is true, given the data – which is what we want to know.

We know that $p(D|H_0)$ is 0.01 – it's the probability of getting a positive, given that the null hypothesis is true.

$P(D|H_1)$ is the probability of getting a positive result, given that the alternative hypothesis (that you do have the disease) is true. This we know is 0.99.

$P(H_0)$ is the probability that you do not have the disease. We know that this is 0.99.

$P(H_1)$ is the probability that you do have the disease. This we know is 0.01.

We plug the numbers into the equation:

$$p(H_0|D) = \frac{p(D|H_0)P(H_0)}{p(D|H_0)p(D) + p(D|H_1)p(H_1)}$$

$$= \frac{0.01 \times 0.99}{0.99 \times 0.01 + 0.99 \times 0.01}$$

$$= \frac{1 \times (0.01 \times 0.99)}{2 \times (0.99 \times 0.01)}$$

$$= \frac{1}{2} = 0.5$$

And we get the answer 0.5(!). That is, when a test which gets the answer right 99% of the time says we have a disease, there is only a 50% chance that we actually have the disease.

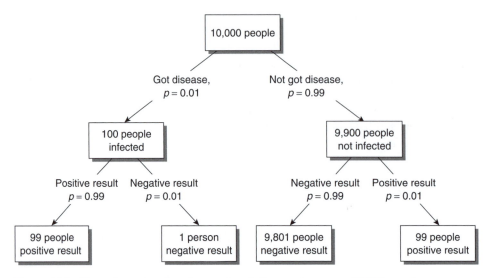

Figure 11.4   Flow chart showing the results of diagnostic test on 10,000 people

This is surprising. (What also might be surprising is that people who administer these tests don't always know this, so they don't know what a positive result means.)

Slow and easy way

We'll now look at the slow and easy way of showing this, just to prove to you that there was no mathematical jiggery-pokery, and it's really true.

Figure 11.4 shows a flow chart of what happened to 10,000 people that we tested. We know that these people have a 1% chance of having the disease. We therefore expect to find 100 people who have the disease, and 9,900 who don't. We know that the test gives the right answer 99% of the time, so of those 100 people 99 get a positive diagnosis.

Of the 9,900 people who don't have the disease, we know that the test gives a positive diagnosis 1% of the time, and therefore we expect 99 of those people have a positive diagnosis.

There are 99 people who have got the disease and have a positive diagnosis; and 99 people who do not have the disease and have a positive diagnosis. The result is that 198 people have a positive diagnosis, of whom only half actually have the disease.

Bayesian analysis is great, isn't it?

Yes, it is. Bayesian analysis tells us what we want to know, that is, the probability of the null hypothesis. This is much better than what 'conventional' statistical analysis tells us, which is the probability of a result of that magnitude (or larger) occurring, given the null hypothesis and, as we have seen, this is not what we want to know (even if we think it is what we want to know).

Optional Extra: Bayesian analysis in other places

You have almost certainly encountered the results of Bayesian analysis, although you might not have been aware of it. If you have an email address, you probably have some sort of spam filter on it, to reduce the amount of junk email you get. Spam filters work using Bayesian methods – they calculate the likelihood that an email is spam by comparing it with other emails that they know to be spam or not spam.

Google uses Bayesian methods to decide which web pages to put at the top of the search results. It doesn't test a null hypothesis, instead it calculates the likelihood that you want a web page, and the more likely it thinks that you will like it, the higher it puts the link.

If Bayesian analysis is so great, why have we written a whole book which emphasises frequentist statistics? We have written about frequentist statistics because Bayesian statistics has a flaw, and frequentists (like us) see it as a rather large one. Looking at the equation above, the flaw is that we must know $p(H_0)$. We have to know the *prior probability* of the null hypothesis being true. That is, before the study has started, we have to effectively guess what the prior probability is, and of course we don't know this. If Jeremy comes up with one prior probability, and Phil comes up with another prior probability, then we will get different *p*-values out of our study.

This is not to say that Bayesian analysis doesn't have a role to play because it is useful in lots of applications. One of them, we have already seen, is diagnostic tests. Another area is in decision making – if we have to decide between two treatments, and the result of our test is not statistically significant, we still have to decide on a treatment. We cannot defer the decision (because we have patients who are waiting). We can also add information such as cost – given that one treatment costs more, it has to be a bit better than the other, to be worthwhile. All this information can be incorporated into a Bayesian analysis, to give a likelihood that one treatment is better than another. An example was Godfrey et al. (2005), who carried out a trial examining two forms of treatment for alcoholism. They concluded that if a quality-adjusted life year were worth £30,000, then one form of therapy would have a 58% chance of being the best, and the other form would have a 42% chance of being the best.

Optional Extra: We're all Bayesians, really

Although we say that there are flaws with Bayesian analysis, in actual fact we all use Bayesian analyses to evaluate statements. Imagine Phil told Jeremy that he had seen Elvis working in the chip shop down the road, and Phil was really, really, 99.999% sure he saw Elvis. Jeremy still would not believe him. Jeremy would not believe Phil, because the *prior probability* that Elvis was in the chip shop was so low, that the null hypothesis (that Elvis wasn't in the chip shop) can be rejected.

In much the same way, if a study had been carried out and it demonstrated that homeopathy was an effective therapy for schizophrenia ($p = 0.01$) we would not believe that homeopathy was an effective cure for schizophrenia. Homeopathic therapy involves giving patients one of a range of substances diluted with distilled water diluted to such an extent that there is most likely none of the active ingredient left in it. There is no way of telling the difference between a homeopathic remedy and distilled water. Our prior probability that a medical treatment which is effectively water can be better than a treatment that *is* water is so low, that we require an awful lot of evidence before we would believe it. (If you were a homeopath and made £30 every time someone bought some of your water and chatted to you for half an hour, your prior probability might be higher.) All Bayes' theorem says in this case is that extraordinary claims require extraordinary evidence.

SUMMARY

Statistical procedures in psychology are driven by conventions. In other words, psychologists have come to believe that some procedures are good, or even, essential things. One example of this is the *p*-value. There are other ways of looking at data, and in this chapter we have given the case against *p*. We have also looked at important, though still sparingly used, techniques such as power analysis and meta-analysis.

Test yourself answers

Test yourself 1

They are all wrong. None of them is true. However, if you did select any of them as being true, you are in good company. Haller and Kraus (2002) carried out a study (in Germany, but we don't think the results would be much different here) in where they put these questions to psychology students, psychology professors and lecturers (who didn't teach statistics) and psychology professors and lecturers who taught statistics. They found that all the students said at least one of the statements was correct; 90% of the lecturers (who didn't teach statistics) said at least one of the statements was correct; and 80% (!) of the lecturers and professors who taught statistics said at least one of the statements was correct.

Test yourself 2

(b) You have only failed to reject the null hypothesis.

12
Report writing

What's in this chapter?

- What goes in a report
- Presenting a report
- Checklist for your final report

KEY TERMS

confidence interval   research hypotheses
data trawling   response rate
hypothesis   statistical hypotheses
plagiarism   story
p-value

INTRODUCTION

You've done the difficult bit. You've analysed your data and found the p-values and you've managed to understand what you've found, so now you just have to write it up. Shame to mess it up now, but it's so easily done. Most readers won't even look at this chapter. It's like 'study skills' lessons – you never go. And the instructions on the new piece of equipment – well, they're for wimps. The first rule of cool is not to look at the instructions until you've broken it. But you know it makes sense to think about your report, and the fact that you're still reading this means that you're already ahead of the game. Follow these simple observations and make sure you don't waste all the work you put into carrying out your project and analysing the data.

I WANT TO TELL YOU A STORY

Writing a report is like most writing in that it has the components of a **story**. It has a context, a motivation, some action, some analysis and a comforting conclusion that also leaves some questions open in case there is a sequel. The best projects buy into a narrative that already exists, play around with some familiar clichés and add a novel twist. There are any number of detective shows on television and each new one has a novel twist even though the storylines are familiar and predictable. Your project is a new version of a familiar story.

The first thing to accept is that it is very unlikely ($p = 0.000000000000001$) that you have made any earth-shattering findings. This is uncommon enough in the hard sciences like physics and chemistry, but in psychology it is almost unheard of. In fact, if you want to wind up your lecturers you can innocently ask them to identify what they believe to be psychology's great findings over the last 100 years. It is difficult, if not impossible, to come up with anything to rival discoveries like DNA and the human genome or inventions like the microchip. If the discipline of psychology is short of great findings you have to get real and accept that your project has not split the psychology atom.

When you become immersed in a project it is common to have a selective focus that tends to see the work as much more important and useful than it really is. This is not to say that your research is pointless, but it is important to realise that the findings alone won't sell it. You have to tell the story very well.

Tip: Start here

Hypotheses are the key to the project. If you have any confusion or ambiguity about them the project will fail.

The main event: hypotheses

Let's cut to the chase here. If you take only one thing from this chapter, take this: the **hypothesis** is the key to a good project. The hypothesis is the heart of the project. It is the motivation for the work and if it is wrong then the whole project falls apart. In every story there has to be a motivation, a key, and main event around which all the action turns. In a project, it is the hypothesis.

It is common for students and even researchers to believe that they are on top of their hypotheses, only for confusion to set in when they come to analyse data and write up the report. If we do things by the book then we should state our hypotheses at the start of the research and keep to them throughout. In the real world, this is not followed and it is common to search for a wide range of data and select the results that make the best story. Oh don't get all upset about it; it is difficult to take precise psychological and behavioural measures, so we commonly take a lot and hope for the best. If we use a five-factor measure of personality – there are lots we could use, but we like Saucier's mini-markers (Saucier, 1994) – and we look for associations with, for example, smoking behaviour we have five chances of a significant result.

Research commonly results in a shedload of data, and it is the task of the researcher to select the most appropriate results and construct the most coherent story with those data. At its worst this can be a cynical exercise in **data trawling** where the researcher tries every which way to get anything that gives a p-value less than 0.05. At best it allows the researcher to look creatively at their data and explore a range of different explanations. These two outcomes sound remarkably similar, but they are separated by the intention of the researcher to either increase our understanding of events, or to get published at any cost.

Let's get back to hypotheses. You started your research with a number of provisional questions. Now you have the data and the analysis you have to be very clear about what you have tested and what you have found. First, you have to be clear about the difference between **research hypotheses** and **statistical hypotheses**. They are not the same thing. For example, if your research project is about the effect of smoking cessation adverts on attitudes and intentions of smokers and non-smokers, your research hypotheses are clear. You can phrase them in conceptual terms and make predictions about the impact of adverts. Your statistical hypotheses are a step removed from this. Your statistical hypotheses are always about your null hypotheses and are on the lines of 'what is the probability of observing these data if the null hypothesis is true?'.

Select the hypotheses that you want to talk about in your project. Be clear about the theoretical hypotheses, and be very clear about what statistical hypotheses you have tested in your data analysis. This sounds very obvious, you say, but it is a common mistake to leave some ambiguity at the very heart of the project or to ask questions of your data that don't match the theoretical questions you posed. The whole point of your study is to test your hypotheses, and if there is the slightest weakness here it will show to the informed reader.

Start in the middle

So, if the hypotheses are the most important part of the report, you have to start there when you come to write the project. Write them out and pin them on the wall. Everything else you write has to be done with these in full view. No, really – do it. Pin them up and keep them in front of you. It is the same trick that smart people use in examinations when they write out the question and leave it at the top of their desk so they keep looking at it while they are writing the essay. It is staggeringly common for students to drift away from the examination question during their essay and converge on one of their own.

Everything you write in the introduction section explains why you have these hypotheses, everything in the method section describes how you tested your hypotheses, everything in the results section analyses the data generated by your hypotheses, and everything in the discussion section comments on what we now know about the hypotheses following the research. Can anything be more important than the hypotheses?

Now that you have fixed the heart of the project and hopefully got it beating, it is possible to move on and prepare the rest of the report. If we follow the strict rules then we now write an introduction, but we are more pragmatic than that. We have a good look at the data and get a grip on the story we are going to tell.

We can take it as read that you have researched the area and that your research was based on theory and your hypotheses have some scientific backing to them. What we have to accept, however, is that the body of psychological evidence is not something that everyone agrees upon. If we take our example of the five-factor model of personality, then it is likely that there have been a range of findings on the topic of smoking and smoking cessation. Our data might fit more into one line of argument than another, so it is not uncommon to keep some of our options open. This is not cheating. It is a feature of research that we do not know what the outcome will be. If we did, there would be no point to the research.

Unless you have the most controlled and simply designed experiment imaginable, it is likely that you have a large array of data and analyses. It is your task now to make the best sense of them and select the ones that make the best story. You do this by looking for the most striking findings from your study. This does not necessarily mean the most significant findings because sometimes null results are more remarkable than significant differences. You have a story to tell so look for the findings that contribute most to your story.

Results

Now that you have you hypotheses stuck on the wall in front of you it might be a good idea to draft your results section. If the hypotheses are the beating heart of the project, then the results are the blood pumping through it. There are some simple do's and don'ts about results sections, and we'll go through the important ones now.

1. Keep it brief. You might have spent days of your life wrestling with SPSS and used up a small rainforest load of paper on the printouts, but no one will be impressed if you show this. All that is required is a description of the most salient data and a clear statement of the statistical outcomes. Throughout this text we have suggested how you might report your results. Use the statistical statement that is appropriate for your design and just state the minimum that is required and no more.

Tip: Beware SPSS

SPSS has a number of very confusing and very long outputs. Make sure you understand everything you present. Don't try and blag it.

2. Be selective from SPSS output. This is an expansion of the above point, but it is very tempting to put in everything from the SPSS, especially the bits you have no idea about. The people who write SPSS make up tests for a laugh just to see if people will put them in their reports. I mean, who will ever refer to 'Roy's largest root' without laughing? If you are not absolutely sure what the output means, do not use it.

Common Mistake: Never paste output from SPSS

Never, ever paste an output table from SPSS directly into your report. SPSS output will contain things:

(a)   that no one is interested in;
(b)   that people who don't use SPSS won't understand;
(c)   that make it look like you have no idea what you are talking about.

If you don't believe us, go and find a published journal article where you could tell that the authors used SPSS for their analysis. And then email the reference to nernernerdyner@jeremymiles.co.uk and we'll put it on the web page – which, as you know, is http://www.jeremymiles.co.uk/usingstatistics

3. It doesn't have to look pretty. I know it makes it look nice if you fill up the report with vividly coloured and strikingly designed graphs and charts, but frankly it looks all wrong. Statisticians don't have coloured pencils. They use numerical indices rather than block graphs. The graphs and charts are very useful for you when you are making sense of the data, but it is not common to use them in reports, or if you do, then only sparingly. If you are going to use them, make sure they make a point and don't just repeat something that is adequately described by numbers.

4. The main event is the confidence interval of the effect and the p-*value of the effect.* Elsewhere we can argue about the value of significance but if you have completed an analysis using the tests in this book then the key statement to present is the **p-value** and the **confidence interval**.

5. Keep a consistent structure. You have stated your hypotheses elsewhere so make sure that you have tested all of them and given them the same weight as you gave them in your introduction.

Tip: Writing for an audience

If you write for *The Guardian* you must use a different style than the one you would use for *The Sun*. For example, a recent research finding about how herrings appear to communicate by expelling air from their swim bladders was presented in different ways by the two papers. *The Guardian* had a droll little piece with the traditional alliteration for a punning headline:

Farting fish fingered

But *The Sun* went for the more direct approach with a headline to match:

Scientists prove fish talk out of their a*s**

WRITING THE REPORT

Once you have completed the above you should be ready to write the report. Our top tip is to *write it quickly*. Get all your notes together and the drafts of each section and then sit and write it as quickly as you can. We find that if you stop and start on any writing project it is very easy to let the argument drift slightly and the style of the argument change.

Our next tip is to be clear about the *style* you are using. Any piece of writing has to have a clear idea of the audience you are writing for. If I try and write a story for *The Sun* I will write it up in a very different style than I would use for *The Guardian*. It is a common mistake to believe that it is easier to write for *The Sun*, but we would suggest that it is more difficult because you have fewer words to present the information and you have to find hooks to engage the reader.

Tip

In summary, when you are writing the report

- Write it quickly.
- Make the style appropriate for your readers.
- Keep it brief.

Your research is not being written for *The Sun* (well, not yet at any rate, though you can dream) but it does have a particular audience and that audience requires a particular style. That style is concise, direct, technical and very focused. It does not allow for any personal asides, jokes or even personal opinions. It is a convention in the UK that we write in the third person, so you don't write 'I think that ...' or 'I found that ...' or 'my results show that ...' etc. You write 'Past research suggests that ...' and 'It was found that ...', and 'The results show ...'.

The one tip you can take from the writing style of *The Sun* is that less is more. Red-top newspapers have very short articles but everything in those articles is to the point. In fact you sometimes don't have to go any further than the headline to find out the whole story. The 'serious' newspapers can sometimes take a double-page spread to tell you no more than you got from 100 words in *The Sun*. The 'serious' newspapers write like that because their readers enjoy reading. They want to spend time over their newspaper and enjoy the experience. This is not the case with academic papers. Readers don't want to spend their Sunday lazily reading through *The British Journal of Very Hard Statistics*. They want the information presented as clearly and concisely as possible. A short report can be an excellent report, as along as it has the right components. A long report might contain padding in the introduction and discussion that makes it *look* better because of the size and the number of references, but has actually lost direction and focus.

Common Mistake: Read reports

To understand the style of a report, you should read reports in journal articles (you'll find them in the library – that's the large grey building with books and stuff in, which they showed you around when you started your course). That's the only way of learning the style.

As a student, you have probably read some textbooks (like this one). Because we know that students read this book, we try to make it interesting and readable. Journal articles don't do that. If you read this book, and compare it with journal articles, you will notice that the style is very different – even from articles that we have written.

Introduction

The introduction is an opportunity to set the context for your research. It gives some background research that covers the concepts and methods used in your project. It is not an opportunity to write a general essay on a psychological theme. The structure of an introduction should be such that when the reader comes to the end of it your hypotheses are not just plausible, they are the most important questions to ask. When the reader finishes the introduction they should already be wanting to know what happens next before they turn the page; imagine their delight when they find that is exactly what you are asking in your research.

If you want to see it in a literary way, you are writing the first chapter of a three-part story. You are introducing the characters, painting a picture of the scene and creating a motivation for the forthcoming action. Sometimes you have to introduce different lines of the argument and then weave them together in the same way that stories sometimes have two or three narratives running along together. You can have as many storylines as you like as long as they all drive inevitably towards your hypotheses.

Here are some general tips for writing your introduction:

1. *Be selective.* You have probably carried out many searches for information and have a box full of papers and notes. There is a lot of redundancy in research and you have to discard as much as nine-tenths of the material you have built up. This is very difficult as you seem to have been wasting your time, but you haven't. You needed to check out all the material in order to get a feeling for the field and to find the research that best fits your project.

2. *Use your own words.* I know this might sound very obvious, but don't cut and paste from the internet and don't copy out chunks from other books or papers without referencing it appropriately. This is called **plagiarism** and is very, very naughty. It fact, it is so naughty that if you are caught you will fail. It's that simple. You have to take great care, because it is easy to make some notes and forget where you got them or how you got them. Unintentional plagiarism is possible, but this is not a defence. 'Will I be caught?' you ask, well may be not, but a new game for lecturers is to type phrases from student reports into Google to see what happens. How do they know which phrases? You should see them cackle with delight when they find the source of the report!

3. *Drill down.* The report is not a flat story but is a fast ride downhill towards the hypotheses. You start with a brief look at the general area before drilling down to the specifics of your study. You introduce the general area only to make sense of the specific topic you have studied and not to discuss the whole field.

4. *Reference all points.* Again this might seem obvious but everything you state must be backed up by past research. For example, if you are carrying out a project on the effects of heavy metal music on mood, you must not make a statement such as 'people believe that fans of heavy metal are violent' without having some research to back this up. Even if something appears self-evident, you must support the statement with past research.

5. *Get someone else to read it.* You will be so immersed in your project that you might not be able to see the glaring flaws in your logic. A common mistake is to keep in some references that are irrelevant to the argument. Maybe they were the first papers you found, but you've moved on and they no longer contribute to the answer. You have to get rid of them and you might need a friend to tell you.

Method

The method is the recipe section of the story. If someone wants to repeat your study, they have to follow your recipe. You need to say what you did, where you did it, who you did it on, and any issues that arose from that. Specifically, you need to identify the following:

1. *Design: What was the structure of the research?* Was the study an experiment? If so, what experimental design did you use and what were the variables? What did you control?

2. *Participants: Who were they and how were they selected?* The details you give of your participants depend on the tasks they have been required to do, but it is often helpful to put in some basic demographics. The most common ones are age and sex. Interestingly, it is very uncommon to collect and report data on class, ethnicity, sexual orientation and religion, even though these variables might well influence the behaviour of the participants. If you are carrying out a reaction-time task then sexual orientation probably has little effect, but if you are carrying out an attitude survey on the sexual content of advertisements then it might well be an important variable. Psychology has little or no interest in class and ethnicity (sadly and surprisingly) so no one will notice if you ignore these important variables, but you can always decide to go outside the narrow psychological box and consider real-life variables.

The selection method is important to record. Were they coerced or bribed or bullied? If you gave out questionnaires, how many were returned, and how many were only partially completed? What is the response rate? This is sometimes difficult to calculate, especially if you have published your questionnaire on the internet. One way of estimating **response rate** might be to add a counter to the site so you can see how many people have clicked on to your page, even though this will only give a very rough estimate of the potential respondents.

3. *Materials: What did you use in your research?* This might be a fancy piece of kit like an inter-galactic neutron disintegrator gun, or it might be a clipboard. If it is a recognised psychometric scale then give details of the scale and reference it. The details should include the standardised scores if these exist for a sample like the one in your research.

4. *Procedure: What did you do?* This is a point-by-point account of what you did. In reality it is a cleaned-up version so you can miss out the many extraneous variables that might have interfered with the results. The reader should be able to replicate your study from this description.

Discussion

The discussion is the key section for getting the best marks. You have to review your research, consider the results, comment on the quality of your evidence and say how your results relate to the theoretical approaches developed in your introduction. One of the difficulties for the writer of a discussion is to be reflective of their work. We commonly justify our position and support what we have done rather than reflect on it with a critical eye. It is important to get the correct balance between self-criticism and self-promotion. There is no value in beating yourself up and going on and on about all the mistakes you made and how awful your data are. There is also no point in spinning a line that says your results are sensational and your work is beyond reproach. If you write it as if the Nobel Prize is just a matter of time you will have overstepped the mark.

All research could be better and nearly all research has some merit (there are exceptions to this second point, but discretion means we won't name names). You need to present what can be reasonably taken from your data and maybe what can't. You can look at the results and explain how they relate to past studies. Maybe you got different outcomes because you carried out the study differently, or used different populations or used different measures of the key variables. The differences between your results and those of past research might be because of error or because you have found out something new. Both possibilities must be considered, though it would obviously be nice if you can dismiss the error explanation.

It is important to recognise that the most important findings might not be the significant ones. We often hope that our studies will 'work', by which we mean they will get a significant result, but often there is a lot of interest to be found in the null results buried in the data.

The first finding of any research project is always 'more research is needed'. Sometimes researchers are discreet about this and only mention it at the end of the report, but it always has to be there. Think of it as a job creation programme, though it is fair to say that there is always something new to find out. With this in mind you have to finish off the story of your report as if you are pitching for a sequel – '*Psychology Research Project 2: The search continues*'. You have looked at some questions, come up with some answers, but there is still some unfinished business. If you have written your discussion correctly, then your further research suggestions will be as inevitable and obvious as your hypotheses were at the end of your introduction.

Common Mistake: Leaving the discussion to the last minute

Discussions are hard to write. You need to think about your project and reflect on it. You need time to decide what further research is needed. If you leave writing your discussion to the last minute you won't be able to write anything useful or sensible, and you will lose a lot of marks.

Title

Thinking of a good title is actually surprisingly hard. Your title should be sufficiently broad that people understand what the report is about, but not so broad that it doesn't narrow it down. Here are some examples:

- Too broad:
  'An experiment on memory'.
- Too narrow:
  'An experiment to see if children remember more words when answering deep-level questions about them, than if shallow-level questions are asked'.
- About right:
  'The effectiveness of levels of processing in aiding children's retention'.

Tip: The colon

When you are writing your title, it is a good idea to put the most important words at the start. However, sometimes this reverses the order of the sentence. If this is the case, you can use a colon. Here are some examples from the most recent (at the time of writing) edition of the *British Journal of Psychology* (February 2006).

Training for vigilance: The effect of knowledge of results format and dispositional optimism and pessimism on performance and stress.

Obsessive-compulsive disorder across developmental trajectory: Cognitive processing of threat in children, adolescents and adults.

Change blindness and visual memory: Visual representations get rich and act poor.

Common Mistake: Trying to be funny

Don't try to be funny in your title. Sorry. It almost always falls flat. And there's very little you can tell us about not being funny.

FINISHING OFF

You've now completed the main parts of the report. All you need to do now is tidy it up and put in the final bits and pieces. These include the abstract, the appendices and the references.

Abstract

There is so much fuss made about the abstract, but it is just a brief summary. It is probably best completed with one sentence from each section of the report: 'The aim of the report was.... It built on research by.... The design was.... The results showed.... The conclusion was...'. Don't get too engaged with this, but don't get it wrong. Think of it as one of those potted book reviews that gives you the whole story in one paragraph. You know the sort of thing: '*Boy meets girl. Girl runs off. Boy napalms Milton Keynes. Girl takes boy back. Boy spends life in Belmarsh.*'

Tip
Try to make your abstract between 100 and 150 words long.

Appendices

These contain any relevant information, such as a blank version of the questionnaire and the consent form. Put each new piece of material in a separate appendix.

References

There are numerous ways to cite references in academic work. Psychology commonly, though not exclusively, uses the American Psychological Association system or some variation on it. We have reproduced a number of references below from different sources, and we have written them in the format used by the American Psychological Association. The important thing to put in any references section is some means of identifying where to find the information that is being referred to. Sometimes people get very engaged about where full stops should be placed and how many spaces there should be between phrases, but we think that is a step too far, and we suspect these people spend their spare time collecting little metal bottle tops. (If you want to be like one of those people, you can read the *Publication Manual* of the American Psychological Association (1995), which lists over 100 different reference sources, and tells you how to cite them.)

Books

Miles, J. & Banyard, P. (2007). *Understanding and Using Statistics in Psychology: A Practical Introduction*. London: Sage.

Book chapters

Koff, E. (1983). Through the looking glass of menarche: What the adolescent girl sees. In S. Golub (Ed.), *Menarche* (pp. 77–86). Lexington, Mass.: Heath.

Reports

Department of Health (1998). *Our healthier nation: A consultation paper*. London: HMSO.

Journal articles

Orne, M. T. (1962). On the social psychology of the psychological experiment: with particular reference to demand characteristics and their implications. *American Psychologist, 17*, 276–783.

Eysenbach, G. & Diepgen, T. L. (1998). Evaluation of cyberdocs. *The Lancet, 352*, 1526.

Magazines

Clarkson, J. (2005, 7 January). Why I drive like Anita Harris. *Boys Toys Monthly,* 30–34.

Conference proceedings

Muir Gray, J. A. (1998). *National Electronic Library for Health.* Paper presented at the Third Annual World Congress of the Internet in Medicine, University of Birmingham.

Websites

Blass, T. (2000). *The Stanley Milgram Website*, Thomas Blass. Available: http://www.stanleymilgram.com/ [2000, 14 July].

(Notice that you need to put the date that you downloaded the page – because pages can change.)

Web downloads

Parks, M. R. & Floyd, K. (1996). Making friends in cyberspace. *Journal of Computer Mediated Communication, 1*(4). Retrieved June 1997 from http://jmc.huji.ac.il/vol1991/issue1994/parks.html

Secondary sources

It is not common to use secondary sources (works that cite the work you are interested in) in projects, or at least it is not common to admit to it. If you do use a secondary source and you decide to come clean (honesty is usually the best policy) then there are conventions for reporting this. If, for example, you find an article on car crime by Clarkson et al. in the general text by Stephenson, the best way to refer to this is either

Clarkson, J. et al. (1990), cited in Stephenson, G. (1992). *The Psychology of Criminal Justice*. Oxford: Blackwell, page 267.
or put 'Clarkson (1990, cited in Stephenson, 1992)' in the report, and just reference the Stephenson book.

CHECKLIST

You can use this checklist as a final examination of your practical report. This is not intended to be an exhaustive set of instructions, rather it contains some of the most common, easily fixed, errors that students make in their report.

- Is the title short and informative?
- Does the abstract give your conclusions, without giving the results of any statistical tests?

- Have you removed all minor details from the abstract?
- Is the abstract 100–150 words, and one paragraph long?
- Does the introduction finish with the aim of the research, and the hypotheses or predictions that are to be tested?
- Have you described the independent variable, and its levels?
- Have you described the dependent variable?
- Have you described your participants in sufficient detail (age, sex)?
- Have you described how your participants were sampled?
- Have you said that you used random sampling? (If you did, you are wrong, so change it.)
- Have you described your materials (not just referred the reader to an appendix)?
- Have you written your materials section as a paragraph?
- Does your procedure contain all the details (from when the participant was approached, to when they were debriefed) which would allow someone else to repeat the experiment?
- If your study is an experiment, have you described how you assigned participants to conditions?
- Have you described how your participants were debriefed?
- Have you described how your dependent variable was calculated? (If it was a questionnaire, how was it scored, for example?)
- Have you labelled all graphs and tables clearly? (Not used abbreviations, and not used variable names from computer printout.)
- Have you used a sensible number of decimal places in your results section?
- Have you reported your statistical tests correctly? Make sure that you have reported the test statistic (*F* or *t*, for example), the df or *N* (and remember that *F* has two sets of df) and the *p*-value.
- Don't confuse $p < 0.05$ and $p > 0.05$ (the fat end of the arrow points toward the larger number, so $p < 0.05$ means that p is less than 0.05.)
- Have you reiterated your results at the start of the discussion?
- Have you referred back to the introduction in your discussion?
- Have you pointed out flaws in your study?
- Have you suggested avenues for future research?
- Have you summarised your findings in your final paragraph?
- Does every reference in your report appear in your references section?
- Do any references appear in your references section, which do not appear in your report?
- Have you put the report in a folder in such a way that all of the text is easily readable?

SUMMARY

So there you have it. Follow the simple rules above and bluff your way to academic success. Follow the format of the report and keep the hypotheses in sight all the time you are writing. The key feature of an excellent report is its coherence; it stays on the case from beginning to end, without deviation or hesitation.

Appendices

These appendices contain tables of critical values that can be used to determine whether the result is statistically significant. As we repeatedly stated in the text, it's almost always better to use some other method (such as a computer) to obtain statistical significance.

APPENDIX 1: Z-SCORES

The table shows the (two-tailed) z-score, for any value of p. p represents the area under the curve, and z is the number of standard deviations from the mean that include this area.

p	z	p	z
0.950	0.06	0.090	1.70
0.900	0.13	0.080	1.75
0.850	0.19	0.070	1.81
0.800	0.25	0.060	1.88
0.750	0.32	**0.050**	**1.96**
0.700	0.39	0.040	2.05
0.650	0.45	0.030	2.17
0.600	0.52	0.020	2.33
0.550	0.60	**0.010**	**2.58**
0.500	0.67	0.009	2.61
0.450	0.76	0.008	2.65
0.400	0.84	0.007	2.70
0.350	0.93	0.006	2.75
0.300	1.04	0.005	2.81
0.250	1.15	0.004	2.88
0.200	1.28	0.003	2.97
0.150	1.44	0.002	3.09
0.100	1.64	0.001	3.29

APPENDIX 2: CRITICAL VALUES FOR THE MANN–WHITNEY U TEST

The observed value needs to be equal or below, in order for the probability value associated with U to be less than 0.05.

	2	3	4	5	6	7	8	9	10	11	12	13	14	15	16	17	18	19	20	21	22	23	24	25
2	—	—	—	—	—	—	0	0	0	0	1	1	1	1	1	2	2	2	2	2	3	3	3	3
3	—	—	—	0	1	1	2	2	3	3	4	4	5	5	6	6	7	7	8	8	9	9	10	10
4	—	—	0	1	2	3	4	4	5	6	7	8	9	10	11	11	12	13	13	14	15	16	17	18
5	—	0	1	2	3	5	6	7	8	9	11	12	13	14	15	17	18	19	20	22	23	24	25	27
6	—	1	2	3	5	6	8	10	11	13	14	16	17	19	21	22	24	25	27	29	30	32	33	35
7	—	1	3	5	6	8	10	12	14	16	18	20	22	24	26	28	30	32	34	36	38	40	42	44
8	0	2	4	6	8	10	13	15	17	19	22	24	26	29	31	34	36	38	41	43	45	48	50	53
9	0	2	4	7	10	12	15	17	20	23	26	28	31	34	37	39	42	45	48	50	53	56	59	62
10	0	3	5	8	11	14	17	20	23	26	29	33	36	39	42	45	48	52	55	58	61	64	67	71
11	0	3	6	9	13	16	19	23	26	30	33	37	40	44	47	51	55	58	62	65	69	73	76	80
12	1	4	7	11	14	18	22	26	29	33	37	41	45	49	53	57	61	65	69	73	77	81	85	89
13	1	4	8	12	16	20	24	28	33	37	41	45	50	54	59	63	67	72	76	80	85	89	94	98
14	1	5	9	13	17	22	26	31	36	40	45	50	55	59	64	69	74	78	83	88	93	98	102	107
15	1	5	10	14	19	24	29	34	39	44	49	54	59	64	70	75	80	85	90	96	101	106	111	117
16	1	6	11	15	21	26	31	37	42	47	53	59	64	70	75	81	86	92	98	103	109	115	120	126
17	2	6	11	17	22	28	34	39	45	51	57	63	69	75	81	87	93	99	105	111	117	123	129	135
18	2	7	12	18	24	30	36	42	48	55	61	67	74	80	86	93	99	106	112	119	125	132	138	145
19	2	7	13	19	25	32	38	45	52	58	65	72	78	85	92	99	106	113	119	126	133	140	147	154
20	2	8	13	20	27	34	41	48	55	62	69	76	83	90	98	105	112	119	127	134	141	149	156	163
21	2	8	14	22	29	36	43	50	58	65	73	80	88	96	103	111	119	126	134	142	150	157	165	173
22	3	9	15	23	30	38	45	53	61	69	77	85	93	101	109	117	125	133	141	150	158	166	174	182
23	3	9	16	24	32	40	48	56	64	73	81	89	98	106	115	123	132	140	149	157	166	175	183	192
24	3	10	17	25	33	42	50	59	67	76	85	94	102	111	120	129	138	147	156	165	174	183	192	201
25	3	10	18	27	35	44	53	62	71	80	89	98	107	117	126	135	145	154	163	173	182	192	201	211

APPENDIX 3: CRITICAL VALUES FOR PEARSON PRODUCT MOMENT CORRELATION

The observed value needs to be equal to or above the critical value listed in the table. If the exact value is not available for your study, then use the next available value.

N	p 0.1	0.05	0.01	0.001
4	0.900	0.950	0.990	0.999
5	0.805	0.878	0.959	0.991
6	0.729	0.811	0.917	0.974
7	0.669	0.754	0.875	0.951
8	0.621	0.707	0.834	0.925
9	0.582	0.666	0.798	0.898
10	0.549	0.632	0.765	0.872
11	0.521	0.602	0.735	0.847
12	0.497	0.576	0.708	0.823
13	0.476	0.553	0.684	0.801
14	0.458	0.532	0.661	0.780
15	0.441	0.514	0.641	0.760
16	0.426	0.497	0.623	0.742
17	0.412	0.482	0.606	0.725
18	0.400	0.468	0.590	0.708
19	0.389	0.456	0.575	0.693
20	0.378	0.444	0.561	0.679
21	0.369	0.433	0.549	0.665
22	0.360	0.423	0.537	0.652
23	0.352	0.413	0.526	0.640
24	0.344	0.404	0.515	0.629
25	0.337	0.396	0.505	0.618
26	0.330	0.388	0.496	0.607
27	0.323	0.381	0.487	0.597
28	0.317	0.374	0.479	0.588
29	0.311	0.367	0.471	0.579
30	0.306	0.361	0.463	0.570
35	0.283	0.334	0.430	0.532
40	0.264	0.312	0.403	0.501
45	0.248	0.294	0.380	0.474
50	0.235	0.279	0.361	0.451
60	0.214	0.254	0.330	0.414
70	0.198	0.235	0.306	0.385
80	0.185	0.220	0.286	0.361
90	0.174	0.207	0.270	0.341
100	0.165	0.197	0.256	0.324
200	0.117	0.139	0.182	0.231
300	0.095	0.113	0.149	0.189
400	0.082	0.098	0.129	0.164
500	0.074	0.088	0.115	0.147
1000	0.052	0.062	0.081	0.104

APPENDIX 4: CRITICAL VALUES FOR SPEARMAN CORRELATION

In order to be significant at the designated level, the value for r_s should exceed the critical value in the table. If the exact sample size is not available, use the next lowest.

N	p 0.05	0.01	0.001
6	0.811		
7	0.754	0.875	0.951
8	0.707	0.834	0.925
9	0.666	0.798	0.898
10	0.632	0.765	0.872
11	0.602	0.735	0.847
12	0.576	0.708	0.823
13	0.553	0.684	0.801
14	0.532	0.661	0.780
15	0.514	0.641	0.760
16	0.497	0.623	0.742
17	0.482	0.606	0.725
18	0.468	0.590	0.708
19	0.456	0.575	0.693
20	0.444	0.561	0.679
21	0.433	0.549	0.665
22	0.423	0.537	0.652
23	0.413	0.526	0.640
24	0.404	0.515	0.629
25	0.396	0.505	0.618
26	0.388	0.496	0.607
27	0.381	0.487	0.597
28	0.374	0.479	0.588
29	0.367	0.471	0.579
30	0.361	0.463	0.570
35	0.334	0.430	0.532
40	0.312	0.403	0.501
45	0.294	0.380	0.474
50	0.279	0.361	0.451
60	0.254	0.330	0.414
70	0.235	0.306	0.385
80	0.220	0.286	0.361
90	0.207	0.270	0.341
100	0.197	0.256	0.324
200	0.139	0.182	0.231
300	0.113	0.149	0.189
400	0.098	0.129	0.164
500	0.088	0.115	0.147

APPENDIX 5: CRITICAL VALUES FOR *T*

The observed value needs to be equal or above the value in the table to be statistically significant.

df	Significance							
	0.2	**0.1**	**0.05**	**0.01**	**0.005**	**0.001**	**0.0005**	**0.0001**
2	1.89	2.92	4.30	9.92	14.09	31.60	44.70	100.14
3	1.64	2.35	3.18	5.84	7.45	12.92	16.33	28.01
4	1.53	2.13	2.78	4.60	5.60	8.61	10.31	15.53
5	1.48	2.02	2.57	4.03	4.77	6.87	7.98	11.18
6	1.44	1.94	2.45	3.71	4.32	5.96	6.79	9.08
7	1.41	1.89	2.36	3.50	4.03	5.41	6.08	7.89
8	1.40	1.86	2.31	3.36	3.83	5.04	5.62	7.12
9	1.38	1.83	2.26	3.25	3.69	4.78	5.29	6.59
10	1.37	1.81	2.23	3.17	3.58	4.59	5.05	6.21
11	1.36	1.80	2.20	3.11	3.50	4.44	4.86	5.92
12	1.36	1.78	2.18	3.05	3.43	4.32	4.72	5.70
13	1.35	1.77	2.16	3.01	3.37	4.22	4.60	5.51
14	1.35	1.76	2.14	2.98	3.33	4.14	4.50	5.36
15	1.34	1.75	2.13	2.95	3.29	4.07	4.42	5.24
16	1.34	1.75	2.12	2.92	3.25	4.01	4.35	5.13
17	1.33	1.74	2.11	2.90	3.22	3.97	4.29	5.04
18	1.33	1.73	2.10	2.88	3.20	3.92	4.23	4.97
19	1.33	1.73	2.09	2.86	3.17	3.88	4.19	4.90
20	1.33	1.72	2.09	2.85	3.15	3.85	4.15	4.84
21	1.32	1.72	2.08	2.83	3.14	3.82	4.11	4.78
22	1.32	1.72	2.07	2.82	3.12	3.79	4.08	4.74
23	1.32	1.71	2.07	2.81	3.10	3.77	4.05	4.69
24	1.32	1.71	2.06	2.80	3.09	3.75	4.02	4.65
25	1.32	1.71	2.06	2.79	3.08	3.73	4.00	4.62
26	1.31	1.71	2.06	2.78	3.07	3.71	3.97	4.59
27	1.31	1.70	2.05	2.77	3.06	3.69	3.95	4.56
28	1.31	1.70	2.05	2.76	3.05	3.67	3.93	4.53
29	1.31	1.70	2.05	2.76	3.04	3.66	3.92	4.51
30	1.31	1.70	2.04	2.75	3.03	3.65	3.90	4.48
35	1.31	1.69	2.03	2.72	3.00	3.59	3.84	4.39
40	1.30	1.68	2.02	2.70	2.97	3.55	3.79	4.32
45	1.30	1.68	2.01	2.69	2.95	3.52	3.75	4.27
50	1.30	1.68	2.01	2.68	2.94	3.50	3.72	4.23
55	1.30	1.67	2.00	2.67	2.92	3.48	3.70	4.20
60	1.30	1.67	2.00	2.66	2.91	3.46	3.68	4.17
65	1.29	1.67	2.00	2.65	2.91	3.45	3.66	4.15
70	1.29	1.67	1.99	2.65	2.90	3.43	3.65	4.13
75	1.29	1.67	1.99	2.64	2.89	3.42	3.64	4.11
80	1.29	1.66	1.99	2.64	2.89	3.42	3.63	4.10
85	1.29	1.66	1.99	2.63	2.88	3.41	3.62	4.08
90	1.29	1.66	1.99	2.63	2.88	3.40	3.61	4.07
95	1.29	1.66	1.99	2.63	2.87	3.40	3.60	4.06
100	1.29	1.66	1.98	2.63	2.87	3.39	3.60	4.05
200	1.29	1.65	1.97	2.60	2.84	3.34	3.54	3.97
500	1.28	1.65	1.96	2.59	2.82	3.31	3.50	3.92
1000	1.28	1.65	1.96	2.58	2.81	3.30	3.49	3.91
∞	1.28	1.64	1.96	2.58	2.81	3.29	3.48	3.89

APPENDIX 6: CRITICAL VALUES FOR THE WILCOXON TEST

To be statistically significant, the value for T must be below the critical value in the table. (Notice that a result cannot be statistically significant at the 0.05 level unless N is at least 7).

N	p 0.1	0.05	0.01
5	0		
6	2	0	
7	3	2	
8	5	3	0
9	8	5	1
10	10	8	3
11	13	10	5
12	17	13	7
13	21	17	9
14	25	21	12
15	30	25	15
16	35	29	19
17	41	34	23
18	47	40	27
19	53	46	32
20	60	52	37

APPENDIX 7: PROBABILITY VALUES FOR THE SIGN TEST

Table of probability values for the sign test. The table contains the exact probability associated with those values for S and N.

| | | | | | | | | S | | | | | | | | |
N	0	1	2	3	4	5	6	7	8	9	10	11	12	13	14	15
5	0.063	0.375	1.000													
6	0.031	0.219	0.688	1.000												
7	0.016	0.125	0.453	1.000												
8	0.008	0.070	0.289	0.727	1.000											
9	0.004	0.039	0.180	0.508	1.000											
10	0.002	0.021	0.109	0.344	0.754	1.000										
11	0.001	0.012	0.065	0.227	0.549	1.000										
12	<0.001	0.006	0.039	0.146	0.388	0.774	1.000									
13	<0.001	0.003	0.022	0.092	0.267	0.581	1.000									
14	<0.001	0.002	0.013	0.057	0.180	0.424	0.791	1.000								
15	<0.001	0.001	0.007	0.035	0.118	0.302	0.607	1.000								
16	<0.001	0.001	0.004	0.021	0.077	0.210	0.454	0.804	1.000							
17	<0.001	<0.001	0.002	0.013	0.049	0.143	0.332	0.629	1.000							
18	<0.001	<0.001	0.001	0.008	0.031	0.096	0.238	0.481	0.815	1.000						
19	<0.001	<0.001	0.001	0.004	0.019	0.064	0.167	0.359	0.648	1.000						
20	<0.001	<0.001	<0.001	0.003	0.012	0.041	0.115	0.263	0.503	0.824	1.000					
21	<0.001	<0.001	<0.001	0.001	0.007	0.027	0.078	0.189	0.383	0.664	1.000					
22	<0.001	<0.001	<0.001	0.001	0.004	0.017	0.052	0.134	0.286	0.523	0.832	1.000				
23	<0.001	<0.001	<0.001	<0.001	0.003	0.011	0.035	0.093	0.210	0.405	0.678	1.000				
24	<0.001	<0.001	<0.001	<0.001	0.002	0.007	0.023	0.064	0.152	0.307	0.541	0.839	1.000			
25	<0.001	<0.001	<0.001	<0.001	0.001	0.004	0.015	0.043	0.108	0.230	0.424	0.690	1.000			
26	<0.001	<0.001	<0.001	<0.001	0.001	0.002	0.009	0.029	0.076	0.169	0.327	0.557	0.845	1.000		
27	<0.001	<0.001	<0.001	<0.001	<0.001	0.002	0.006	0.019	0.052	0.122	0.248	0.442	0.701	1.000		
28	<0.001	<0.001	<0.001	<0.001	<0.001	0.001	0.004	0.013	0.036	0.087	0.185	0.345	0.572	0.851	1.000	
29	<0.001	<0.001	<0.001	<0.001	<0.001	0.001	0.002	0.008	0.024	0.061	0.136	0.265	0.458	0.711	1.000	
30	<0.001	<0.001	<0.001	<0.001	<0.001	<0.001	0.001	0.005	0.016	0.043	0.099	0.200	0.362	0.585	0.856	1.000
31	<0.001	<0.001	<0.001	<0.001	<0.001	<0.001	0.001	0.003	0.011	0.029	0.071	0.150	0.281	0.473	0.720	1.000
32	<0.001	<0.001	<0.001	<0.001	<0.001	<0.001	0.001	0.002	0.007	0.020	0.050	0.110	0.215	0.377	0.597	0.860
33	<0.001	<0.001	<0.001	<0.001	<0.001	<0.001	<0.001	0.001	0.005	0.014	0.035	0.080	0.163	0.296	0.487	0.728

APPENDIX 7: (CONTINUED)

N	s															
	0	1	2	3	4	5	6	7	8	9	10	11	12	13	14	15
34	<0.001	<0.001	<0.001	<0.001	<0.001	<0.001	<0.001	0.001	0.003	0.009	0.024	0.058	0.121	0.229	0.392	0.608
35	<0.001	<0.001	<0.001	<0.001	<0.001	<0.001	<0.001	0.001	0.002	0.006	0.017	0.041	0.090	0.175	0.311	0.500
36	<0.001	<0.001	<0.001	<0.001	<0.001	<0.001	<0.001	<0.001	0.001	0.004	0.011	0.029	0.065	0.132	0.243	0.405
37	<0.001	<0.001	<0.001	<0.001	<0.001	<0.001	<0.001	<0.001	0.001	0.003	0.008	0.020	0.047	0.099	0.188	0.324
38	<0.001	<0.001	<0.001	<0.001	<0.001	<0.001	<0.001	<0.001	<0.001	0.002	0.005	0.014	0.034	0.073	0.143	0.256
39	<0.001	<0.001	<0.001	<0.001	<0.001	<0.001	<0.001	<0.001	<0.001	0.001	0.003	0.009	0.024	0.053	0.108	0.200
40	<0.001	<0.001	<0.001	<0.001	<0.001	<0.001	<0.001	<0.001	<0.001	0.001	0.002	0.006	0.017	0.038	0.081	0.154

APPENDIX 7a

		DF				
		1	2	3	4	5
P	0.05	3.84	5.99	7.81	9.49	11.07
	0.01	6.63	9.21	11.34	13.28	15.09
	0.001	10.83	13.82	16.27	18.47	20.51

APPENDIX 8: CRITICAL VALUES FOR THE F DISTRIBUTION

Critical values are given for $p=0.05$ and $p=0.01$. The calculated value must exceed the critical value, for the result to be statistically significant at the stated level. If the your exact value for your df isn't available, use the next lowest values of df.

df_2	df_1							
	1		2		3		4	
p	0.05	0.01	0.05	0.01	0.05	0.01	0.05	0.01
3	10.13	34.12	9.55	30.82	9.28	29.46	9.12	28.71
4	7.71	21.20	6.94	18.00	6.59	16.69	6.39	15.98
5	6.61	16.26	5.79	13.27	5.41	12.06	5.19	11.39
6	5.99	13.75	5.14	10.92	4.76	9.78	4.53	9.15
7	5.59	12.25	4.74	9.55	4.35	8.45	4.12	7.85
8	5.32	11.26	4.46	8.65	4.07	7.59	3.84	7.01
9	5.12	10.56	4.26	8.02	3.86	6.99	3.63	6.42
10	4.96	10.04	4.10	7.56	3.71	6.55	3.48	5.99
11	4.84	9.65	3.98	7.21	3.59	6.22	3.36	5.67
12	4.75	9.33	3.89	6.93	3.49	5.95	3.26	5.41
13	4.67	9.07	3.81	6.70	3.41	5.74	3.18	5.21
14	4.60	8.86	3.74	6.51	3.34	5.56	3.11	5.04
15	4.54	8.68	3.68	6.36	3.29	5.42	3.06	4.89
16	4.49	8.53	3.63	6.23	3.24	5.29	3.01	4.77
17	4.45	8.40	3.59	6.11	3.20	5.18	2.96	4.67
18	4.41	8.29	3.55	6.01	3.16	5.09	2.93	4.58
19	4.38	8.18	3.52	5.93	3.13	5.01	2.90	4.50
20	4.35	8.10	3.49	5.85	3.10	4.94	2.87	4.43
25	4.24	7.77	3.39	5.57	2.99	4.68	2.76	4.18
30	4.17	7.56	3.32	5.39	2.92	4.51	2.69	4.02
35	4.12	7.42	3.27	5.27	2.87	4.40	2.64	3.91
40	4.08	7.31	3.23	5.18	2.84	4.31	2.61	3.83
45	4.06	7.23	3.20	5.11	2.81	4.25	2.58	3.77
50	4.03	7.17	3.18	5.06	2.79	4.20	2.56	3.72
60	4.00	7.08	3.15	4.98	2.76	4.13	2.53	3.65
70	3.98	7.01	3.13	4.92	2.74	4.07	2.50	3.60
80	3.96	6.96	3.11	4.88	2.72	4.04	2.49	3.56
90	3.95	6.93	3.10	4.85	2.71	4.01	2.47	3.53
100	3.94	6.90	3.09	4.82	2.70	3.98	2.46	3.51
200	3.89	6.76	3.04	4.71	2.65	3.88	2.42	3.41
500	3.86	6.69	3.01	4.65	2.62	3.82	2.39	3.36

References

Abelson, P. (1995). *Statistics as principled argument*. Hillsdale, NJ: Erlbaum.

Adams, D. (1980) *The restaurant at the end of the universe*. London: Pan.

Adams, S. (1997). *The Dilbert principle*. London: Boxtree.

Alexander, F. E., Anderson, T. J., Brown, H. K., Forrest, A. P., Hepburn, W., Kirkpatrick, et al. (1999). 14 years of follow up from the Edinburgh randomised trial of breast cancer screening. *The Lancet, 353*, 1903–1907.

Altman, D. G. (1991). *Practical statistics for medical research*. London: Chapman & Hall.

Altman, D. G. & Bland, J. M. (1983). Measurement in medicine: the analysis of method comparison studies. *The Statistician, 32*, 307–317.

American Psychological Association (1995). *Publication manual of the American Psychological Association*. Washington, DC: APA.

Banyard, P. & Hunt, N. (2000). Reporting research: something missing? *The Psychologist, 13*(2), 68–71.

Banyard, P. & Shevlin, M. (2001). Responses of football fans to the relegation of their team from the English Premier League: PTS? *Irish Journal of Psychological Medicine, 18*, 66–67.

Barrow, J. (2005). *The infinite book*. London: Vintage.

Bem, D. J. (1972). Self-perception theory. In L. Berkowitz (Ed.), *Advances in experimental social psychology,* Vol. 6 (pp. 1–62). New York: Academic Press.

Bender, K. G., Azeem, N. & Morrice, J. (2000). Schizophrenia and birth order in Pakistan. *Schizophrenia Research, 44*(2), 113–120.

Birleson, P. (1981). The validity of depressive disorder and the development of a self rating scale: a research report. *Journal of Child Psychology and Psychiatry, 22*, 73–88.

Bland, J. M. & Altman, D. G. (1986). Statistical methods for assessing agreement between two methods of clinical measurement. *The Lancet,* 307–310.

Bland, J. M. & Altman, D. G. (1999). Measuring agreement in method comparison studies. *Statistical Methods in Medical Research, 8,* 135–160.

Carlson, E. B. & Putnam, F. W. (1993). An update on the Dissociative Experiences Scale. *Dissociation, 6,* 16–27.

Cochran, W. G. (1977). *Sampling techniques* (3rd ed.). New York: Wiley.

Cohen, J. (1983). The cost of dichotomization. *Applied Psychological Measurement, 7,* 249–253.

Cohen, J. (1988). *Statistical power analysis for the behavioral sciences.* Hillsdale, NJ: Erlbaum.

Cohen, P. (1994). The earth is round ($p < 0.05$). *American Psychologist, 49*(12), 997–1003.

Craik, F. I. M. & Tulving, E. (1975). Depth of processing and the retention of words in episodic memory. *Journal of Experimental Psychology: General, 104,* 268–294.

Crawford, J. R. & Howell, D. C. (1998). Comparing an individual's test score against norms derived from small samples. *The Clinical Neuropsychologist, 12*(4), 482–486.

Cronbach, L. J. (1951). Coefficient alpha and the internal structure of tests. *Psychometrika, 16,* 297–334.

Deary, I. J., Whiteman, M. C., Starr, J. M., Whalley, L. J. & Fox, H. C. (2004). The impact of childhood intelligence on later life: Following up the Scottish Mental Surveys of 1932 and 1947. *Journal of Personality and Social Psychology, 86*(1), 130–147.

DeCarlo, L. T. (1997). On the meaning and use of kurtosis. *Psychological Methods, 2,* 292–307.

Diener, E., Emmons, R., Larsen, J. & Griffin, S. (1985). The satisfaction with life scale. *Journal of Personality Assessmemt, 5*(2), 164–172.

Dorahy, M. J., Middleton, W. & Irwin, H. J. (2005). The effect of emotional context on cognitive inhibition and attentional processing in dissociative identity disorder. *Behaviour Research and Therapy, 43,* 555–568.

Dumville, J. C., Hahn, S., Miles, J. N. V. & Torgerson, D. J. (2006). The use of unequal randomisation ratios in clinical trials: a review. *Contemporary Clinical Trials, 27,* 1–12.

Dunn, O. J. (1961). Multiple comparisons among means. *Journal of the American Statistical Association, 56,* 52–64.

Embretson, S. & Hershberger, S. L. (Eds) (1999). *The new rules of measurement.* Hillsdale, NJ: Erlbaum.

Feldman, P. J., Cohen, S., Doyle, W. J., Skoner, D. P. & Gwaltney, J. M. (1999). The impact of personality on the reporting of unfounded symptoms and illness. *Journal of Personality and Social Psychology, 77,* 370–378.

Field, A. P. (2005). *Discovering Statistics Using SPSS.* (2nd ed.). London: SAGE Publications.

Frick, R. W. (1997). The appropriate use of null hypothesis significance testing. *Psychological Methods, 1,* 379–390.

Furnham, A. & Gasson, L. (1998). Sex differences in parental estimates of their children's intelligence. *Sex Roles, 38*(1–2), 151–162.

Gale, M. & Ball, L. J. (2006). Dual-goal facilitation in Wason's 2-4-6 task: What mediates successful rule discovery? *Quarterly Journal of Experimental Psychology,* 59, 873–885.

Gigerenzer, G. (1993). The Superego, the Ego, and the Id in statistical reasoning. In G. Keren & C. Lewis (Eds), *A handbook for data analysis in the behavioral sciences: Methodological issues* (pp. 311–339). Hillsdale, NJ: Erlbaum.

Gigerenzer, G. (2002). *Calculated risks: How to know when numbers deceive you.* New York: Simon & Schuster.

Gigerenzer, G. (2004). Mindless statistics. *Journal of Socio-economics, 33,* 584–606.

Gigerenzer, G. & Murray, D. J. (1987). *Cognition as intuitive statistics.* Hillsdale, NJ: Erlbaum.

Gigerenzer, G., Swijtink, Z., Porter, T., Daston, L., Beatty, J. & Krüger, L. (1989). *The empire of chance. How probability changed science and everyday life.* Cambridge: Cambridge University Press.

Godfrey, C. G. & UKATT Trial Team (2005). Cost effectiveness of treatment for alcohol problems: findings of the randomised UK alcohol treatment trial. *British Medical Journal, 331,* 544–550.

Goodwin, P. J., Leszcz, M., Ennis, M., Koopmans, J., Vincent, L., Guther, H., Drysdale, E., Hundleby, M., Chochinov, H. M., Navarro, M., Speca, M., Masterson, J., Dohan, L., Sela, R., Warren, B., Paterson, A., Pritchard, K. I., Arnold, A., Doll, R., O'Reilly, S.E., Quirt, G., Hood, N. & Hunter, J. (2001). The effect of group psychosocial support on survival in metastatic breast cancer. *New England Journal of Medicine, 345*(24), 1719–1726.

Haddon, M. (2003*). The curious incident of the dog in the night-time.* London: Jonathan Cape.

Haller, H. & Kraus, S. (2002). Misinterpretations of significance: a problem students share with their teachers? *MPR-Online, 7*(1), 1–20.

Harding, R. & Golombok, S. E. (2002). test-retest reliability of the measurement of penile dimensions in a sample of gay men. *Archives of Sexual Behavior, 31*(4), 351–357.

Hughes, A., Galbraith, D. & Torrance, M. (2005, 4–6 November). Promoting self-esteem, self efficacy, motivation, and aspirations in adolescent students: an intervention study. Paper presented at the British Psychological Society Psychology of Educational Annual Conference, Durham.

Hulme, C., Hatcher, P. J., Nation, K., Brown, A., Adams, J. & Stuart, G. (2002). Phoneme awareness is a better predictor of early reading skill than onset-rime awareness. *Journal of Experimental Child Psychology, 82*(1), 2–28.

Keren, G. (1993). Between- or within-subjects design: A methodological dilemma. In G. Keren & C. Levis (Eds), *A handbook for data analysis in the behavioral sciences, Vol 1: Methodological issues*. Hillsdale, NJ: Erlbaum.

Kish, L. (1965). *Survey sampling*. New York: Wiley.

Kozak, B., Strelau, J. & Miles, J. N. V. (2005). Genetic determinants of individual differences in coping styles. *Anxiety, Stress and Coping, 18*(1), 1–15.

MacFarlane, J., Holmes, W., Gard, P., Thornhill, D., MacFarlane, R., Hubbard, R. & van Weel, C. (2002). Reducing antibiotic use for acute bronchitis in primary care: blinded, randomised controlled trial of patient information leaflet. *British Medical Journal, 324*(7329), 91.

Mackenzie, D. (2004). Vital statistics. *New Scientist, 2453,* 36–38.

Mann, H. B. & Whitney, D. R. (1947). On a test of whether one of two random variables is stochastically larger than the other. *Annals of Mathematical Statistics, 18,* 50–60.

Maxwell, S. E. & Delaney, H. D. (2004). *Designing experiments and analyzing data: a model comparison perspective*. Mahwah, NJ: Erlbaum.

McCann, S. J. H. (2001). The precocity-longevity hypothesis: Earlier peaks in career achievement predict shorter lives. *Personality and Social Psychology Bulletin 27*(11), 1429–1439.

McCann, S. J. H. (2003). Younger achievement age predicts shorter life for governors: Testing the precocity-longevity hypothesis with artifact controls. *Personality and Social Psychology Bulletin, 29*(2), 164–169.

McGarrigle, J. & Donaldson, M. (1974). Conservation accidents. *Cognition, 3,* 341–350.

Miles, J. (2005). Central limit theorem. In D. Howell & B. Everitt (Eds), *Encyclopaedia of statistics in behavourial science*. Chichester: Wiley.

Miles, J. N. V. & Shevlin, M. E. (2001). *Applying regression and correlation*. London: Sage.

Miles, J., Shevlin, M. & McGhee, P. (1999). Gender differences in the reliability of the EPQ? A bootstrapping approach. *British Journal of Psychology, 90*(1), 145–154.

Morrison, C. M. & Ellis, A. W. (2000). Real age of acquisition effects in word naming and lexical decision. *British Journal of Psychology 91*, 167–180.

Neave, N. J., Emmett, J. R., Moss, M., Ayton, R., Scholey, A. B. & Wesnes, K. (2004). The effects of protective helmet use on physiology and cognition in young cricketers. *Applied Cognitive Psychology, 18*(9), 1181–1193.

Newstead, S. E. (2004). Time to make our mark. *The Psychologist, 17,* 20–23.

Newstead, S. E. & Dennis, I. (1994). Examiners examined: The reliability of exam marking in psychology. *The Psychologist, 7,* 216–219.

Nunnally, J. & Bernstein, I. (1992). *Psychometric Theory, 3rd ed.* New York: McGraw-Hill.

Pearl, J. (2000). *Causality: models, inference and reasoning.* Cambridge: Cambridge University Press.

Pearson, K. (1900). Mathematical contributions to the theory of evolution VII. On the correlation of characters not quantitatively measurable. *Philosophical Transactions of the Royal Society of London, Series A, 195,* 1–47.

Roberts, M. J. & Russo, R. (1999). *A student's guide to analysis of variance.* London: Routledge.

Roney, J. R., Mahler, S. V. & Maestripieri, D. (2003). Behavioral and hormonal responses of men to brief interactions with women. *Evolution and Human Behavior, 24*(6), 365–375.

Rossi, J. S. (1997). A case study in the failure of psychology as a cumulative science: the spontaneous recovery of verbal learning. In L. L. Harlow, S. A. Mulaik & J. H. Steiger (Eds), *What if there were no significance tests?* Hillsdale, NJ: Erlbaum.

Rutherford, M. D., Baron-Cohen, S. & Wheelwright, S. (2002). Reading the mind in the voice: A study with normal adults and adults with asperger syndrome and high functioning autism. *Journal of Autism and Developmental Disorders, 32*(3), 189–194.

Salsburg, D. (2001). *The lady tasting tea: How statistics revolutionized science in the twentieth century.* New York: W. H. Freeman and Co.

Saucier, G. (1994). Mini-markers: A brief version of Goldberg's unipolar Big-Five markers. *Journal of Personality Assessment, 63,* 506–516.

Schmidt, F. L. (1996). Statistical significance testing and cumulative knowledge in psychology: implications for the training of researchers. *Psychologicial Methods, 1,* 115–129.

Schmidt, F. L. & Hunter, J. E. (1997). Eight common but false objections to the discontinuation of significance testing in the analysis of research data. In L. L. Harlow, S. A. Mulaik & J. H. Steiger (Eds), what if there were no significance tests? (pp. 37–64). Mahwah, NJ: Lawrence Erlbaum Associates.

Scott, S. & Duncan, C. (2004). *Return of the Black Death: The World's Greatest Serial Killer.* Chichester: Wiley.

Senn, S. J. (2003). Dichotomania. *British Medical Journal, 327* (http://bmj.bmjjournals. com/cgi/content/full/327/7428/0-h).

Sheskin, D. J. (2003). *The handbook of parametric and nonparametric statistical procedures.* Boca Raton, FL: Chapman & Hall/CRC.

Smits, D., De Boeck, P. & Vansteelandt, K. (2004). The inhibition of verbally aggressive behaviour. *European Journal of Personality, 18,* 537–555.

Stigler, S. W. (1980). Stigler's law of eponymy. *Transactions of the New York Academy of Science, 39,* 147–157.

Streiner, D. L. & Norman, G. R. (2003). *Health measurement scales: A practical guide to their development and use.* Oxford: Oxford University Press.

Swift, W., Hall, W., Didcott, P. & Reilly, D. (1998). Patterns and correlates of cannabis dependence among long-term users in an Australian rural area. *Addiction, 93,* 1149–1160.

Tversky, A. & Kahneman, D. (1971). Belief in the law of small numbers. *Psychological Bulletin, 76,* 105–110.

Vaughan, R., Morrison, L. & Miller, E. (2003). The illness representations of multiple sclerosis and their relations to outcome. *British Journal of Health Psychology, 8*(3), 287–301.

Wainer, H. (1999). One cheer for hull hypothesis significance testing. *Psychological Methods, 4,* 212–213.

Welch, B. L. (1938). The significance of the difference between two means when the population variances are unequal. *Biometrika, 34,* 29–35.

Wetherell, M. A., Crown, A. L., Lightman, S. L., Miles, J. N. V., Kaye, J. & Vedhara, K. (2006). The 4-dimensional stress test: psychological, sympathetic-adrenal-medullary, parasympathetic and hypothalamic-pituitary-adrenal responses following inhalation of 35% CO_2. *Psychoneuroendicronology, 31,* 736–747.

White, P., Lewith, G., Hopwood, V. & Prescott, P. (2003). The placebo needle: is it a valid and convincing placebo for use in acupuncture trials? A randomised, single-blind, cross-over pilot trial. *Pain, 106*(3), 401–409.

Whitehead, J. (1993). Sample-size calculations for ordered categorical data. *Statistics in Medicine, 12,* 2257–2271.

Wilcox, R. R. (1997). *Introduction to robust estimation and hypothesis testing.* London: Academic Press.

Wilcoxon, F. (1945). Individual comparisons by ranking methods. *Biometrics, 1,* 80–83.

Wiseman, R. & Greening, E. (2005). 'It's still bending': Verbal suggestion and alleged psychokinetic ability. *British Journal of Psychology, 96,* 115–127.

Wright, B., Ashby, B., Beverley, D., Calvert, E., Jordan, J., Miles, J. N. V., Russell, I. & Williams, C. (2005). A feasibility study comparing two treatment approaches for Chronic Fatigue Syndrome in Adolescents. *Archives of Disease in Childhood, 90,* 369–372.

Zimmerman, D. W. (2004). A note on preliminary tests of equality of variances. *British Journal of Mathematical and Statistical Psychology, 57*(1), 172–181.

Index